READINGS IN ANTHROPOLOGY OF HUMAN MOVEMENT
Edited by Drid Williams

1. *Anthropology and Human Movement: The Study of Dances*, by Drid Williams
2. *Anthropology and Human Movement: Searching for Origins*, by Drid Williams

Anthropology and Human Movement

Searching for Origins

Drid Williams

*Readings in Anthropology of
Human Movement, No. 2*

The Scarecrow Press, Inc.
Lanham, Maryland, and London
2000

SCARECROW PRESS, INC.

Published in the United States of America
by Scarecrow Press, Inc.
4720 Boston Way, Lanham, Maryland 20706
http://www.scarecrowpress.com

4 Pleydell Gardens, Folkestone
Kent CT20 2DN, England

British Library Cataloguing in Publication Information Available

Library of Congress Cataloging-in-Publication Data

Williams, Drid, 1928–
    Anthropology and human movement : searching for origins / Drid
Williams, [editor].
        p.   cm. — (Readings in anthropology of human movement ; no. 2)
    Includes bibliographical references and indexes.
    ISBN 0-8108-3707-2 (cloth : alk. paper)
    1. Dance—History. 2. Sign language—History. I. Title. II. Series.
GV1595.W53   1999
    306.4′84—dc21
                                                                99-33951
                                                                CIP

⊖™ The paper used in this publication meets the minimum requirements of
American National Standard for Information Sciences—Permanence of
Paper for Printed Library Materials, ANSI/NISO Z39.48–1992.
Manufactured in the United States of America.

CONTENTS

PREFACE

> Intellectual movements crystallize in persons and places, countries and university departments. They become embodied or located. They continue their spread to other persons, or places, or into other intellectual fields (Ardener 1989[1977]: 194).

Unlike the first volume in the series (*Anthropology and Human Movement, 1: The Study of Dances*) this book shifts the reader's attention from ethnography to the placement of sign languages and dances in historical perspective. Overall, *Searching for Origins* deals with a widespread problem concerning time/space and the world-historical context regarding the study of human movement. Like *The Study of Dances*, it covers a wide geographical area and several distinctly different peoples. Unlike the first book, it deals with two distinct types of structured systems of human action.

In the beginning 'Essays' section, South African dance forms are discussed by Sylvia Glasser (1991). Following her work are essays on two kinds of sign language: American Sign Language [ASL] by an historian (Douglas Baynton 1995), and Assiniboine (Nakota) sign language (one of many systems of Plains Sign Talk [PST]) by Brenda Farnell (1995). Last but not least, readers will find Theresa Buckland's essay on traditional English ceremonial and social dance forms (1994).

Although Joann Keali'inohomoku addressed the problem of origins with reference to dances in Vol. 1 (1997: 15-36), the concept is still overlooked. Perhaps it is considered to be "too theoretical," seeming far removed from the realities of everyday movement usage. As we shall see, the problem of origins is not far removed. It has greatly affected the literature on traditional dancing and, in the case of sign languages, it touches many people's lives daily — so much so that it became necessary to provide alternative foundations for new concepts. With these, future students have the option of replacing the misconceived viewpoints discussed by Glasser, Baynton, Farnell and Buckland.

Aware of similar difficulties regarding concepts of origin in studies of primitive religion over thirty years ago, Evans-Pritchard remarked:

> We may, indeed, wonder why they [social anthropologists and other writers on primitive religion generally] did not take as their first field of study the higher religions about whose history, theology, and rites far more was known than of the religions of the primitives, thus proceeding from the better known to the less known. They may to some extent have ignored the higher religions to avoid controversy and embarrassment in somewhat delicate circumstances ... but *it was chiefly because they wanted to discover the origin of religion*, the essence of it, and they thought that this would be found in very primitive societies. However some of them may have protested that by 'origin' they did not mean earliest in time but simplest in structure, the implicit assumption in their arguments was that *what was simplest in structure must have been that from which more developed forms evolved*. This ambiguity in the concept of origin has caused much confusion in anthropology (Evans-Pritchard 1965: 16 - italics added).

Similarly, it was (and still is) widely believed that the origins and essence of dancing and signing will be found in 'primitive' societies. Ambiguities in the concept of origin still cause much confusion in the anthropology of human movement.

Although problems of origins aren't solely confined to studies of sign languages and dances, the implicit assumptions made by many writers about the relationship between alleged 'simple structures' and 'primitive' systems of human movement are widespread in the literature about dancing, where the idea of a simple to complex continuum often dictates the format of many pseudo-historical books on the dance.[1] [p. 249]

These books typically begin with sections on African, Caribbean or Australian Aboriginal forms of dancing. They invariably end with sections on the ballet or contemporary modern concert-dancing. A general premise fundamental to many of these books reads like this:

> Before man learned how to use any instruments at all, he moved the most perfect instrument of all, his body. He did this with such abandon that *the cultural history of prehistoric and ancient man is, for the most*

part, nothing but the history of dance. We must understand this literally. Not only is prehistory mostly dance history, but dance history is mostly prehistory. Like a giant monolith, the dance stands in the midst of the changing forms of human expression (van der Leeuw 1963: 13 - italics added).

Van der Leeuw's book was first published in English approximately forty years ago, thus it is not surprising that some people today still think as this author does. Many people believe that the ultimate origins of the ballet are to be found, if not somewhere in Africa, then in Aboriginal Australia or some other "stone-age" society. If those holding such beliefs *do* entertain doubts about the origins of contemporary Euro-American dance forms in Africa, Australia, or elsewhere, they tend merely to move the locus of imagined origins to peoples who painted the caves in Lascaux or to the inhabitants of ancient Greece.

No matter where the presumed origins of dancing are located, inferences are made regarding stylistic and other types of continuity from some speculative beginning until now. While it is true, for example, that Bushman trance-dancing (discussed in a later section) is chronologically older than the ballet, it does not follow that there are *direct* lines of continuity connecting Bushman trance-dancing with modern forms of dancing.

To remedy the problem of oversimplified concepts of time, students will find that they must seriously re-think the subject regarding classification and categories. They must accept the possibility that social theory and politics in the form of governmental and educational policies literally define whole populations of dancers and signers. A different perspective is needed. For example, the political situation in South Africa was not the same two hundred years ago as it is today:

In the eighteenth century, considerable cross-fertilisation occurred between colonists, indigenous populations and slave populations. ... Back then, segregation was a matter of social class. *It was not legislated*, thus continuous cultural exchange took place between different groups of people (see Glasser, p. 25 - italics added).

Neither colonial forms of dancing nor indigenous dancing in South Africa were frozen in time. There is no such thing as van der Leeuw's unchanging "giant monolith" of dances anywhere in the world. Dances change, but the ideas people have about them often do not. Like dances, governmental and educational policies change, but some of the ideas that support the policies often do not.

When it was finally put in place, *apartheid* (legislated separatism in South Africa) was strongly supported by evolutionary theory and ideas. *Apartheid* was a comparatively recent political development in South Africa. Now, it no longer exists as an overt governmental policy, but misconceived theories of social evolution still do.

According to Baynton, American attitudes toward deafness and sign languages changed in the mid-nineteenth century when Darwinian evolutionary theory re-defined human nature:

> Baynton describes how evolutionary discourses that defined human body movement as 'animal-like' and 'primitive' provided justification for educational theories and policies which denied deaf people the opportunity to be educated in their native sign languages. I am reminded how a similar rhetoric of "civilizing the savages" led to the ban on American Indian languages in government boarding schools of the same period with disastrous consequences for many individuals thus alienated, and for the languages themselves, most of which are now seriously endangered. A prevailing conception of gesture as [the] "primitive precursor to speech" meant that users of Plains Sign Language were readily classified as "savages" on a presumed social evolutionary scale. In her appreciative essay in response to Baynton's article (1995: 174-189), Williams notes that the same set of beliefs and ideologies have adversely affected dancers and the study of dancing in western cultures. Here is an unlikely arena, then, where Deaf persons, Plains Indians, and dancers find common ground (Farnell 1995: 135-136).

Expectations

Students can expect to confront diverse populations of people and meet authors from different disciplines: social anthropologists, philosophers, historians, archæologists, biologists and classical scholars contribute to this book. Stu-

dents will encounter dissimilar political and biological ideologies, and they are expected to cope with vague concepts
of the past. They will discover classificatory problems in
books of reference and find themselves obliged to re-examine the nature of archæological, historical and sociocultural
anthropological evidence. They are also encouraged to re-
examine the grounds for ideas they initially brought into the
classroom with them. Correcting an all-pervasive problem
isn't easy. However, correctives are necessary if the aim is to
understand sign languages and dances in greater depth and
with reasonable accuracy.

As a whole, this book represents a dedicated effort to help
students come to terms with some of the myths surrounding
concepts of origin and human movement. I do not flatter
myself that it was (or is) a single-handed job. In later chapters of the book, readers will find lengthy quotations from
the works of scholars who have dealt with specific aspects
of the subject, e.g., Chapman (pp. 156-7); Farnell (pp. 166-
68); Lawler (pp. 205-206); Best (pp. 138-141); Steiner (p. 159);
Bohannan (pp. 159-162) and Lewis-Williams (pp. 200-202).

The long citations are included because it is important for
students to have opportunities honestly to *interact with received authorities in the forms in which the ideas were originally
written*. Too often, an instructor's summaries of long passages
containing an original author's arguments are hurriedly
memorized for an exam, then promptly forgotten. Here, I
attempt to supply a format for approaching intellectual problems that encourages students to develop their own capacities to summarize and *to think for themselves*. If students already know how to summarize and think for themselves,
then these skills can only be enriched during what for them
becomes a valuable review process.

This teaching text provides an interdisciplinary intellectual context that invites students to hone their own mental
skills. Students say they are more willing to consult an original author's text when they find they are capable of understanding the contents of long passages, such as those which
appear in this book.

The remaining chapters of the book are perhaps best used in classroom or seminar sessions. I hope, however, that the original works will be read in their entirety in a spirit of discovery.

Teaching Techniques Are Crucial

Long experience provides me with ample proof that significant numbers of undergraduate and graduate students lack the critical skills necessary for comprehending (far less competing in) scholarly fields, making teaching techniques decisive factors with reference to success or failure in this regard. The same teaching techniques that I developed for use in graduate classes to ensure the development of critical skills are used in this book.

One of these consists of having class members, in turn, *read aloud* a long passage which is then followed by an exegesis of the passage and group discussion. Through this process, *students gradually learn to read differently*. They learn how to find what is relevant to the field of study. They learn to ask and to answer questions. The précis exercises serve to reinforce the teaching techniques.

I have tried to keep to those teaching methods that alert novices at any level to the fact that, for example, information in distinguished reference books often actively *conceals* many issues that are crucial to understanding the field. For example, how are readers new to anthropology and human movement supposed to handle awkward classificatory headings, such as "tribal dance," "ethnic dance" and others? An average mixture of undergraduate and graduate students in the United States, at any rate, rarely possesses prior knowledge of such terminological difficulties. They aren't familiar with the intricacies of, say, historical method in contrast to archæological or anthropological method and theory. Sometimes, they do not have clear pictures of what evidence consists in any of these disciplines. Moreover, if there *are* students in a class who have had adequate theoretical, classificatory, and methodological preparation, they stand to benefit from the repetition because they are given opportunities to bring previously gained knowledge to bear in different contexts.

The second section, 'Predispositions of Thought' was conceived as a long, connected essay concerning many of the flagrant confusions that exist with reference to ideas of evolution, subjectivity and objectivity, progress, primitive, ethnic, and universality, as they pertain to the study of dancing and sign languages. There are other ways of looking at the contents, of course, since I do *not* propose to clarify all the confusion nor do I feel it necessary to write my own solutions to the problems presented in the first section of essays.[2] My purpose was to produce a teaching text that would enable students successfully to find their own individual paths through the maze of blunders and false starts they inherit from the past.

Besides reprinted essays, chapters and excerpts from books, there are short biographical notes of authors, précis and "time-line" exercises (pp. 193-96), designed primarily to make history into a living process for individual students rather than a dead repository for random selections of events.

Notes, précis, etc. are included for the same reasons they were used in *Anthropology and Human Movement, 1*. Teachers require adequate benchmarks whereby their students' grasp of assigned materials can be accurately assessed. *Students need clear guidelines* with which they can chart their progress through previously unknown intellectual territories.

Macro-History, Micro-History and Ideology

The predominant idea throughout is to promote a more enlightened understanding of the major question that inspired this book:

> *HOW ARE THE MICRO-HISTORIES OF SIGN LANGUAGES AND DANCES FITTED INTO THE MACRO-HISTORY OF THE HUMAN RACE?*

How can we effectively deal with intellectual problems inherited from the past?[3] What should we do, for example, with naive theories of unilineal evolution, the best example of which for dancing was produced by the musicologist, Curt Sachs, who begins with "what he calls the 'mating dances' of mountain chickens in British Guyana, proceeds to stilt birds in Australia, thence to Wolfgang Köhler's apes on Tenerife" (Williams 1991: 89-90, summarizing Sachs's unilinear evolutionary theory of the origins of dancing).

Social evolutionary theory encourages the cultivation of viewpoints about dancing as an inferior activity because its origins are thought to be rooted in the movements of birds, apes and human 'primitives'. One of the reasons for the past (and continuing) popularity of Sachs's book is that he wrote during a crisis in thought that occurred at the end of the nineteenth and the beginning of the twentieth centuries. He wrote just after the period when Darwin's evolutionary theory became an ideology.

> What Darwin did was take early-nineteenth century *political* economy and expand it to include all of *natural* economy. Moreover, he developed a theory of sexual selection in evolution ... in which the chief force is the competition among males to be more appealing to discriminating females. This theory was meant to explain why male animals often display bright colors or complex mating dances (Lewontin 1991: 10).

Darwin's theory is one of the most successful and popular theories ever to have emerged in the sciences. "No aspect of human life is untouched by Darwin's theory of evolution, modified in various ways to apply to economics and politics, to the explanation of the origins and the significance of art, and even to the history of ideas themselves" (Goodwin 1994: vii).

> Darwinism sees the living process in terms that emphasize competition, inheritance, selfishness, and survival as the driving forces of evolution. These are certainly aspects of the remarkable drama that includes our own history as a species. But it is a very incomplete and limited story, both scientifically and metaphorically, based on an inadequate view of organisms; and it invites us to act in a limited way as an evolved species in relation to our environment, which includes other cultures and species. *These limitations have contributed to some of the difficulties we now face* ...(Goodwin 1994: xii - italics added).

We do not, as David Pocock (1994[1973]) put it, "float free" of our historical selves. The facts that bind us to our sociolinguistic histories, personal or otherwise, become clearly evident when the difficulties facing students of human movement are addressed. How can we reconcile the limitations of social evolution and traditionally orthodox 'scientific' points of view with the lived realities of human actions in our own and other cultures?

Organization

Anthropology and Human Movement, 2: Searching for Origins is divided into three major sections: I: Essays, II: Predispositions of Thought, and III: Intellectual Resources. The second section, 'Predispositions', includes Chapter 5: Records and References, Chapter 6: Objectivity and Subjectivity, Chapter 7: Universality and Chapter 8: Time. The third section, 'Resources', includes Chapter 9: Ancient Dances, Chapter 10: Movement Literacy/Evidence and Chapter 11: The Basic Structures of Argument.

The first of the four essays in Section I deals with the political nature of dancing in South Africa and, by implication, elsewhere. The second summarizes significant changes in American attitudes toward deaf-signing during the nineteenth and early twentieth centuries, indicating how policymakers' concepts of humanity influenced educational policies in schools for the Deaf.[4] The third addresses two issues: different culture-specific ways of thinking about time/space and gesture and the general notion of embodiment. The fourth essay addresses the problem of origins with reference to culture-specific dance forms offering excellent guidelines for the kind of painstaking research that is necessary when students prepare to undertake research. Each essay provides 'spring-boards', so to speak, for remaining chapters.

Section I: Essays

1. Is Dance Political Movement? (Glasser 1991)

Sylvia Glasser emphasizes the fact that Darwin's theories of evolution reinforced European attitudes of racial and cul-

tural superiority toward the dances of indigenous populations. The culture of the indigenous black population was

> perceived as simple, undeveloped and generally on a lower level of
> 'civilization' than that of European colonists. Their music and dance
> was seen as primitive and not worthy of understanding or emula-
> tion. These attitudes have persisted and are still to be found to this
> day (p. 26, this volume).

She challenges readers with a situation in South Africa as it
existed in the late 1980s, but circumstances then surrounding the dance in South Africa still exist in questions about
what to keep and what to throw away. Glasser's work raises
the issue of 'process' vs. 'preservation'.

The battles that take place over these ideas are ubiquitous
with reference to the study of dances. Fairbank provides interesting insights regarding China: [5]

> As a result of the recent directives to restore national culture, the re-
> newed political interest in minority groups, and the large-scale re-
> search project in dance being conducted at this time, the investiga-
> tion and collection of ethnic dance material throughout China has
> become highly organized under the present government. There are
> two distinct groups of researchers involved. One group, the 'preser-
> vationists', is principally concerned with preservation and documen-
> tation, while the chief interest of the other group, the 'processors', is
> in the collection of materials for teaching and choreographic use. ...
> All collection and standardization procedures are extremely influ-
> enced by *jigong* (processing), *meihua* (beautification) and *xheng-li* (to
> arrange and put in order)...[6]
> As one researcher explained, this national effort to collect and dis-
> seminate minority and folk dances is not simply for archival purposes,
> "but to develop a new dance form in order to express and enrich
> modern life" (Fieldnotes 1983). This ethnic material must not only
> appeal to a general audience, but must also be morally 'correct'[7] and
> flattering to minority populations. Consequently, anything drawn
> from the field and introduced to classrooms or theaters must pass
> certain tests of morality, aesthetic appeal and political approval from
> a Han/communist point of view before it can be introduced to the
> masses (Fairbank 1985: 169).

Here, we find aggressive governmental policies directed toward cultural appropriation and the direct assimilation of

minority groups by a dominant political group. The Chinese *change* the dances of their minority groups to fit policies based on nationalist ideologies.

Unlike China, however, "The architects of *apartheid* saw cultures as bounded, fixed, homogeneous entities. ... They reified cultural traditions" (p. 31). In South Africa, governmental policies weren't aimed at cultural appropriation and nationalization. In that country, governmental policies legislated separatism. In spite of all this, indigenous forms of dancing not only grew, but flourished.

Whether *xheng-li* in China (aimed toward standardization), or *apartheid* in South Africa (aimed toward racial exclusion), political ideologies like these are embodied. They have distinct locations, and, as we shall see, they have far-reaching consequences in people's daily lives.

2. "Savages and Deaf-Mutes." Evolutionary Theory and the Campaign Against Sign-Language (Baynton 1994)

Fully available in his recent book (1996), Douglas Baynton's admirable work is succinctly summarized in this essay. "Here is an author who makes people who lived in the past (oralists, manualists and Deaf populations in the United States) emerge from the pages and seem real" (Williams 1994: 174). One can imagine how countless students all over the United States felt when they came to school one day to discover that the manual sign language in which they were proficient was no longer to be used in classes. From that time on, they had to learn to communicate orally. How shocking, painful and discouraging that must have been; yet, those students had to endure the changes. Why?

The oralist movement in Deaf education ... "[W]as symptomatic of a new understanding of human history—and of the place of sign language in that history " at the end of the nineteenth century ... forcefully reminding us again how so-called 'abstractions' in the form of profound ideas about the nature and character of humanity are transformed into sets of beliefs and/or ideologies that affect what we think and do, and (perhaps more important) what we think we ought to do, individually and socially (Williams 1994: 176).

The rationale for the massive change brought about in thousands of Americans' lives was that signing itself signified some kind of *regression*:

> That is, evolutionary analogies, explanations and ways of thinking were ubiquitous. Psychologists theorized mental illness as evolutionary reversion. Criminologists defined "the criminal type" as a throwback. Social policies were defended or attacked on the basis of their ostensible likelihood to further or stunt evolution. Even sin came to be described as "a falling back into the animal condition" (Baynton pp. 43-4, this volume).

Baynton's writing encourages clear thinking about the past — thinking that is based on historical evidence — not speculation. His essay generates intriguing questions. For example, 1. (on p. 50) Is *historical* inferiority the same or different than the notion of *inherent* inferiority? 2. (on p. 56) Is it not ironic that the result of policies of discrimination against African-American deaf students meant that they probably "received a better education than most deaf white students?" Baynton concludes:

> Speech had become the "greatest of all objects" as Alexander Graham Bell expressed it. To "ask the value of speech" he believed, "is like asking the value of life" (1884: 178). The value of speech was, for the oralists, akin to the value of being human. To be human was to speak. To sign was to step downward in the scale of being and become a 'savage'.
>
> In that formulation — an unfortunate by-product of evolutionary theory — lies much of the reason for the decline of manualism and the rise of oralism at the end of the nineteenth century (pp. 67-8).

How much have ideas about evolution changed? What is the world of movement like for younger generations of students who read this book? Are their ideas about speech and signing (or speech and dancing) significantly different from those of their predecessors? Do ideas about movement remain unchanged? And, what of the 'savages' to whom dancers and the Deaf alike are constantly compared?

3. Where Mind Is a Verb: Spatial Orientation and Deixis in Plains Indian Sign Talk and Assiniboine (Nakota) Culture (Farnell 1995)

In Brenda Farnell's work, we find ourselves in the same framework of evolutionary bias that Glasser's and Baynton's descriptions of dancing and deaf-signing emphasize:

> [La Mont] West's work [in 1956] was pioneering because sign languages were not considered by linguists and educators at that time to be real languages -- a battle that is still going on in the education of the Deaf today. In conjunction with a long-standing cultural bias against the body generally, sign languages were considered to be simple codes, probable precursors to spoken language in the evolutionary scheme of things. Indeed considerable interest had been shown in PST by nineteenth-century anthropologists such as E.B. Tylor, precisely because they seemed to provide indisputable evidence of a primitive state (p. 80, this volume).

We are introduced to the direct effects that changes in theory and policy have on the style of living of whole populations of people. "A brief glimpse into the lived experience of the shape of the circle in terms of human relationships and the sense of loss due to the altered shape of contemporary living spaces ..." (Farnell, p. 84, this volume). In the words of Emma Lamebull:

> [L]ike in a tipi we always sat in a circle and looked at each other's faces. When we ate we sat in a circle. When we talked and visit each other, tell stories, we sat in a circle, and when we looked at each other [we] could tell when this person was feeling bad, what his feelings were 'cause you could see their faces. And after the white people came, well then they took our kids to school and instead of looking at each other, they're looking at the back, at the back of heads—you don't see their face no more, you don't know if they're feeling bad or, if they don't feel good you can't comfort them because you can't see their faces. And then the teacher stands up there, teaching you, and in-

stead of trying to make you learn lessons, they teach you your lessons but they learn you how to compete—they learn you to be higher
than this one—you study harder and you get A's and they do things
for you because they learn you how to compete. Even these animals,
we learn to, they learn their children to kill them when they need it—
when they need to eat. When the white people came they turn that
into competing—they wanna see who killed the biggest elk or the
biggest buffalo or the longest fish (pp.84-5).

It will always remain a mystery to me how theory and practical living can be *separated*, as if one existed without the other.
One of the most revealing insights in Farnell's essay, however, is contained in her discussion of Nakota space/time
(pp. 82-86, this volume). Here, we discover the most important reason why the Assiniboine were incomprehensible
to their American colonizers — and the reverse.

Look at Figure 5 (p. 259), remembering that the cardinal
directions represent "the four [tracks of] the winds" to the
Assiniboine, which means that "certain things come toward
a person in contrast to the Euro-American conventional picture of the four directions as lines moving outward from a
given point" (p. 88).

Thus we do not find any equivalent to the time line in ASL, wherein
past time signs use the space *behind* the line of the body, *present* time
signs are located *at* the body, and *future* time signs are *in front*, consistent with the way in which the English language locates time spatially (Baker and Cokely 1980, cited in Farnell 1995: 97 - italics added).

Reading this, I was forcibly reminded of a direct encounter with spatial concepts unlike those of English-speakers a
few years ago while teaching at Moi University in Kenya.
Makiya Lesarge [mah-KEE-yah leh-SAR-gay], was a Maasai
moran (warrior), enrolled at the university in undergraduate
social anthropology:

In a class discussion of orientational metaphors, we talked about
'front/back', and I had explained how English-speaking people generally associate the future with 'front' and the space directly ahead of

them. 'Past' to an English-speaker is 'back' or 'behind'. 'Now' is 'here', where I stand, where my axis of gravity happens to be. As I talked I noticed that Makiya had a withdrawn, puzzled look on his face. I asked him what was the matter. He replied, "I don't think that way," to which I replied, "That's all right. Can you explain how you do think about all this?"

There was a long silence. Then he said, "You go towards the future. I don't. My future comes to me. Death comes to me. I stand. Time moves past, around, over and through me. I don't go into it" (Williams 1993: 85-6).

Relevant to the situation at the time in northeastern Kenya are the circumstances in which Makiya lived: his family graze their cattle in an area sixty-two miles north of Isiolo, Kenya where Somali bandits regularly raid. Maasai war-dances prepare the *ilmurran* [plural of *moran*] for war, thus they perform the dances in deadly earnest. They might be killed, but if they perform well, it is not Makiya who will die, but his Somali enemy.

Human beings may indeed occupy the same *material* universe, but that does not mean that their relationship to nature and their sociolinguistic surroundings are the same. Spoken languages and body languages bind human beings to one another; yet, as we have just seen, they also divide.

4. Traditional Dance: English Ceremonial and Social Forms (Buckland 1994)

In her introduction, Theresa Buckland orientates her readers by providing (a) definitions of 'traditional' dancing, and (b) a lucid discussion of previous scholarship, showing how research into traditional dance forms began in England. She then systematically discusses the kinds of written source materials that are necessary for anthropologists and/or historians to consult if they wish to carry out research in this field. Although her work pertains specifically to English traditional dancing, it is not difficult to see that work on national dancing in other countries would begin in the same way. We can imagine the same kinds of source materials existing for Swedish, French, Italian, Israeli or other national or regional forms of traditional ceremonial and/or social dancing.

On pages 109, 110 and 114 (this volume), Buckland makes an attractive distinction between dances *beyond* living memory, and dances *within* living memory, respectively, illustrating in two sections the kinds of sources that are available in each category. Her essay provides valuable guidelines for investigation, highlighting the important differences between reports of events that are *pseudohistorical* and those that are not.

Many people would argue, of course, that historical events are wholly subjective, that they cannot be validated, and that each individual may have different views of past events. The crucial difference lies in the fact that real historical accounts are firmly established in plausible claims accompanied by compelling supporting evidence. Pseudohistory is distinguished by implausible claims and a significant lack of supporting evidence.

If someone wants to argue that modern forms of dancing are direct inheritors of dancing in the ancient past, then they must examine the evidence for such a theory — *and produce it, if it exists*. However, pseudohistorians are rarely interested in historical or evolutionary facts. Like Curt Sachs (p. 8, this volume), they are more interested in a kind of evolutionary 'quality' or 'flavor'. They seem uninterested in making the considerable efforts required of an historiographer. On the whole, they frequently seem more intent upon promoting a universalist (or some other) agenda, rendering their whole enterprise suspect.

For example, no one knows why the "theory of cultural survival" Buckland talks about (p. 105) was so popular at the turn of the century, and nowhere in the writings of Cecil Sharp and his associates can we find the "pagan origins theory" for English dances supported by real evidence.

At the end of the twentieth century it behooves us to examine *how* we search for the origins of African, Assiniboine, South African and Euro-American dance forms and sign languages.

> Dumont suggests, "Let us suppose that our society and the society under study both show in their system of ideas the same two elements A and B. That one society should subordinate A to B and the other B to A is enough for considerable differences to occur in all their conceptions. In other words, the hierarachy present in a culture is essential for comparison" (1987: 7 - cited in Williams 1995: 51).

The spaces in which human acts occur are more than simple physical spaces. They are simultaneously physical, conceptual, moral, and ethical spaces. The people who generate and occupy these spaces are subjects in their own spoken and body language(s). These complexities should prevent people from arranging dances on a simple-to-complex line of evolution.

Ardener's remarks about intellectual movements that "crystallize in persons and places, countries and university departments" are true (epigraph, p. 1). Ideas *do* become "embodied." They persist. Because of this, they are difficult to change, but it is incumbent on us to try.

Drid Williams, Editor

THOUGHT EXERCISES
(Optional)

1. Evans-Pritchard makes several valuable points in the cited passage on page 2. Can any of these points be applied to the study of sign languages and/or dances?

2. Social evolutionary theory encourages people to think about dancing and signing as "inferior activities" (p. 8). Why? What difference does it make?

3. In the passages below, we find that Darwin's theories of evolution (a) "reinforced European attitudes of racial and cultural superiority"; (b) were "symptomatic of a new understanding of human history" and the place of Deaf signing in that history; (c) created a "framework of evolutionary bias" regarding indigenous peoples in the Americas and (d) spawned a "theory of cultural survival" and a "pagan origins theory" for which no real evidence can be found; i.e.,

(a) "Glasser emphasizes the fact that Darwin's theories of evolution reinforced European attitudes of racial and cultural superiority towards the dances of indigenous populations [of South Africa]" (pp. 9-10).

(b) "The oralist movement in Deaf Education [in America] ...was symptomatic of a new understanding of human history---and of the place of sign language in that history at the end of the nineteenth century" (p. 12).

(c) "In Farnell's work, we soon find ourselves in the same framework of evolutionary bias that we encountered in Glasser's and Baynton's descriptions of dancing and deaf-signing" (p. 13).

(d) "...no one knows why the "theory of cultural survival" ...was so popular [in England] at the turn of the century, and nowhere ...can we find the "pagan origins theory" for English dances supported by real evidence" (p. 17).

On the basis of your reading so far, could you successfully defend this proposition: *Theory and practice can usefully be separated.*

SECTION I
ESSAYS

CHAPTER 1

Sylvia Glasser: Is Dance Political Movement?

SHORT BIOGRAPHICAL NOTE

Sylvia Glasser was born in South Africa. She holds a Diploma from the London College of Dance and Drama and a B.A. with majors in English Language and Classical Life and Thought from the University of Witwatersrand, Johannesburg. Her Master's thesis, *Teaching Children Dance*, was conferred by the University of Houston in Clear Lake, Texas, in 1977. She founded *Moving Into Dance* (a non-segregated dance company and school) in Johannesburg in 1978. In 1992 she established a one-year Community Dance Teachers' Training course for marginalized youth from black townships. She did a three year course in social anthropology at the University of the Witwatersrand from 1987 to 1990 as a mature student. It was there that she met David Hammond-Tooke, Deborah James, David Webster and David Lewis-Williams who were to have a profound influence on her thinking about so-called 'primitive' and/or 'ethnic' dances.

Glasser has taught and choreographed in Canada and the United States and she was a Visiting Fellow at the University of New South Wales (St. George's campus) in Sydney, Australia, in the nineteen-eighties. She has written several articles, among them, 'Fusing the Divided' (Australian Association of Dance Education Conference Proceedings, 1991); 'On the Notion of "Primitive" Dance' [*JASHM*, 1993], 'Appropriation and Appreciation' [Paper for the Society of Dance History Scholars and the Committee on Research in Dance Conference, 1993] and 'Transcultural Transformations', *Visual Anthropology*, 8(2-4): 287-310, 1996.

The following text is a reproduction (retaining English spelling and including minor additions and changes by the editor) of **Glasser, Sylvia. 1991.** Is Dance Political Movement? *Journal for the Anthropological Study of Human Movement* [JASHM] 6(3): 112-122.

[**N.B.** The version in *JASHM* was reprinted with permission from *The Dance Journal*, School of Dramatic Art, Witwatersrand University. The edited version is reprinted by permission of the Editors of *JASHM*].

IS DANCE POLITICAL MOVEMENT?

The Dilemma of Dance in Society

There are two opposing views currently debated in South Africa among the dance community. One holds that 'dance' is political. The contrary opinion is that 'dance' is essentially a-political, occupying a separate domain and is in no sense connected with political matters.

Adherents of the first view would argue that particularly in South Africa (and probably universally), 'dance' or indeed, *any form of cultural expression* is inextricably interwoven into the socio-political, economic and religious fabric of peoples' lives.

Adherents of the second view believe that politics and art should be separated, echoing traditional attitudes towards mixing sport and politics. They say that 'dance' is solely a form of entertainment. Interestingly, it is often those having political power in the society at large who support the idea that art and 'dance' is *not* political, while those who don't have political power (offices, appointments, etc.) tend to support the idea that 'dance' is political.

Another way of conceptualising these two views is to ask whether the arts "mirror" life. That is, do they portray and magnify the realities of life, or do they represent an escape from reality — a fantasy world?

Terminology

Before continuing with a discussion of these issues, some terminological questions need clarification. It is difficult, for example, to discuss dancing or dances in isolation because they are often associated with other forms of the performance arts, i.e. opera, drama and story-telling. Not only that, the word, 'art' is problematic as it tends to suggest a domain of experience that exists on a separate level of reality.

I use the term 'cultural expression' instead of 'art' because it seems less exclusive. Apart from that, in indigenous African cultural forms of expression, dance and music are inextricably linked. The music is part of the dance and vice-versa. Georgina Gore's insights into similar problems in West Africa are apposite:

> To speak of West African dance is in fact a misnomer. As has been well documented (Blacking 1983: 89; Grau 1983: 32; Kaeppler 1985: 92-4; Middleton 1985: 168; Spencer 1985: 140; Williams 1991: 5, 59), the ethnocentricly European term 'dance' is not applicable to systems of structured human body movement of non-European peoples, who have their own terms of reference for conceiving of such activities. For example, in southern Nigeria most ethnic groups have a generic term which includes dance among other activities which are construed as intrinsically sociable and usually rhythmic. The Bini word *iku* refers to 'play', 'dance', 'games' and the Igbo *egwu* to 'play', 'games', 'dance', 'music', song. In Bini the word for 'to dance' is *gbe*, which also denotes 'to beat', while in the related Isoko language *igbe* means 'dance'. The specific meaning of each of these expressions is context-dependent. Individual dances do, however, have their own names ... (Gore 1983: 59).

The word 'traditional' also needs clarification: it is used to refer to that kind of South African dancing which has its source in rituals and rites of passage (birth, initiation, harvests, death) of the rural, black population. These forms have undergone changes due to interactions with neighbouring groups of rural people, as well as transformations in response to migrant labour and proletarianisation.

Defining 'Political' in Relation to 'Dance'

If we are to discuss whether or not 'dance/music' is political, we must establish the sense in which the word 'political' is being used. The narrow, specific usage of 'political' is connected with the state and/or government and its organisation at various levels. There is, however, a more diffuse, broader usage: "belonging to or taking sides in politics; relating to a person's or organisation's status or influence" (OCD). It is in the broader sense that the word, 'political' is used in this essay.

It is easy to dismiss the notion of music as political if one uses the narrow construal of political — to "communicate ideologies and specific ideas," however, the broader political role of music lies in the notion that "aesthetics instigates the changed forms of consciousness needed to generate practical changes in society" (Erlman 1982: 1). Others also see a political function of music, as its performance "generates feelings and relationships between people that enable positive thinking and action in fields that are not musical" (Blacking 1981: 35).

These ideas can be applied to dancing in the same sense as to music in that *dances can act as catalysts for political thought and action*. Also, dances are political in the sense that attitudes toward them or aesthetic values relating to the dance are both forged and influenced by prevailing modes of political action at particular times in history. Moreover, the actual structure — the forms of dances and the ways in which these are transformed is influenced by political actions and attitudes. There were certainly political influences at work in connection with a recent choreography, 'Tranceformations', for the Moving into Dance Company (see Glasser 1996).

Although I argue that dances are political, I'm not saying that they are *only* political. The political aspect is merely one facet of a multitide of elements that contribute to dance formation and expression. To argue that dances are political doesn't ignore the many other functions of the dance, such as individual aesthetic expression, entertainment, recreation, communication and such. Nor do I attempt to minimise the essential roles played by individual performers, teachers or choreographers in creating new dance forms.

I would want to say, however, that although individuals involved in the creative process may not be conscious of political motivations, their position in South African society is politicised for them through the influence of colonialism and *apartheid*, even though these have undergone vast changes in recent years.

The Dance and Culture

Any aspect of the dance needs to be understood in relation to a broad view of culture. That is, 'culture' can be defined as "the state of being cultured, i.e. enlightened, having excellent taste acquired through aesthetic and intellectual training." However, in contrast, 'culture' in its anthropological definition means "the total pattern of human behavior and its products embodied in thought, speech, action and artifacts dependent upon humanity's capacity for learning and transmitting knowledge through the use of tools, language and systems of abstract thought" (WID). Having a broad view of culture therefore means assuming the anthropological definition.

For my purposes, I would want to point out that culture not only connotes a set of symbols, values and beliefs of a people, but their varying responses to circumstances. These circumstances encompass not only the material or economic aspects of culture, but their socio-political activities.

While southern African culture may be thought of or talked about as a whole, groups that exist within it (or any other society) should not be assumed to be the same. To a certain extent, groups within the same society will share aspects of the whole culture, but there is usually great diversity among the smaller groups that comprise the whole. "Just as groups are unequally ranked in terms of wealth and power, so cultures are differently ranked" (Clark 1976: 11). Even within the social categories or classes of culture there will be continuous flux and transformation.

For example, the conflict between classes is often fought at the level of culture and cultural formations are often class-based. However, in South Africa, where one can conceptualise certain cultural forms as class-based to a certain extent (e.g. the ballet as against all other forms of dancing), the concept of a class-based culture such as a 'working class' culture is complicated by black/white oppositions and the entire historical process of colonisation.

Colonial Influences

Colonial attitudes affected the extent and direction of cultural cross-fertilisation in southern Africa. Colonial settlers coming to South Africa brought their dances with them from Europe. Dancing for these Europeans was a form of social communication, recreation and entertainment in the form of court or 'folk' dances. On the other hand, for indigenous South Africans the dance (which included music) was an integral part of their social, religious and political rituals and ceremonies. The dilemma I mentioned earlier — whether 'dance' should be classified as separate from or integrated into other spheres of life — existed in no uncertain terms in the different roles dances occupied in Euro-centred and indigenous cultures. The relationship between these two broad categories of culture, however, hasn't always remained the same.

In the eighteenth century, considerable cross-fertilisation occurred between colonists, indigenous populations and slave populations. 'Coloured'[1] musicians were very influential in forging a popular western 'Cape-performance' culture. Back then, segregation was a matter of social class. *It was not legislated*, thus continuous cultural exchange took place between different groups of people. During a period of about two hundred years in the western Cape when segregation was customary rather than legislated, a popular performance culture developed which was "based on Afrikaans and common to white as well as Coloured people" (Coplan 1983: 10-15). 'Coloured' slaves and free men would perform on rural farms or country dances at official balls, as well as in "racially mixed seaside taverns and dancehall canteens" (Coplan 1985: 10).

In contrast, the history of both social and theatrical dances of the European settlers and their descendants in southern Africa during the latter part of the nineteenth and twentieth centuries has been characterised largely by the *lack* of adoption, absorption or adaptation of local indigenous dance forms. In general, colonial attitudes, especially at the height of British imperialism, were characterised by disdain towards indigenous cultures and populations.

Darwin's theories of evolution reinforced European attitudes of racial and cultural superiority for them and beliefs about inferiority for the indigenous populations. The latter were perceived as 'simple' and 'undeveloped' — generally located on a lower level of civilisation. Their music and dances were seen as primitive, i.e. not worthy of understanding or emulation. These attitudes have persisted and although not backed by legislation or as widely held as they once were, they can still be found today.

Dance communities were not immune. The ethnocentrism of a large percentage of the dance community allowed them to see indigenous black dances as "repetitive and boring." Instead of learning to appreciate the structural subtleties, the rhythmic complexity, the intricate footwork, sudden shifts of weight and the visual counterpoint of juxtaposed body parts, they resorted to racist clichés. Although Johnny Clegg with Juluka and Savuku, Amaponda and groups such as Ladysmith Black Mambazo's, as well as shows such as *Sarafina* have brought African music and dancing to a wide white population, helping to change attitudes, there is a long way to go before entrenched prejudices are replaced by real knowledge and understanding. On the positive side, during the two decades 1970-1990, a small but growing number of choreographers and dance teachers in southern Africa have been working with racially non-segregated dance groups. They have incorporated indigenous elements into their work.

Dances for Children and Dance Companies

When ballet became popular once again in England in the early part of this century,[2] the colonies and dominions followed the trend. Until recently, ballet-dancing was a predominantly elitist activity taught mainly to white children (in the Cape to Coloured children as well). Since both education and residential areas have been segregated, the majority of South

African children have not had access to ballet, modern concert, or other European forms of dancing. Most of the syllabi
taught by the various examining bodies for ballet in South
Africa have been formulated without consideration for the
cultural and socio-economic backgrounds of the majority of
children in the nation. When state-subsidised ballet companies were formed in the early 1960s, they were modelled on
western European prototypes. Although there were some
ventures into indigenous culture through the use of myths
or stories, the form in which this material was expressed was
still based on western aesthetic criteria.

One of the most obvious examples of how politics in this
country has explicitly affected the dance is in the Separate
Amenities Act. For over twenty years there were racially
exclusive Performing Arts Councils, hence racially exclusive
ballet companies. The Cape (always politically more liberal)
had a ballet company which was not exclusively white.

One of the first areas where the colour-bar was broken was
in the state-controlled institutions of the Performing Arts
Councils. PACT's [Performing Arts Council of the Transvaal]
recently formed Dance Company (contemporary modern
dance forms) could not have existed as it presently does two
decades ago because of politics — not because of artistic or
financial considerations. It almost seems superfluous to point
out that the cultural boycott has also affected the dance community, in particular the followers of modern dance.

Dance and the Church

Under the colonial regimen, white missionaries were
largely responsible for both the conversion and education of
indigenous black populations. Most missionaries saw traditional dancing as part of the pagan rituals which they believed must be suppressed. The converted Christian black
people who were forbidden to dance in their customary way
at communal occasions channeled their need for social
musicalisation into Christian congregational singing (Coplan
1985: 29). For these Christians, dancing became separated

from their everyday social and religious life. Traditional South African dancing became the sole preserve of non-Christian black people for some time.

In the early twentieth century, with the advent of established separatist African churches, not only were traditional musical structures introduced into hymn singing, but traditional style dances were used as a form of communal worship. The establishment of separatist churches can be viewed as a form of political protest of black Christians against the totally Euro-centred forms of worship the missionaries imposed in church. Traditionally, dances and music were often (though not always) the means through which trance-like states were reached through which mediums communicated with the ancestors. By re-introducing dancing into worship, the African people were re-affirming the values of their cultural traditions (Blacking 1981: 37*ff*).

Syncretic Forms of Cultural Expression

The formation of many indigenous, syncretic music/dance forms in the slum-yards, townships, hostels and compounds, which started in the last part of the nineteenth century and has continued until the present, can be seen largely as a response to political actions as well as economic conditions. With the discovery of diamonds and gold, there was a demand for a plentiful supply of manual labour. Restrictive legislation culminating in the 1913 Land Act, together with the imposition of hut tax and natural disasters, resulted in a severe shortage of land and cash for rural black people. Migrancy became an increasing necessity for survival. The effect on dancing was that not only did traditional rural forms of cultural expression change through urban contact, but the new urban forms incorporated rural elements.

Although I make no attempt to examine all of these syncretic indigenous dance/music forms, a few will be discussed for the purpose of showing how they embody a complex set of values which may include the political.

Slumyards Give Birth to *Marabi*

The creation of a large number of crowded urban slum-yards in Johannesburg in the early twentieth century was a result of restrictive legislation and poverty. Situated in these slum-yards, the *shebeens* provided a source of income as well as social meeting points. Regular weekend parties with music and dancing were an essential part of the *shebeen* (roughly, 'club' - 'gathering place'). A new class of semi-professional *shebeen* musicians arose. Their music assimilated elements including traditional African, Afro-western, Afrikaans, folk music, American ragtime and jazz into a single urban style called *marabi*. *Marabi* dances which could be performed alone or with a partner were not rigidly structured, but improvised, with the performers drawing on traditional African and western forms of dancing. They used whatever repertoire of movements they knew, exchanged, or picked up. Anthropologically speaking, the new dance form was a true *bricolage*.

Marabi became more than a form of music or dance. It became synonymous with a new culture that arose in the slum-yards. This culture, including the dancing, of course, grew out of a general response to the deprivation and the exclusion of black people. It is important to place this form of cultural expression in its total context: the *shebeens* were illegal, yet people continued to participate frequently in *marabi* music and dancing. Thus, this *marabi* culture can be seen as an expression of resistance. That is, people saw no social stigma in going to jail as a result of raids during *marabi* parties at *shebeens*. By being an integral part of the *shebeen*-based *marabi* culture, the dances and dancing can be seen to be a part of the "resistance to a cruel system" (Themba 1972: 108).

Marabi was not only a form of resistance, "it was also the [embodiment of] the desire of a largely unschooled and un-westernised urban African [population] to modernise by absorbing new cultural elements within a familiar structure" (Coplan 1985: 107). Here, we can see how important it is to examine the location and the context of a dance in order to understand the full significance of its performance. It should not be forgotten that for many of the *shebeen* frequenters, the *marabi* dance was a form of socialising — a way to meet people.

Iscathamiya — Many Messages

Iscathamiya developed out of many other forms of music/dance, including traditional *Ngoma* songs and dances,[3] Zulu wedding songs and dances, Christian hymnody, and American minstrel and ragtime music and dances. It is the very diversity of these sources that enables Erlmann to demonstrate how *Iscathamiya* or its predecessor *mubube* could express — could contain within it — such dissimilar messages as working-class consciousness, urban status, Christianity, rural nostalgia, pan-ethnic African nationalist ideology and Zulu nationalism (Erlmann 1987: 2).

Iscathamiya competitions were (and still are) popular with Zulu migrant workers of the industrial centres of Johannesburg and Durban. The way in which a particular group danced or sang was a way of identifying that group by its members and those outside. The groups had a choice: they could compete in weekly competitions against each other or they could perform together to express their solidarity as black workers for organisations such as the Industrial and Commercial Unions. Whereas the traditional element in *Iscathamiya* has been seen by many as reactionary, Erlmann (1987) points out that the persistence of traditional elements could be an expression of opposition by the migrant workers to capitalism.

The characteristic 'step' of *Iscathamiya* also developed as a response to social change — more specifically, to a change of attire from rural to urban dress. As one of Erlmann's informants puts it, "This is where the 'step' comes from. The 'step' and *ngoma* are different. The difference is that the 'step' allows you to dance with a tie, a suit. ... But with *ngoma* you cannot perform it with a tie, wearing a suit" (From an interview of Mtshali by Erlmann 1977: 21).

Stick Fighting Transformed Into *Isishameni*-Style Dancing

Clegg (1981) describes how traditional stick-fighting matches (in which participants followed rules and no one was hurt), were changed into real life-destroying contests. In the Natal Midlands the appropriation of land and the resulting scarcity of this resource (as well as jobs) led to intense competition between traditional stick-fighting districts. As an increasing number of people were killed by stick-fighting, another cultural response was needed, and it took the form of dance competitions. Many new dances were developed in the *Isishameni* style.

While the development of these dances and the competitions can be viewed as a response to social, political and economic factors, it should not be forgotten that they also provide entertainment and recreation to performers and onlookers, as well as sustaining a sense of sheer physical exuberance and well-being for the dancers. Dance forms can be created for many reasons and dances can have many 'functions' with reference to the larger societies in which they exist.

Apartheid⁴ and Dancing

The architects of *apartheid* saw cultures as bounded, fixed, homogeneous entities. They emphasized the more obvious, superficial differences between people and, they reified cultural traditions. The preservation of traditional cultures as discrete entities, frozen in time, was in keeping with their policies of racial exclusiveness. Tribalism and ethnic purity were promoted as parts of "separate development." Tribal dancing was seen as something that should be preserved in its pure forms and any signs of urban or western influence were seen as a form of cultural bastardisation (James 1990).

As a reaction against government-enforced cultural differentiation and the policy of 'divide and rule', many of the opponents and victims of *apartheid* regarded any emphasis on cultural differences or ethnicity with suspicion. Terminology such as 'ethnic dance', 'tribal dance' or even 'traditional dance' in South Africa have become emotionally loaded concepts. It is not only the words or the terminology of dance classification that have been affected: cultural unity and solidarity are inevitably stressed in response — sometimes at the expense of uniqueness and diversification.

Indeed, the variety of dance forms which exists among different southern African language groups has often been ignored or devalued. They are not seen in terms of their richness as cultural heritages. On the one hand, we have white ethnocentrism and attitudes of cultural superiority — differences seen as rigid, unyielding areas of control. On the other, we have black suspicion of government-promoted 'tribal' dances and dancing coupled with an holistic worldview.

Politics more often than not simply distorts the intricate issues involved, blurring the realities of situations through facile generalisations. People think they must have 'x' or 'y', but not both. Politics create polemics. People feel obliged to oversimplify in order to survive. If the real message is that 'x' and 'y' are complex — not reducible to digitised choices — politics almost never provides satisfying solutions, because *there are no simple solutions*—no simple answers.

The Dance and Protest Theatre

What South Africans call 'protest theatre' is undoubtedly political. Dancing and music have been central to productions expressing the frustration and anger, as well as the aspirations, of the victims of *apartheid* at venues such as the Afrika Cultural Centre, the Funda Centre and the Market Theatre in Johannesburg, as well as the People's Space and Baxter Theatres in Cape Town. Movement and music were as important as the spoken word in productions such as Workshop 71's 'Crossroads', Maponya's 'Hungry Earth', Junction Avenue's 'Sophiatown', Manaka's 'Goree', the Dhloma Theatre Collective's 'Burning Embers' and Ngema's 'Sarafina', among many others.

National and Regional Dances

National variations in folk-dancing are widely found throughout the world. Italian folk dances differ from Slavonic dances, the former having much more elevation than the latter, which have an earthy quality, skimming smoothly over the ground. Within countries, there are regional differences: for example, the dignified, controlled dances from northern Italy (Trescone or Furlana), in contrast to the freer, more relaxed Saltarello and fiery, passionate Tarantella of southern Italy. Similar regional variations exist in South African dances: the undulating, almost lyrical movements of Venda *domba* dancing has different dynamics from the stamping moves reminiscent of the military which characterise the *umgonga* style of Zulu dancing (Clegg 1981: 11).

To carry the cross-cultural analogy further, countries such as Poland, Russia, Spain, Israel and Senegal (all possessing strong dance traditions) have formed professional theatrical folk or 'national' companies which tour throughout the world and have been enthusiastically received. Indigenous South African dances provide ample material for an exciting professional folk dance company. Dances from all the regions could be included and theatricalised if necessary so that one would not be promoting ethnic differences in a divisive sense, but rather acknowledging the values of cultural diversity.

Dancing as Non-Vocalised Communication

The question is often asked, how can 'dance' which is a "non-verbal" art,[5] be political? It is precisely the fact that movement, rather than speech, is used as the vehicle of communication that makes dancing such a powerful tool of expression, in particular for an oppressed people. As I have pointed out, dance/music often expresses sentiments of resistance for a people who are denied verbal, literary expressions of their thoughts and feelings.

There are many cases of dances which are not cases of "harmony" but of disharmony at many levels. The Kalela dance of the Bisa

(Mitchell 1956) is an example, and this is by no means the only instantiation of its kind that can be found. Whole dance forms (e.g. American modern dancing — the theatrical kind) contains elements of social dissonance as its subject matter ... (Williams 1991: 123).

Because dances are not vocalised, they are semantically ambiguous, especially to people who are unfamiliar with the body languages and symbolism used by the dancers. Ideas that might be censored and forbidden in vocalised forms may be suggested through dancing them.

In the Zambian Copperbelt, the workers took part in regular recreational dances, but, as part of the *kalela* dance (Mitchell 1956), they expressed their dissatisfaction with conditions in the mines and made insulting jokes about their white bosses. Their criticisms would have been unacceptable in verbal forms. If doubt still exists about the strong political element in dancing and dances, one needs to look no farther than recent protest marches and demonstrations, in particular the *toyi-toyi*, which is a central part of political protest in South Africa.

Dances and dancing are not only expressions of political feelings, they also influence the perceptions of their participants and viewers, contributing to the transformation of socio-political systems. In South Africa, *where* you dance, *with whom* you dance, *what kind* of dances you perform and *your attitudes toward dancing* will say something about you as a political being, as well as saying something about you as a performer/artist.

I have not attempted to reduce the dance to politics here. Rather, I want to acknowledge that politics are an integral part of the social, economic and religious lives of all peoples. I argue that 'dance' *is* political and for many people, it is 'political movement' which means that we cannot rightly reduce dancing in any form to the status of recreation and entertainment. As South Africa and its politics become normalised, it is possible that dances and dancing will become de-politicised, or the focus of the politicisation may change.

As ethnocentrism gives way to a real openness and willingness to understand and appreciate, so will suspicion give way to cooperation and collaboration in the dance community. In this way, the dance can be seen not only to reflect society, but to influence its very nature in important ways.

[S.G.]

PRECIS 1

[1]There are two opposing views currently debated in [2]South Africa among the dance community. One holds [3]that 'dance' is political. The contrary opinion is that [4]'dance' is essentially a-political, occupying a separate [5]domain and is in no sense connected with political matters.

[6]Adherents of the first view would argue that particu-[7]larly in South Africa (and probably universally), 'dance' [8]or indeed, *any form of cultural expression* is inextricably [9]interwoven into the socio-political, economic and reli-[10]gious fabric of peoples' lives. Adherents of the second [11]view believe that politics and art should be separated, [12]echoing traditional attitudes towards mixing sport and [13]politics. They say that 'dance' is solely a form of en-[14]tertainment. Interestingly, it is often those having politi-[15]cal power in the society at large who support the idea [16]that art and 'dance' is *not* political, while those who [17]don't have political power (offices, appointments, etc.) [18]tend to support the idea that 'dance' is political.

[19]Another way of conceptualising these two views is to [20]ask whether the arts "mirror" life — do they portray [21]and magnify the realities of life — or do they represent [22]an escape from reality — a fantasy world?

[23]Before continuing with a discussion of these issues, [24]some terminological questions need clarification. It is [25]difficult, for example, to discuss dancing or dances in [26]isolation because they are often associated with other [27]forms of the performance arts, i.e. opera, drama and [28]story-telling. Not only that, the word, 'art' is problem-[29]atic as it tends to suggest a domain of experience that [30]exists on a separate level of reality.

[31]I use the term 'cultural expression' instead of 'art' be-[32]cause it seems less exclusive. Apart from that, in indig-[33]enous African cultural forms of expression, dance and [34]music are inextricably linked. The music is part of the [35]dance and vice-versa. Georgina Gore's insights into [36]similar problems in West Africa are apposite:

> [37]To speak of West African dance is in fact a misnomer. As [38]has been well documented ... the ethnocentricly Euro-[39]pean term 'dance' is not applicable to systems of struc-[40]tured human body movement of non-European peoples, [41]who have their own terms of reference for conceiving of [42]such activities. For example, in southern Nigeria most [43]ethnic groups have a generic term which includes dance [44]among other activities which are construed as intrinsi-[45]cally sociable and usually rhythmic. The Bini word *iku* [46]refers to 'play', 'dance', 'games' and the Igbo *egwu* to [47]'play', 'games', 'dance', 'music', song. In Bini the word [48]for 'to dance' is *gbe*, which also denotes 'to beat', while [49]in the related Isoko language *igbe* means 'dance'. The [50]specific meaning of each of these expressions is context-[51]dependent. Individual dances do, however, have their own names ...

[52]The word 'traditional' also needs clarification: it is used [53]to refer to that kind of South African dancing which [54]has its source in rituals and rites of passage (birth, ini-[55]tiation, harvests, death) of the rural, black population. [56]These forms have undergone changes due to interac-[57]tions with neighbouring groups of rural people, as well

[58]as transformations in response to migrant labour and proletarianisation.

[59]If we are to discuss whether or not 'dance/music' is [60]political, we must establish the sense in which the word [61]'political' is being used. The narrow, specific usage of [62]'political' is connected with the state and/or govern-[63]ment and its organisation at various levels. There is, [64]however, a more diffuse, broader usage: "belonging to [65]or taking sides in politics; relating to a person's or [66]organisation's status or influence" .... It is in the [67]broader sense that the word, 'political' is used in this essay.

[68]It is easy to dismiss the notion of music as political if [69]one uses the narrow construal of political — to "com-[70]municate ideologies and specific ideas," however, the [71]broader political role of music lies in the notion that [72]"aesthetics instigates the changed forms of conscious-[73]ness needed to generate practical changes in society" [74]... Others also see a political function of music, as its [75]performance "generates feelings and relationships be-[76]tween people that enable positive thinking and [77]action in fields that are not musical" ...

[78]These ideas can be applied to dancing in the same sense [79]as to music in that *dances can act as catalysts for politi-*[80]*cal thought and action*. Also, dances are political in the [81]sense that attitudes toward them or aesthetic values [82]relating to the dance are both forged and influenced [83]by prevailing modes of political action at particular [84]times in history. Moreover, the actual structure — the [85]forms of dances and the ways in which these are trans-[86]formed is influenced by political actions and attitudes.

Find Definitions

•apposite [line 36]; •a-political [line 4]; •proletarianisation [line 58]; •inextricably [lines 8 and 34]; •aesthetic [lines 72, 81]; •culture(-al) [lines 8, 33]; •catalyst(s) [line 79]; •misnomer [line 37]; •ethnic [line 43].

Having completed definitions for the 86 lines of the précis, are you sure you understand these? ••syncretic [subheading on p. 28]; ••construal [line 2, p. 23]; ••superfluous [line 7 on p. 27]; •• reify (-ed, -ies) [line 3, p. 31]; ••*bricolage (bricoleur)* [line 16 on p. 29]. The latter will require an anthropology dictionary, or an alternative reference source. It refers to a concept first used in anthropology by Claude Lévi-Strauss.

Answer These Questions

I. A. [line 31]: Why does the author use the term "cultural expression" instead of "art"?

B. [lines 1-18]: Briefly state the two opposing views about the dance in South Africa, then state where *you* stand regarding these views.

C. [lines 23-4]: If someone asked you *why* "terminological questions [for the dance] need clarification," what would *you* answer? Which side of the issue, as presented, do you think makes more sense? Why? Do American dancers and writers have the same problems? If you say 'yes', tell why. If you say 'no', tell why.

D. [lines 59-77]: **(a)** Do you think dances are political? **(b)** How effective is Glasser's use of music as an analogy to dance with reference to politics? Finally, **(c)** would *you* have used music or another performing art to illustrate the point she tries to make?

II. There are approximately 525 words in the above précis exercise. *Using no more than 125 words and no less than 80 words,* summarize the 86 line passage. This means you will write a précis of it. Do the work on a separate piece of paper, making sure you indicate word count on the final product.

SECTION I
ESSAYS

CHAPTER 2

Douglas Baynton: "Savages and Deaf-Mutes:" Evolutionary Theory and the Campaign Against Sign Language

SHORT BIOGRAPHICAL NOTE

Douglas C. Baynton is a former American Sign Language inter-preter who has a Ph.D. in History from the University of Iowa. Currently, he is an Assistant Professor of History and American Sign Language at the University of Iowa.

He is the author of *Forbidden Signs: American Culture and the Campaign Against Sign Language* (University of Chicago Press, 1996). Other previous publications include 'A Silent Exile on This Earth: The Metaphorical Construction of Deafness in the Nineteenth Century' (*American Quarterly* 44 - June 1992) and the essay reprinted in this collection.

Recently (1997-98), he was a Fellow at the National Museum of American History of the Smithsonian Institution in Washington D.C. His current research focuses on citizenship debates at the turn of the century; i.e., women's suffrage, immigration policy and African-American civil rights. He explores the use of disability as a justification for inequality, not just for disabled people, but covertly for women and minority groups as well. His thesis is that disability is a fundamental signifier for relations of power. As such, it must be re-situated from the margins to the center of scholarship in the Humanities.

The following text is a reproduction of **Baynton, Douglas. 1995.** "Savages and Deaf-Mutes:" Evolutionary Theory and the Campaign Against Sign Language. *Journal for the Anthropological Study of Human Movement* [JASHM] 8(4): 139-173, 1995. The text is reprinted by permission of the Editors of *JASHM*.

[N.B. We should like to acknowledge the fact that an earlier and shorter version of this essay appeared in 1992 in a collection edited by John Van Cleve entitled *Deaf History Unveiled: Interpretations from the New Scholarship*. Gallaudet University Press].

"SAVAGES AND DEAF-MUTES:" EVOLUTIONARY THEORY AND THE CAMPAIGN AGAINST SIGN LANGUAGE

A late nineteenth century movement to prohibit sign language in the schools dramatically transformed the education of deaf people in the United States. From 1817, when the first American school for deaf pupils was founded, until the 1860s, nearly all educators of the deaf considered sign language indispensable.[1] Several generations of teachers not only used "the noble language of signs," as teachers often termed it, but devoted much effort to using it well (Turner 1848: 78). They respected and admired sign language, cultivated their signing skills with care and pride, and wrote learned treatises on its nature and proper use. Beginning in the 1860s, however, a new generation waged a campaign to replace the use of sign language in the schools with the exclusive use of lip-reading and speech. The reasons for the turn against sign language were many and complex, but among them was the influence of the new theories of evolution. Evolutionary theory fostered a perception of sign languages as inferior to spoken languages, fit only for "savages" and not for civilized human beings.

In the latter decades of the century, two hostile camps developed within the field of deaf education, with the mostly older "manualist" educators defending the use of sign language against their mostly younger "oralist" adversaries. Most schools began offering oral training in the 1860s and 1870s, but this was not the crux of the issue for oralism's advocates. They insisted not only that training in oral communication be offered, but that all classes be conducted *solely* by oral means. Oralists charged that the use of sign language damaged the minds of deaf people, interfered with the ability of deaf children to learn English, and reduced the motivation of deaf children to undertake the difficult but, in their view, crucial task of learning to communicate orally. They sought the complete abolition of sign language in the schools, in hopes that it would then disappear from use outside of the schools as well.[2]

In the larger sense, the oralist movement failed. Sign language continued to be used and vigorously defended by the deaf community. Deaf parents passed sign language on to their children, and those children who were deaf passed it on to their schoolmates. Indeed, even most schools that were trying to discourage the use of sign language found they could not do without it entirely, reserving it for the always substantial number of older "oral failures." Oral communication was simply too impractical for many deaf people, and sign language too cherished by the deaf community, for the latter to disappear completely.[3]

Oralism nevertheless did have a profound impact on deaf education. By the turn of the century, nearly 40 percent of American deaf students sat in classrooms from which sign language had been entirely banned; over half were taught orally for at least part of the day (Bell 1899: 78-9). By the end of World War I, nearly 80 percent of deaf students were taught entirely without sign language (see the *Volta Review* 1920: 372). Oralism remained orthodoxy until the 1970s when sign language began to return to the classroom.

The advocacy of oralism was not new in the late nineteenth century. Oralism had been promoted in the United States before the 1860s, but with little success (Lane 1984: 281-336). Why did manualism remain dominant throughout most of the nineteenth century, only succumbing to the oralist challenge at the end of the century? What had changed?

The campaign against sign language in deaf education was not an isolated phenomenon unconnected to larger developments in American culture. Rather, it was symptomatic of a new understanding of human history — and of the place of sign language in that history — that accompanied the rise of evolutionary theory in the late nineteenth century.

A New Past

This new understanding of human history was evident in the 1899 keynote address by the president of Amherst College, John M. Tyler, to the summer convention of the American Association to Promote the Teaching of Speech to the Deaf. America would "never have a scientific system of education," Tyler insisted to his audience of oralist teachers and supporters, "until we have one based on the history of man's development, on the grand foundation of biological history." Therefore, the "search for ... goal[s] of education compels us to study man's origin and development," he contended, and he then outlined for his listeners the two major theories of that origin and development (Tyler 1899: 19-21). The first was the creationist theory, the belief that "man was immediately created in his present form, only much better morally, and probably physically, than he now is. Man went downhill; he fell from that pristine condition." The second was the theory of evolution. Tyler felt confident that he could "take for granted" the truth of the theory of evolution and that most of his listeners had "already accepted it" (Tyler 1899: 19-21 and 26).

Here was a crucial cultural change that separated those first generations of teachers who used sign language from the later generations who attempted to do away with sign language. Most of the former came of age before the publication of Charles Darwin's *Origin of Species* (1859), and had constructed their understanding of the world around the theory of immediate creation. Most of those opposed to the use of sign language belonged to a younger generation whose world view was built upon an evolutionary understanding of the world.

While natural selection (the mechanism Darwin advanced in 1859 to explain how evolution worked), was not widely accepted in the United States until after the turn of the century, the general idea of evolution itself quickly found widespread acceptance (Bowler 1989, Greene 1981, Ellegard 1990 and Hofstadter 1955).[4] Evolutionary thinking pervaded American culture during the years that oralism became dominant in deaf education. That is, evolutionary analogies, explanations and ways of thinking were ubiquitous. Psychologists theorized mental illness as evolutionary reversion. Criminologists defined "the criminal type" as a throwback.

Social policies were defended or attacked on the basis of their ostensible likelihood to further or stunt evolution. Even sin came to be described as "a falling back into the animal condition."[5]

Evolutionary theory set the terms of debate in deaf education as well. It was no coincidence that oralist theory began to transform deaf education in the United States during the same period that evolutionary theory was radically changing how Americans defined themselves and their world. The most important aspect of that change for deaf people and their education occurred in attitudes toward language — specifically the relative status and worth of spoken and gesture languages.

New Responsibilities

Tyler continued his address by admonishing his audience of teachers that the recent discovery of the laws of evolution gave them important new responsibilities. While humanity was "surely progressing towards something higher and better," there was no guarantee that it would continue to do so (1899: 22). Echoing a neo-Lamarckian interpretation of evolutionary theory common at the time, one that was especially popular in the United States, Tyler explained that continued human evolutionary progress would require active effort (Bowler 1989:296-99). The human race would continue its onward and upward course only if certain "bequests from our brute and human ancestors" were consciously eliminated. Quoting from an unidentified poem, he exhorted his listeners to "Move upward, working out the beast/And let the ape and tiger die" (Tyler 1899: 22 and 26).

Just as the adult must put away childish things, Tyler explained, so must the human slough off that which is brutish. By studying the characteristics that separated the higher animals from the lower and tracing "how Nature has been training man's ancestors at each stage of their progress," teachers could find vital "hints as to how we are to train the child today." If, in short, they could "find what habits, tendencies, and powers Nature has fostered, and what she has sternly repressed" then they would know what they ought to encourage and what to repress. It was crucial, Tyler insisted, to "make our own lives and actions, and those of our fellows, conform to and advance" what had been the upward "tendency of human development in all its past history [else our] lives will be thrown away"(1899: 22-26).

Tyler's speech would have held no surprises for his listeners. His ideas were the common currency of educated and popular discourse by 1899. Nothing he said would have seemed the slightest bit radical or unusual to his audience of oralist teachers. Indeed, it would have confirmed beliefs already firmly held and (to their eyes) explicitly associated with their work — an association that concerned the relationship, for their generation, between speech and gesture, on the one hand, and humanity and lower evolutionary forms of life on the other.

Condillac and the History of the Species

It was commonly speculated throughout the nineteenth century that humans had relied upon some form of sign language before they had turned to spoken language (see Hewes 1973: 5; Diamond 1959: 265; Sommerfelt 1954: 886-892 and Tylor 1878: 15). The idea seems to have originated with the French philosopher Etienne Bonnot de Condillac in the mid-eighteenth century. When Condillac historicized Locke's empiricist epistemology, taking Locke's explanation of the psychological development of the individual and projecting it onto the history of the human species, he naturally directed his attention to the question of the origin and development of language. In a section of his *Essay* (1746) subtitled "On the Origin and Progress of Language" Condillac began with the conventional affirmation that reason and speech were gifts from the Creator to "our first parents." Having satisfied orthodoxy, he then went on to speculate about how language might have been invented by people if by some chance it had been necessary to do so — say, if two untutored chil-

dren had survived the great flood alone and had had to create a new language between them. Suggesting this hypotheti-
cal circumstance allowed Condillac to theorize, from a basis
of sensualist philosophy, that such children would first be
limited to inarticulate cries, facial expressions, and natural
gestures in their communication with each other.[6]

In the *Essay*, Condillac supposed that gestures — or what
he called the "language of action" — would be confined to
the early stages of linguistic and intellectual development,
and because of its inferiority would gradually be superseded
by speech. However, as the German historian Fischer has
recently pointed out (1993: 431-33), Condillac markedly re-
vised this view in his *Grammar* (1775), after visiting the Institution for Deaf-Mutes in Paris where he conversed with its
founder, the Abbé de l'Epée.

He came to believe that the "language of action" was not
necessarily inferior to speech in what it could communicate,
and that it could be "extended sufficiently to render all the
ideas of the human mind." What Fischer called "this
revolutionary view" about the independence of language
efficiency from its medium was also the view of most nineteenth-century American manualists, with one important
difference. Unlike Condillac, the manualist assertions that
language was originally a gift from God were not mere for-
malities, but matters of fundamental belief.

By the nineteenth century, the question of the origin of language had become an important topic of philosophical discussion. Condillac's theory of the primacy of gesture had
found a great many adherents. Manualist teachers, most of
them college-educated men, were well aware of the discussion. As experts on sign language, they were naturally interested in the possibility that gestures preceded speech, and
they frequently alluded to the theory in their professional
journals and conferences. They were pleased by, and took
pride in, the idea that "sign or gesture language is of great
antiquity," that "many philologists think that it was the original language of mankind," and that sign language might have

been "in the designs of Providence, the necessary forerunner of speech."[7]

As evangelical Protestants, manualists interpreted the theory in terms of Biblical history. According to their creationist understanding, humanity had come into the world essentially in its present form. They disagreed on finer points, for instance the precise nature of the first humans. Some held to the literal story in Genesis, arguing that God had created Adam and Eve with a complete language ready for use. Others sought to adapt the Biblical account to recent intellectual trends, treating it more loosely, suggesting that God had originally given humans the capacity for language and had left them to develop that capacity themselves over time.

Of those who believed that language developed over time, many argued that some form of gesture or sign language must have been used before spoken language (see Peet, 1855: 20 for extended discussion, and Valade 1873: 31). But, even though humans were thought perhaps to have developed in some ways since the creation, such as in language, it was widely held that humans had remained the same morally and intellectually — or that these faculties had actually degenerated (Peet 1855: 15 and Tyler 1899: 20). The idea that sign language preceded speech did not imply inferiority within the framework of the manualists' Protestant beliefs — indeed, it was a mark of honor.

Different Interpretations

Oralist educators of the late nineteenth century, however, would show an even greater interest in the idea that sign language preceded speech, and give a very different interpretation to its significance. To the manualist generation, "original language" meant "closer to the Creation." It held different connotations for post-Darwin oralists, for whom it meant, instead, closer to the apes. According to the theory of evolution, humanity had risen rather than fallen. It was the end product of history rather than its beginning. In an evolutionary age, language was no longer an attribute inherent in the human soul, one of an indivisible cluster of abilities that included reason, imagination, and the conscience, conferred by God at the Creation. It was, instead, a distinct ability achieved through a process of evolution from animal ancestors. Sign language came to be seen as a language low in the scale of evolutionary progress, preceding in history even the most "savage" of spoken languages and supposedly forming a link between the animal and the human. The "creature from which man developed in one direction, and the apes in another," probably used rudimentary forms of both gesture and speech, as one writer in *Science* speculated. While in humans the "gesture language was developed at first," speech later supplanted it. On the other hand, "in the apes the gesture-language alone was developed" (Jastrow 1886: 555-56).

Linguists of the late nineteenth century commonly applied to language theory what has been called "linguistic Darwinism." Inferior languages died out, they argued, and were replaced by superior languages in the struggle for existence (Stam 1976: 242-250). Gestural communication seemed to have been an early loser. The American philologist, William Dwight Whitney, for example, believed that human communication once consisted of "an inferior system of ... tone, gesture, and grimace;" it was through the process of selection and survival of the fittest that the voice has gained the upper hand" (Whitney 1876: 291).

The Stigma of Inferiority

The languages of early humans could not be directly studied, of course. No fossils are left recording speech, gesture or expressions of the face. Anthropologists,[8] however, began in the latter decades of the nineteenth century to see the so-called "savage races" as examples of earlier stages of evolution. Assuming a model of linear evolutionary progress, they depicted them — Africans, American Indians, Australian Aborigines and others — as "living fossils" left behind by the more rapidly progressing cultures (see Bowler 1989: 233 and Hoxie 1989: 115-145). This way of understanding evolution provided them with an ostensible means of studying early human cultures and language.

An eminent British social anthropologist Edward B. Tylor, for example, noted in his *Researches Into the Early History of Mankind* that

> Savage and half-civilised races accompany their talk with expressive pantomime much more than nations of higher culture, [indicating that] in the early stages of the development of language ... gesture had an importance as an element of expression, which in conditions of highly-organised language it has lost (Tylor 1878: 15 and 44).

Although Tylor took a great interest in gestural languages and was apparently familiar with British Sign Language [BSL] besides having friends who were deaf, he held to the prevailing evolutionary assumption that sign language was a primitive — and therefore inferior — form of communication.[9]

Garrick Mallery, a retired U.S. Army colonel who studied American Indian cultures for the Bureau of Ethnology at the Smithsonian Institution, was probably the foremost expert in the nation on Indian sign languages. His articles and lectures were sometimes reprinted in the *American Annals of the Deaf*. Along with anthropologists, he believed that while early humans had probably not used gestures to the complete exclusion of speech, it was likely that "oral speech remained rudimentary long after gesture had become an art."

While Mallery associated sign language use with a lower stage of evolution, he nevertheless had a genuine fascination and respect for sign languages, as Tylor did. He defended aboriginal users of sign language against charges that they employed gestures only because their spoken languages were deficient. The common traveler's story that some aboriginal spoken languages were not sufficient by themselves to permit conversations after dark was not true, he insisted. He argued that the use of sign language was largely a function of the number of disparate languages spoken within a region since, he thought, the primary use of sign language was inter-tribal communication. Many of these ideas have been (and are being) amended, of course. In a recent and fascinating book, Farnell has corrected the long-held assumption that Indian Sign Language (or Plains Sign talk, [PST] as it is more properly called) functioned only as a *lingua franca* for intertribal communication (Farnell 1995b: 1-3). She discovered that among the Assiniboine people of northern Montana, at least, PST is an integral part of the language for everyday interactions and especially for formal story-telling.

Still, Mallery viewed the transition to speech as a clear indication of human progress. For example, the invention of writing influenced people to "talk as they write" and therefore to gesture less. He speculated that gesture signs were most common among people who hunted ("the main occupation of savages") because of the need for stealth. Sign language was then used in other contexts simply by force of habit. To Mallery, it was undeniable that the use of gestures existed in "inverse proportion to the general culture." He concluded that the most notable criterion for distinguishing between "civilized" and "savage" peoples was to be found "in the copiousness and precision of oral language, and in the unequal survival of the communication by gesture signs which, it is believed, once universally prevailed" (Mallery 1880b: 13 - reprinted in Sebeok 1978).[10] Mallery did not believe, however that sign languages were *inherently* inferior or primitive. Indeed, he argued that they could potentially express any idea that spoken languages could. Nearly one hundred years before modern linguists rediscovered sign language and began to take them seriously as authentic languages, Mallery spoke confidently of "conclusive proof that signs constitute a real language." His argument, rather, was that sign languages were *historically* inferior — that is, they were relatively undeveloped because less used in recent times than spoken languages.

The distinction between *inherent* inferiority and *historical* inferiority that Mallery made, however, was not often observed by popular writers or the critics of sign language in deaf education. For most people, sign language was simply the inferior language of inferior peoples, thus the language used by deaf people became increasingly linked in the public mind with the languages of "savages." References such as Tylor's to "the gesture-signs of savages and deaf-mutes" (1878: 547) became commonplace in both popular and scholarly publications.

Darwin himself wrote of gestures as a form of communication "used by the deaf and dumb and by savages" (1872: 61). After noting that sign languages were "universally prevalent in the savage stages of social evolution," Mallery suggested that it was likely that "troglodyte" humans communicated "precisely as Indians or deaf-mutes" do today (1880b: 12-14).

A contributor to *Science* magazine commented that sign languages were used by "the less cultured tribes, while the spoken language is seen in its highest phase among the more civilized," adding that sign language was also used "in the training of the deaf and dumb" (Jastrow 1886: 556). A reporter for the *New York Evening Post*, in an article on the prolific gestures of Italian immigrants, noted that

> Philosophers have argued that because among most savages the language of gesture is extensive ... [the use of gesticulation with or in lieu of speech is a] sign of feeble intellectual power, and civilization must needs leave it behind (cited in Fox 1897: 398 and 400).

He pointed out that deaf people as well as American Indians also use gestures to communicate.

The Idea of Progress

One might expect the literature of deaf education to deal in more concrete terms with issues related to the actual lives of deaf people, but here, too, the association of sign language with peoples considered to be "inferior" colored all discussions. Oralist teachers worried that sign language was "characteristic of tribes low in the scale of development" (Gordon 1899: 206). Gardiner B. Hubbard, president of the Clarke Institution (one of the first oral schools) complained that the sign language of deaf people "resembles the languages of the North American Indian and the Hottentot of South Africa" (1868: 5). J.D. Kirkhuff of the Pennsylvania Institution asserted that "as man emerged from savagery, he discarded gestures for the expression of his ideas," thus it followed that deaf people ought to discard them as well, and it fell upon their teachers to "emancipate the deaf from their dependence upon gesture language" (Kirkhuff 1892: 139).

A leading oralist in England, Susanna E. Hull, wrote that since spoken language was "the crown of history," to use sign language with deaf children was to "push them back in the world's history to the infancy of our race." Since sign language was the language of "American Indians and other savage tribes," she asked, "shall sons and daughters of this nineteenth century be content with this?" (Hull 1877: 236). According to Katherine Bingham, the sign language of deaf people was identical to the gestures used by "a people of lowest type" found to exist "in the ends of the earth where no gleam of civilization had penetrated" (1900: 22).

The theory that speech supplanted sign language in an evolutionary competition was so common that the oralist Emma Garrett could make an elliptical reference to it as early as 1883, assuming her readers would understand the allusion: "If speech is better for hearing people than barbaric signs, it is better for the deaf; being the 'fittest, it has survived'" (Garrett 1883: 18). In 1910, oralists were still arguing the same point in the same way; that it was wrong "to leave [deaf people] a few thousand years behind the race in the use of that language of signs from which human speech has been evolved" (Crouter *n.d.*, from the Gallaudet Archives).

Manualists had been well aware, of course, that American Indians used sign language. In fact, delegations of Indians were occasional visitors to schools for the deaf where they conversed with deaf students and teachers in pantomimic signs. On one such occasion at the Pennsylvania Institution in 1873, as Mallery explained it,

> it was remarked that the signs of the deaf-mutes were much more readily understood by the Indians than were theirs by the deaf-mutes, and that the latter greatly excelled in pantomimic effect (1880a: 7).

Mallery thought this was not surprising "when it is considered that what is to the Indian a mere adjunct ... is to the deaf-mute the natural mode of utterance."[11]

While manualists often compared the sign language of deaf people to that of American Indians, in the same paragraph they were apt to compare it to the high art of pantomime cultivated by the ancient Romans, or note the syntactical features it shared with ancient Latin, Greek, Hebrew or Chinese languages (Peet 1868: 4 and 6-7).[12] If sign language appeared to have been used more in the past than in the present, this did not imply inferiority to them in the same way it would for the oralist generation. When the manualists thought of "progress," it was social progress, an accumulation of knowledge and accomplishment, not an improvement in the actual physical and intellectual capacities of human beings. As Harvey Peet affirmed for his colleagues in 1855:

> We find in our philosophy no reason to reject the Scriptural doctrine, that the first man was the type of the highest perfection, mental and physical, of his descendants. Races of men sometimes improve, but, in other circumstances, they as notoriously degenerate. It is at least full as philosophical to suppose the inferior races of men to have been degenerate descendants from the superior races, as to suppose the converse (Peet 1855: 16).

Competing Theories

One theory of history for the manualists' generation was that civilizations rose and fell rather than climbed continuously. Languages and peoples did not ascend ever higher over the course of history, but rather had their birth, growth and culmination, "like the language of the Hebrews for instance, or the splendid tongues of Greece and Rome" (Peet [Isaac] 1890: 214). Languages could not perpetually progress, for the "tendency of every language is toward change, decay, and ultimate extinction as a living organism" (Wilkinson 1881: 167). The examples of Sanskrit, Hebrew, Greek and Latin were evidence that all languages changed over time and finally "passed into that doom of death and silence which awaits alike the speaker and the speech" (Wilkinson 1881: 167). Languages changed, but they could as well decline as improve. There was no reason to assume that present languages were better than past ones.

Americans who came of age in the late nineteenth century looked to a different past than this. Because sign language was supposed to have been superseded long ago by speech, it was to their way of thinking necessarily inferior. As such, it deserved extinction. An oralist in 1897, pointing out that manualists had often commented upon the similarities between the sign languages of American Indians and deaf people, suggested that he would not question the truth of this observation nor deny that it was worth noting. He would attribute to the observation, however, a very different significance than had his predecessors. While "savage races have a code of signs by which they can communicate with each other," he wrote, surely "we have reached a stage in the world's history when we can lay aside the tools of savagery" (Wright 1897: 332-3). Because of progress in enlightenment, schools were "fortunately able now to give our deaf children a better means of communication with men than that employed by the American Indian or the African savage" (Wright 1897: 333-4).

And just as sign language had been supplanted by speech in the advance of civilization, so too was the use of sign language in deaf education — like all the ideas of "a cruder and less advanced age" (1897: 334) — being rendered unnecessary by progress.

If oralists associated sign language with Africans who, in evolutionary terms were considered to be "savages," then what did they do when they encountered African-American deaf students? Information specifically on the education of black deaf children is difficult to come by. The subject was rarely raised at conferences or addressed in school reports and educational literature. At least in the American south, however, where schools for the deaf (like schools for the hearing) were typically segregated, oral education was clearly not extended to blacks on the same basis as whites.

For example, at the 1882 meeting of the Convention of American Instructors of the Deaf, after the superintendent of the North Carolina Institution had given a report on the new oral program established in his school, he was asked, "has any experiment been made in the institution to teach colored children?" The superintendent replied

> [I]n a separate building, one mile from the main institution, there are thirty colored children ... with a separate teacher in charge. No instruction has been given in articulation, and none will be given at present (Discussion 1882: 105-6).

African-American Deaf Students

Five southern schools for black deaf students were listed in the *American Annals of the Deaf* annual directory in 1920, those located in North Carolina, Texas, Maryland, Virginia and Oklahoma. Most of the schools were never listed — for example, the Georgia and Mississippi schools, both established in 1882 — because, even though they were physically separated from the main school, they were not formally independent but rather "colored departments" under the direction of the white school (See *Annals* 1882: 125-6).

In 1920, the Virginia State School for Colored Deaf and Blind Children and the Oklahoma Industrial Institution for the Deaf, Blind and Orphans of the Colored Race, were the only two schools in the United States that still described themselves as "manual." By this time, all other schools for the deaf described themselves as "oral" or "combined." White schools in Virginia and Oklahoma were listed as "combined," with the majority of their students being taught orally.

North Carolina did teach slightly over half of its black students orally, but four out of five of its white students were so taught. Maryland used oral methods with two of the twenty-four black deaf students it had in its student population, but oral methods were used with 110 out of 129 white students. The Texas Deaf, Dumb and Blind Institute for Colored Youths had converted from "manual" to "combined" about ten years earlier; nevertheless, by 1920, it was still teaching fewer than a third of its students by oral methods, while at the Texas school for white deaf students, nearly three-fourths of the students were taught orally. In addition, the school reported that only one of its twelve teachers was an oral teacher and that the oral class consisted of thirty pupils — a size that would effectively preclude successful teaching by oral methods in the view of oral teachers then, and today. In contrast, the Texas school for white students had an average of ten pupils in their oral classes, which was the typical size in other state schools for oral classes.[13]

Apparently, overcrowded classes were a general problem at black schools in the South. A black deaf teacher from the North Carolina school, Thomas Flowers, expressed to the 1914 convention of teachers his hope that soon, "certain discouraging features will be lifted from the teachers of the colored deaf" so that "the work will then give results." Among these discouraging features were poor facilities, low pay for teachers and "the large and miscellaneous classes" (1915: 100).

A survey of black schools for the deaf finally appeared in the *Annals* (see Settles 1940) much later than the period under consideration here. That survey reported that of sixteen segregated schools or departments for black deaf children, eleven were still entirely manual. While other schools throughout the south joined northern schools in pushing deaf people to "rise" (as they saw it) "to full humanity" by abjuring sign language, this was apparently not considered significant for deaf people of African descent. Because of the continued use of sign language in the classroom, however, the ironic result of this policy of discrimination may have been that southern deaf African-Americans, in spite of the chronic underfunding of the schools, received a better education than most deaf white students.

The provision of oral or manual education according to race may not have prevailed to the same degree in the North, but the evidence is harder to find and more circumstantial, since there were no separate schools for blacks there. Thomas Flowers had been a student in the oral program at the Pennsylvania Institution from 1886 to 1895 where, as he later wrote, the teachers "saw beyond this dusky skin of mine, into my very soul." Since, in 1908, he wrote that he had been the first black student to graduate from the Pennsylvania Institution and the first deaf student to graduate from Harvard University, he does not, however, appear to have been a typical case.[14]

When, at the 1914 convention, the superintendent from North Carolina averred that "North Carolina was the first state in establishing institutions for the colored race, although other states are falling into line," Philip Gillett (superintendent of the Illinois school) immediately rose to protest: "Illinois has had an institution for colored deaf-mutes for over thirty years." With heavy sarcasm he added that this institution was in fact the same one that white students attended. Black students, he was proud to say, "have always attended on precisely the same basis and have the same advantages that the whites have had" (*Discussion*, 1882: 105-6).

On the other hand, the Clarke Institution in Northampton, Massachusetts, the pre-eminent oral school in the country, makes no mention in its annual reports of accepting black pupils or training black teachers during this period, and, in 1908, it appears to have affirmed a policy of excluding blacks. During that year, an African-American woman made inquiries about entering the Clarke School training program for teachers. The principal of the school, Caroline Yale, wrote to Mrs. Alexander Graham Bell, who had inquired on the young woman's behalf, to express doubts about accepting the student. The Clarke School had "never had an application for a colored student in our Normal department before," she wrote, and she doubted "whether with the large number of southern teachers which we have this could be done." She was "certain that some of our southern girls would violently object" and worried that "we should very likely lose some or all of them" (Yale 1908).

This limited and circumstantial evidence is far from conclusive. In any case, before the great migration of African-Americans to the North after the First World War, there were relatively few black people living in the northern states. Given the low incidence of deafness marking a percentage of the total population, few black children would have attended northern schools for the deaf. The Washington D.C. school for the deaf, however, had eight or nine black students out of a total of sixty students in 1886. According to Gallaudet,

> in the sleeping apartments and at the table they are separated in deference to the caste prejudice, which still continues in our country to a certain extent, but in the classes they come together (see Gordon 1892: 12).

Gallaudet gave no indication, however, of whether they were generally taught by the same methods or followed the same course of study.

The Construction of Evolutionary Progress

Race was not the only issue involved in the hierarchical construction of evolutionary progress. As a linguistic atavism, sign language was portrayed not only as a throwback to "savagery" and "barbarism," but, worse yet, as a return to the world of the beast. One of the effects of evolutionary theory, after all, was to change the way that people answered the question, "What is it that separates us from the animals?" Animals have always been the "ultimate other" for human beings. Throughout history, people have defined themselves in relation to them. Every culture keeps available a large stock of answers to the question of what makes humans unique: for example, humans possess reason, histories and cultures; they can feel pain and suffer; they have self-consciousness and consciences; they use tools and alter their environments. One could compile a very long list of such attempts (and they are intriguingly persistent attempts) definitively to distinguish humanity from every other species of creature (see Thomas 1983; Midgely 1979; Turner 1980 and Singer 1975: 192-222).

"What separates us from the animals?" is a question of rich potential for the student of human culture. Much of how a people define themselves, their sense of individual and cultural identity, can be found in their answers to this most basic of questions — what Thomas Huxley called "the question of questions for mankind" (cited in Roberts 1988: 51). For the manualists of the early to mid-nineteenth century, the possession of an immortal soul was the pre-eminent characteristic that distinguished humans from all other species. Contained within the concept of the soul were other, subsidiary signs of human uniqueness, faculties such as language, morality and reason, which humans had and animals did not. These however, were conceived to be secondary to (and existing merely as a result of) the human soul.

The manualist teacher Luzerne Rae, for example, in 1853, described thoughts and feelings as the "spiritual children of the spirit," meaning that they were manifestations of spirit and therefore spiritual themselves (1853: 157-8). Language, on the other hand, was the "sensible form" of the spiritual. That is, it made the spiritual accessible to the senses and was the material expression of the higher, non-material realm. Language, then, whether in its aural or visual form, did not take place within spirit, but was merely the outward means of communication between spiritual beings who existed perforce in a physical state. It was only the "embodiment" of thoughts and feelings into language that could "enable them to pass through the senses." Language was physical (Rae called it "the body of thought") and therefore secondary and derivative. Spirit was primary and original (1853: 157-8).

a. Language

Language was conceived to be an important characteristic of humanity, but it did not define humanity. It was merely the visible expression of the invisible essence within. In 1850, the manualist Harvey Peet allowed that "language is one of the surest tests of humanity," but hastened to add that "language" was by no means the equivalent of "speech." Deaf

education had been rarely attempted in the past, he explained, because until recently, "the power of speech seemed
the only difference between reasoning beings and animals
devoid of reason" (1855: 19; also see Peet 1850: 107). While
spoken and gestural languages were undeniably different

> in material, in structure, in the sense which they address, and in the
> mode of internal consciousness, [nevertheless the] man whose lan-
> guage is a language of gestures ... is still, not less than his brother
> who possesses speech, undeniably a man. ... Another prerogative that
> distinguishes man from the most sagacious of the mere animal cre-
> ation ... yet higher than language ... is religion (Peet 1855: 9 and 20-
> 24).

While language was of great importance, it remained secondary — and 'religion' for him consisted pre-eminently in
the knowledge of a Creator and of the immortal soul within.

The foremost task of the Reverend Collins Stone, a
manualist teacher at the Hartford school, was "imparting to
the deaf and dumb a knowledge of the soul." He accomplished this, he explained, by calling the attention of his students to the ways in which they differed from the things and
creatures around them: "there is something in the child which
they do not find in trees, animals, or anything else." This
"wonderful 'something' is not his body, or any part of it."
Within this "something" resided intelligence, imagination,
the ability to use language, and the moral sense. It conferred
immortality. Once the pupils understood that it is "this that
'thinks and feels' and makes us differ from the animals and
things about us," they are then "prepared to be told that the
power that manifests itself in these different ways is called
the soul." Without that knowledge, the uninstructed deaf
person was reduced "to the level of mere animal life," capable only of "mere animal enjoyment" (Stone 1848:137-141).
This definition of education was widely shared by the teachers of Stone's generation.

Woodruff lamented that without education, the deaf person was "looked upon, by many, as well-nigh a soulless being, having nothing in common with humanity but his physi-

cal organization, and even that imperfect" (1848: 195). With an education made possible by the use of sign language, Henry Camp wrote, deaf people could be "raised from their degraded condition — a condition but little superior to that of the brute creation — and restored to human brotherhood" (Camp 1848: 214-15). For J. A. Ayres, the "right development of moral and religious character is the most important part of all education." With the use of sign language, "the deaf-mute is restored to his position in the human family, from which his great loss had well nigh excluded him, and is enabled to hold communion with man and with God" (Ayres 1848: 223). Coming to know God was the greatest aim of education, and one could not know God without first knowing about the soul. If deaf people were not "led to conceive of a thinking agent within them, distinct from their corporeal existence," then they could "form no correct conception of God, who is spirit" (Peet, I.L. 1851: 212).

The historian, Paul Boller, among many others, has written of the "shattering effect" that evolutionary theory had on "traditional religious thought about ... the uniqueness of man" (Boller 1850: 212). While traditional religious beliefs about the place and nature of humankind were certainly challenged and altered, the belief in the uniqueness of the human continued unabated. Explanations for that uniqueness were adjusted to meet new realities, and by the late nineteenth century the most common explanation for why humans were fundamentally different from other animals was no longer that they possessed a soul, but that they possessed articulate speech (or alternatively, intelligence, of which speech was both the crowning achievement and necessary concomitant). As Thomas Huxley, the great defender of Darwin's theory, wrote, "reverence for the nobility of manhood will not be lessened by the knowledge, that Man is ... one with the brutes, for he alone possesses the marvelous endowment of intelligible and rational speech" (Huxley 1906: 104).

The belief that speech is the crucial attribute that separates humans from the animals is by no means associated exclusively with evolutionary thought. The idea was hardly new — it goes back at least to ancient Greece, and can be found throughout the nineteenth century in European and American literature. However, during the first half of the nineteenth century in America, the possession of a soul became the predominant expression of fundamental difference between humans and animals. During the latter half of the century the emphasis shifted to the possession of speech.

b. The Concept of Soul

Part of the reason for this shift was the argument, made by Darwin in the *Descent of Man*, that the faculties that earlier had been placed under the higher and unifying concept of the soul (which were explained by the existence of the soul and had appeared clearly to separate humans from the animal kingdom), were in fact present in less developed form in other animals. Abilities that had previously been regarded as unambiguously human were instead explained as more highly evolved forms of abilities that had first appeared at earlier stages of evolution. The idea of a soul, Darwin (and others) argued, was no longer necessary to explain them (Darwin 1896: 65-96).

The soul was not, at any rate, easily adapted to an evolutionary explanation of the human past. To speak of the possession of a soul as the characteristic that separated the human from the animal and at the same time to speak of humans developing from animals was problematic at best. At what point did humans acquire souls? Did immortal souls evolve like other attributes, or had they been specially created at some point and infused into creatures previously not human?

The concept of a soul certainly can be, and has been, by many religious thinkers reconciled with evolutionary theory. However, in the same way that the "argument from design" — that is, the theory that the adaptation of living things to their environment was evidence of a designing intelligence — was rendered unnecessary and marginalized by evolutionary theory (though of course it could not be disproved), so was the soul made unnecessary as an explanation for human capabilities.

In addition, evolutionary theory was but one aspect of a general movement toward scientific naturalism in public discourse. In both scientific and public discourse, the soul as an explanation for human nature diminished rapidly in importance. As nineteenth-century American Christians had been used to speaking of the term, the soul was neither convenient to think of as a product of evolution nor amenable to scientific description. See Roberts (1988: 176-79 and 205-207); Carter (1971: 85-107); Moore (1979: 232-33, 266-67 and 336-37); Pearson (1916: 4-23) and Oldroyd (1980: 250-52). Speech, on the other hand, was both.

Focus on Speech

Huxley wrote that an important part of the explanation for the "intellectual chasm between the Ape and the Man" involved the senses and muscles necessary for the "prehension and production of articulate speech."

> Possession of articulate speech is the grand distinctive character of Man [and a] man born dumb [he continued] would be capable of few higher intellectual manifestations than an Orang or a chimpanzee, if he were confined to the society of dumb associates (Huxley 1906: 95-96).

Sociologists such as Cooley agreed that the "achievement of speech is commonly and properly regarded as the distinctive trait of man, as the gate by which he emerged from his pre-human state" (Cooley 1909: 70; see also Giddings 1916[1898]: 238-241). Books designed for high schools and academies echoed the point: "animals have a variety of natural cries. Speech belongs to man alone" (Overton 1908[1891]: 298). Educators of the deaf also began to allude to this reformulation of human uniqueness.

An oral teacher at the Pennsylvania Institution entered into her monthly report the observation that despite the difficulties of oral training, speech was "one of the distinguishing characteristics between man and the lower order of animals — we think it is worth the labor costs" (Garrett 1882). The founder of Chicago's McCowen Oral School for Young Deaf Children thought that learning to speak was "the highest act of human evolution" and wrote about the lack of speech as a condition from which deaf children could "gradually rise" (McCowan 1907: 258-59). One of the founders in 1867 of the Clarke Institution wrote that "the faculty of speech more than the faculty of reason, puts mankind at a distance from the lower animals" (Dudley 1884: 7). He elsewhere suggested that deaf people who used sign language felt themselves to be less than human. When he visited a school in which sign language was used, the children looked at him

> with a downcast pensive look which seemed to say, 'Oh, you have come to see the unfortunate; you have come to see young creatures human in shape, but only half human in attributes; you have come here much as you would go to a menagerie to see something peculiar and strange' (Dudley 1882: 7).

He contrasted the demeanor of these children with that of a young girl he had met who had recently learned to speak: "the radiant face and the beaming eye showed a conscious-ness of elevation in the scale of being. It was a real eleva-tion" (1882: 7).

Not only was speech the mark of the human, but sign lan-guage was increasingly the mark of the brute. Benjamin Pettingill (a teacher at the Pennsylvania Institution) in 1873 found it necessary to defend sign language against charges that it was nothing more than "a set of monkey-like grimaces and antics" (1873: 4). A manualist teacher at the Kendall School, Sarah Porter, complained twenty years later that the common charge against the use of sign language — "You look like monkeys when you make signs" — would be "hardly worth noticing except for its ... incessant repetition" (Porter 1894: 171). A teacher from Scotland wrote to the *An-nals*, saying that it was wrong to "impress [deaf people] with the thought that it is apish to talk on the fingers" (Dodds

1899: 124). But there were many who agreed with an oralist educator who was of the opinion that "these signs can no more be called a language than the different movements of a dog's tail and ears which indicate his feelings" (Wright 1897: 338-8). Also see Gallaudet, E.M. (1881).

Expression and Emotion

The work of Charles Bell, author of *The Anatomy and Philosophy of Expression* (1885[1806]) and foremost authority of his time on the physical expression of emotions, rested on the premise that humans had been created with specific muscles intended for the sole purpose of expressing emotional states. The ability to reveal the emotions through expression, he believed, was a gift from the creator, a natural channel for human souls to communicate with one another unimpeded by artificial conventions. It was, as Thomas H. Gallaudet phrased the idea, "the transparent beaming forth of the soul" (1848: 80, and see also Richards 1987: 230-34). In 1848, the manualist educator, Charles Turner, could claim that "the aspect of the brute may be wild and ferocious ... or mild and peaceful ... but neither in the fury of the one, nor the docility of the other, do we see anything more than natural instinct, modified by external circumstances" (1848: 77).

His readers would not have been perplexed or surprised by his belief that "man alone possesses the distinctive faculty of expression." Only the human being possessed a soul, and facial expressions were "the purposes of the soul ... impressed upon the countenance." His observation, therefore, that facial expression was an indispensable concomitant to sign language and that sign language owed "its main force and beauty to the accompanying power of expression" was intended, and would be understood, as high praise (Turner 1848: 77). T. H. Gallaudet agreed, marveling that "the Creator furnished us [with] an eye and countenance, as variable in their expressions as are all the internal workings of the soul" (1848: 81).

The expressions of the face, as a means of communicating feelings and thoughts, were seen as both distinctly human and wonderfully eloquent. Instructors of this generation, for example, delighted in telling of sign masters who could recount Biblical tales using facial expression alone so skillfully that their deaf audiences could identify the stories (Turner 1848: 77-8 and also Lane 1984: 174-5).

Darwin's *Expression of the Emotions in Man and Animals*, however, signaled that important changes in attitudes toward facial expression were underway. In his frame of reference, expression was not a God-given gift nor a mark of humanity nor the outward expression of the unique workings of the human soul. Darwin criticized previous works on the subject, arguing that those who, like Bell, tried to "draw as broad a distinction between man and the lower animals" as possible by claiming that emotional expression was unique to humanity, did so out of the mistaken assumption that humans "came into existence in their present condition." Instead, he insisted, humans shared many expressions in common with animals, and the origins of human expression were to be found in their animal ancestors. Indeed, the similarities between humans and other animals in this regard was itself additional evidence that humans "once existed in a much lower and animal-like condition" (Darwin 1965[1872]: 10). In short, facial expression was no longer distinctly human, but, like gesture, a mere vestige of our animal past.

It was not long before popular writers were commenting on the "special facility" that apes have for "the more lowly forms of making one's self understood" — that is, the use of "gesture-language" and "facial muscles as a means of expression" (Jastrow 1886: 555-56). Teachers of the deaf expressed the change in attitude as well. An anonymous letter to the *Annals*, signed 'A Disgusted Pedagogue' criticized the use of sign language in the schools because it caused teachers to "grimace and gesticulate and jump" (Anon. 1873: 263). A manualist teacher complained of oralists who ridiculed signers for their "monkey-like grimaces" (Pettingill 1873: 4). Facial expression and gestures both were spoken of as the "rudimentary and lower parts of language' as opposed to speech, which was "the higher and finer part" (Howe, *et al* 1866: liii-liv). Deaf people were advised to avoid "indulging in the horrible grimaces some of them do lest they be accused of "making a monkey" of themselves (Unsigned 1890: 91). A writer in *Science* used a somewhat different metaphor, writing of students at a school for the deaf as "inmates making faces, throwing their hands and arms up and down. ... The effect is as if a sane man were suddenly put amidst a crowd of lunatics" (Engelsman 1890: 220). Given the theory of the time that insanity was a kind of reversion to an earlier stage of evolution, the metaphor may well be related to the comparisons with animals (Gilman 1988: 129-32).

The belief that gestures preceded speech in human history, then, took on radically different meanings once evolution became the dominant way of understanding the past. For the manualists, the ability to use sign language had been — no less than the power of speech — an ability contained within the soul. It was a gift that the "God of Nature and of Providence has kindly furnished" so that deaf people might come to know that they possessed a soul and were thereby human (Gallaudet, T.H. 1848: 86). Hearing people also benefited from the use of gesture. Why did the Creator grant to humans the wonderful ability to communicate with face and gesture, T.H. Gallaudet asked, if not "to supply the deficiencies of our oral intercourse, and to perfect the communion of one soul with another?" (1848: 80).

For the oralist generation, however, sign language came to be in itself a sub-human characteristic. What had been the solution to the problem of deafness became the problem. By the turn of the century, it was "the grand aim of every teacher of the deaf to put his pupils in possession of the spoken language of their country" (Hull 1898: 109). Speech had become the "greatest of all objects" as Alexander Graham Bell expressed it. To "ask the value of speech," he believed, "is like asking the value of life" (1884: 178). The value of speech was, for the oralists, akin to the value of being human. To be human was to speak. To sign was to step downward in the scale of being.

In that formulation — an unfortunate by-product of evolutionary theory — lies much of the reason for the decline of manualism and the rise of oralism at the end of the nineteenth century.

[D.C.B.]

PRECIS 2

¹A late nineteenth century movement to prohibit sign ²language in the schools dramatically transformed the ³education of deaf people in the United States. From 1817, ⁴when the first American school for deaf pupils was ⁵founded, until the 1860s, nearly all educators of the deaf ⁶considered sign language indispensable. Several generations of teachers not only used "the noble language ⁸of signs," as teachers often termed it, but devoted much ⁹effort to using it well ... They respected and admired ¹⁰sign language, cultivated their signing skills with care ¹¹and pride, and wrote learned treatises on its nature and ¹²proper use. Beginning in the 1860s, however, a new generation waged a campaign to replace the use of sign ¹⁴language in the schools with the exclusive use of lip-¹⁵reading and speech. The reasons for the turn against ¹⁶sign language were many and complex, but among ¹⁷them was the influence of the new theories of evolution. Evolutionary theory fostered a perception of sign ¹⁹languages as inferior to spoken languages, fit only for ²⁰"savages" and not for civilized human beings.

²¹In the latter decades of the century, two hostile camps ²²developed within the field of deaf education, with the

[23]mostly older "manualist" educators defending the use [24]of sign language against their mostly younger "oralist" [25]adversaries. Most schools began offering oral training [26]in the 1860s and 1870s, but this was not the crux of the [27]issue for oralism's advocates. They insisted not only [28]that training in oral communication be offered, but that [29]all classes be conducted solely by oral means. Oralists [30]charged that the use of sign language damaged the [31]minds of deaf people, interfered with the ability of deaf [32]children to learn English, and reduced the motivation [33]of deaf children to undertake the difficult but, in their [34]view, crucial task of learning to communicate orally. [35]They sought the complete abolition of sign language [36]in the schools, in hopes that it would then disappear [37]from use outside of the schools as well. In the larger [38]sense, the oralist movement failed. Sign language con-[39]tinued to be used and vigorously defended by the com-[40]munity. Deaf parents passed sign language on to their [41]children, and those children who were deaf passed it [42]on to their schoolmates. Indeed, even most schools that [43]were trying to discourage the use of sign language [44]found they could not do without it entirely, reserving [45]it for the always substantial number of older "oral fail-[46]ures." Oral communication was simply too impracti-[47]cal for many deaf people, and sign language too cher-[48]ished by the deaf community, for the latter to disap-[49]pear completely.

[50]Oralism nevertheless did have a profound impact on [51]deaf education. By the turn of the century, nearly 40 [52]percent of American deaf students sat in classrooms [53]from which sign language had been entirely banned; [54]over half were taught orally for at least part of the day. [55]By the end of World War I, nearly 80 percent of deaf [56]students were taught entirely without sign language [57]Oralism remained orthodoxy until the 1970s when sign [58]language began to return to the classroom.

[59]The advocacy of oralism was not new in the late nine-
[60]teenth century. Oralism had been promoted in the
[61]United States before the 1860s, but with little success
[62]Why did manualism remain dominant throughout most
[63]of the nineteenth century, only succumbing to the oralist
[64]challenge at the end of the century? What had changed?

[65]The campaign against sign language in deaf education
[66]was not an isolated phenomenon unconnected to larger
[67]developments in American culture. Rather, it was symp-
[68]tomatic of a new understanding of human history —
[69]and of the place of sign language in that history — that
[70]accompanied the rise of evolutionary theory in the late
[71]nineteenth century.

[72]This new understanding of human history was evident
[73]in the 1899 keynote address by the president of Amherst
[74]College, John M. Tyler, to the summer convention of
[75]the American Association to Promote the Teaching of
[76]Speech to the Deaf. America would "never have a sci-
[77]entific system of education," Tyler insisted to his audi-
[78]ence of oralist teachers and supporters, "until we have
[79]one based on the history of man's development, on the
[80]grand foundation of biological history." Therefore, the
[81]"search for ... goal[s] of education compels us to study
[82]man's origin and development," he contended, and he
[83]then outlined for his listeners the two major theories of
[84]that origin and development ... The first was the cre-
[85]ationist theory, the belief that "man was immediately
[86]created in his present form, only much better morally,
[87]and probably physically, than he now is. Man went
[88]downhill; he fell from that pristine condition." The sec-
[89]ond was the theory of evolution. Tyler felt confident
[90]that he could "take for granted" the truth of the theory
[91]of evolution and that most of his listeners had "already
[92]accepted it" ...

[93]Here was a crucial cultural change that separated those [94]first generations of teachers who used sign language [95]from the later generations who attempted to do away [96]with sign language. Most of the former came of age [97]before the publication of Charles Darwin's *Origin of Spe-*[98]*cies* ... and had constructed their understanding of the [99]world around the theory of immediate creation. Most [100]of those opposed to the use of sign language belonged [101]to a younger generation whose world view was built [102]upon an evolutionary understanding of the world.

[103]While natural selection (the mechanism Darwin ad-[104]vanced in 1859 to explain how evolution worked), was [105]not widely accepted in the United States until after [106]the turn of the century, the general idea of evolution [107]itself quickly found widespread acceptance .... Evo-[108]lutionary thinking pervaded American culture during [109]the years that oralism became dominant in deaf edu-[110]cation. That is, evolutionary analogies, explanations [111]and ways of thinking were ubiquitous. Psychologists [112]theorized mental illness as evolutionary reversion. [113]Criminologists defined "the criminal type" as a throw-[114]back. Social policies were defended or attacked on the [115]basis of their ostensible likelihood to further or stunt [116]evolution. Even sin came to be described as "a falling [117]back into the animal condition."

[118]Evolutionary theory set the terms of debate in deaf [119]education as well. It was no coincidence that oralist [120]theory began to transform deaf education in the United [121]States during the same period that evolutionary theory [122]was radically changing how Americans defined them-[123]selves and their world. the most important aspect of [124]that change for deaf people and their education oc-[125]curred in attitudes toward language — specifically the [126]relative status and worth of spoken and gesture lan-guages.

Find Definitions

•evolution(-ary) [lines 17-18, 70, 89, 91, 102, 104, 106, 107-8, 110, 118, 121]; •natural selection [line 103]; •pristine [line 88]; •orthodox(-y) [line 57]; •indispensable [line 6]; •manualist (-ism) [lines 23, 62]; •oralist (-ism) [lines 24, 27, 29, 38, 50, 57, 59-60, 63, 78, 109, 119]; •analogy(-ies) [line 110]; •ostensible [line 115]; •ubiquitous [line 111].

Having completed definitions for the 126 lines of the précis, are you sure you understand these? ••atavism [line 2, para. 4, p. 58]; ••irony(-ic) [para. 3, line 11, p. 56]; ••syntactical (-ically) [line 7 from bottom of p. 53]; ••elliptical [line 3, para. 3, p. 52]; ••troglodyte [line 5, para. 2, p. 51]; ••neo-Lamarckian [line 6, para. 3, p. 44].

Answer These Questions

I. A. What were the "two hostile camps" in deaf education at the turn of the century and what were the main lines of their debate? [lines 22-37]

B. Did oralism succeed? [line 37-8]. Why not? [lines 38-49]

C. What change brought about the oralist challenge? [lines 65-71]

D. Many people want to separate the world of ideas and human intellect from 'the real world'. Do you think the separation is valid or useful? What evidence does Baynton provide to refute the belief that ideas and theories can be usefully separated from the real world?

II. There are approximately 1000 words in the above précis exercise. *Using no more than 400 words and no less than 250 words*, summarize the 126-line passage. This means you will write a précis of it. Do the work on a separate piece of paper, making sure you *indicate word count* on the final product.

THOUGHT EXERCISES
(Optional)

1. Compare and contrast the ways in which Baynton talks about evolutionary theory and the ways in which Glasser talks about evolutionary theory.

2. Although neither Baynton nor Glasser speak of evolutionary theory in terms of "macro-history," *evolutionary theory is a macro-historical theory of the origins of the human race.* From the reading you have done so far, do you think it is a good idea to tie the history of southern African dance forms to the history of the human race? Do you think it is a good idea to tie the teaching of deaf education to the history of the human race? If you think it is a good idea, briefly explain why. If you think it is an undesirable idea, briefly explain why.

3. Baynton states,

> While natural selection (the mechanism Darwin advanced in 1859 to explain how evolution worked), was not widely accepted in the United States until after the turn of the century, the general idea of evolution itself quickly found widespread acceptance ... Evolutionary thinking pervaded American culture during the years that oralism became dominant in deaf education. That is, evolutionary analogies, explanations and ways of thinking were ubiquitous (p. 43, this volume).

In the Preface (p. 8), Williams cites this passage from the writings of an eminent biologist:

> Darwinism sees the living process in terms that emphasize competition, inheritance, selfishness, and survival as the driving forces of evolution. These are certainly aspects of the remarkable drama that includes our own history as a species. But it is a very incomplete and limited story, both scientifically and metaphorically, based on an inadequate

view of organisms; and it invites us to act in a limited way as an evolved species in relation to our environment, which includes other cultures and species. These limitations have contributed to some of the difficulties we now face (Goodwin 1994: xii).

a. What connections, if any, do you see between the two statements? That is, compare and contrast Baynton's statement with Goodwin's.

b. What status do you think evolutionary thinking has in the United States as the twentieth century comes to a close?

SECTION I
ESSAYS

CHAPTER 3

Brenda Farnell: Where Mind Is a Verb: Spatial Orientation and Deixis in Plains Indian Sign Talk and Assiniboine (Nakota) Culture

SHORT BIOGRAPHICAL NOTE

Brenda Farnell is presently an Associate Professor in the Anthropology Department, University of Illinois, Urbana-Champaign. She came there from the University of Iowa where she was a Visiting Professor, having earned her Ph.D. in sociocultural anthropology at Indiana University (Bloomington). Born in England, she also holds a Teaching Diploma from I. M. Marsh College of Physical Education of Liverpool University, a Diploma in Dance and Dance Education from the Laban Centre for Movement and Dance of London University and an M.A. in the Anthropology of Human Movement from New York University.

Her research interests include ethno-poetics and performance in Plains Indian Sign Language, Assiniboine oral narrative, deixis, and dances of the Northern Plains. She is the author of *Do You See What I Mean: Plains Indian Sign-Talk and the Embodiment of Action* and an interactive multi-media CDRom, *Wiyuta: Assiniboine Storytelling with Signs* [University of Texas Press, Austin, 1994]. Recent papers include 'Ethno-Graphics and the Moving Body', *MAN* 29(4): 929-974, 1994; 'Movement Writing Systems' in *The Worlds Writing Systems*, (W. Bright and P. Daniels, Eds.), Oxford University Press, 1996 and 'Metaphors We Move By', *Visual Anthropology* 8(2-4): 311-336, 1996. She is an Editor of the *Journal for the Anthropological Study of Human Movement* [JASHM], and has written several articles for the journal since it began in 1980.

The following text is a reproduction of **Farnell, Brenda. 1995.** Where Mind Is a Verb: Spatial Orientation and Deixis in Plains Indian Sign Talk and Assiniboine (Nakota) Culture. IN *Human Action Signs in Cultural Context: The Visible and the Invisible in Movement and Dance* (B. Farnell, Ed.), Metuchen, New Jersey: Scarecrow Press, pp. 82-111. The text is reprinted by permission of Scarecrow Press.

WHERE MIND IS A VERB: SPATIAL ORIENTATION
AND DEIXIS IN PLAINS INDIAN SIGN TALK
AND ASSINIBOINE (NAKOTA) CULTURE

Many Nakota speakers, who live on the Northern Plains of North America, accompany their speech in everyday action and interaction and in storytelling performances with gestures that belong to a system known as the Plains Indian Sign Language or Plains Sign talk (PST). PST was formerly a *lingua franca* among the Plains tribes. Today, only a few people are sufficiently skilled to use sign talk without speech, and most often, speech and signs occur together, interweaving meaning between both media, in action that is as complex as it is beautiful.

In this chapter, I first discuss the existence of a "rhetoric of demise" with regard to PST, which, while not entirely incorrect, has served to make continued use of the sign language largely invisible to outsiders. The contemporary use of PST in conjunction with speech, however, also presents an interesting theoretical problem for linguistic anthropology given the generally accepted distinction between verbal and non-verbal communication. A brief examination of signed and spoken data addresses this problem by showing how some key symbolic forms provide semantic resources that are common to the use of both spoken language and signed language in Assiniboine culture. In addition, deictic devices that organize space/time in language are shown to be shared by both media, and not restricted to spoken language. An actor-centered theory is suggested that seeks to embody the notion of deixis and so overcome the problematic Cartesian division between language viewed as non-material product of mind separate from a moving body.

A Rhetoric of Demise

One of the criticisms some Native Americans have of the anthropological record is that it consistently tells them that they and their traditions are dying out; "Why does no one talk about the changes in the white man's culture that way?" they ask. "You don't live like your great-grandparents did either." Their complaint is justified and insightful. When American ethnologists began to document the ways of life of Native American peoples during the nineteenth and early twentieth centuries, the general assumption was that those cultures were doomed to extinction or assimilation given the inevitable onslaught of "progress."

Whether ethnologists aligned themselves with assimilationists or actively engaged in assisting Indian peoples to retain their lands and way of life, an understandably pessimistic outlook prevailed. The drastic economic, political, and social changes that were being imposed on indigenous peoples a century ago (and since) created a rhetoric that was predominantly one of loss and regret, among Indians and ethnologists alike. In that climate, documentation of pre-contact and pre-reservation culture became a priority, and these writings often presented an idealized and normative view of pre-contact aboriginal cultures, frozen in time. When current conditions were included, the focus tended to be on the Indian as victim, and little attention was paid to the remarkable flexibility of indigenous peoples and their accommodation to ongoing cultural change that had, in fact, long been a feature of Plains Indian life. Unwittingly perhaps, ethnologists contributed to the anti-Indian political rhetoric of their own society: if the only good Indian was not a dead Indian, then the next best thing in terms of a more comfortable political accommodation to racist government policies was at least a dying Indian culture. The Indian-as-victim metaphor left out of the record the strategies of resistance, the imaginative assimilations of new ideas with older practices, and ways that traditional symbols and practices were being actively reinterpreted to accommodate new meanings (Fowler 1987).

Ironically, however, the assumption that customs were "dying out" has, in unexpected ways, provided some distinct advantages for later scholars. For example, Gen. Hugh

L. Scott, retired army veteran of the Plains wars and amateur ethnologist, became convinced that PST—that unique gestural *lingua franca* of the Plains—was dying out. So in 1930 he persuaded the U.S. Congress to authorize the making of a film record as soon as possible, thereby providing one of the earliest and the most extensive film records of Plains sign talk in use.[2]

In the film, General Scott is not wearing the uniform of the army but that of the Boy Scouts of America. Although fascinated by, and knowledgeable about PST, Scott nevertheless believed that its ultimate value and only hope of survival lay in its potential application as an international communication system for that most Anglo-Saxon of boys' institutions—the Boy Scouts of the world—who, of course, appropriated and romanticized many elements of a supposedly Indian forest lore and brotherhood. Had it not been for this odd combination of preservationist, political, and altruistic motivations, the film of the sign council and its accompanying film dictionary of signs would never have been produced.

Twenty years later, in the 1950s, it was anthropologist Alfred Kroeber who noted that PST was falling into disuse, and he urged Carl Voegelin to find a student who could undertake a linguistic study of it before it was too late (Kroeber 1958). Consequently, La Mont West Jr. embarked on a pioneering study of the language from the perspective of descriptive linguistics. West moved around the Northern Plains at a rapid pace during the fall of 1956, collecting data from twenty-five reservations and ninety-seven sign talkers in only fifty days, including travel time. Many of West's informants were elderly, and certainly the sign language as a *lingua franca* was in decline by the 1950s because English was gradually taking over the inter-tribal function. But it cannot have been dying out quite as rapidly as was assumed to be the case, for it is otherwise doubtful that West could have accomplished his project with such ease and speed. I suspect that the impression of impending extinction came from the fact that the contexts in which PST was still used were no longer quite so visible to outsiders. As a public intertribal language it had been clearly visible at events where non-Indians were present: at treaty councils, in trading contexts, for public oratory, and among Indian army scouts who were often drawn from tribes speaking several different languages (Dunley 1982). The historical record focuses on those contexts and the impression is given that quite separate languages are involved—as if speech switches off as the sign language switches on. Ignored were contexts in which signs continued to be used among people who *did* speak the same language and for whom the sign talk was an integral part of their linguistic repertoire.

West's work was pioneering because sign languages were not considered by linguists and educators at that time to be real languages—a battle that is still going on in the education of the Deaf today.[3] In conjunction with a long-standing cultural bias against the body generally, sign languages were considered to be simple codes, probable precursors to spoken language in the evolutionary scheme of things. Indeed considerable interest had been shown in PST by nineteenth-century anthropologists such as E.B. Tylor, precisely because they seemed to provide indisputable evidence of a primitive state. The predominance of iconic or representational gestures in sign languages was viewed by some as evidence of an earlier stage of development when language was a direct representation of nature prior to the development of arbitrariness in the spoken language sign.[4] The possibility that the so-called "savages" might be more sophisticated than Europeans because of their systematic skill in the linguistic use of both movement and sound, was certainly ignored.

In 1984, when I explored the possibility of turning my library study of PST into field research, the general opinion among Plains scholars was that this long-standing and distinctive language was now dead—a "lost" tradition, along with the buffalo hunting economy and buckskin dress of bygone days. Fortunately, I was encouraged (and stubborn enough) to go and see for myself, and I started with a visit to an elderly Assiniboine woman from Fort Belknap, Montana, who apparently "waved her hands around a lot" when she was telling stories.[5] I was delighted to recognize from the nineteenth-century documentation that she was indeed using the sign language as she talked, and we later began to work together making video recordings of her stories and other vocabulary in both signs and spoken Nakota.

I thought I must have found the only remaining sign talker on the Plains, but I began to notice that other Nakota speakers in the community also frequently accompanied their speech with gestures belonging to that system. Upon mentioning this observation, I was told, "Of course, it's part of the language," and my remark was considered to be rather obvious if not altogether stupid. This alerted me to the consideration that the conception of a "Plains sign language" as a distinct and primarily intertribal language, is grossly misleading. It may be a product of what Roy Harris (1981) has called "the language myth": the artifactualization of languages as "fixed codes." Instead, there exists, in the Assiniboine case at least, a continuum, moving from an informal use of gestures that accompany or replace speech in everyday interactions, to more formalized contexts such as storytelling performances (and sign songs and hymns). In former times, and where deafness exists today, the continuum extends to the use of a widely conventionalized intertribal system that can exclude speech altogether. People draw on an available repertoire of gestures that can be used with or without spoken language according to individual knowledge, personal preference, skill, and context. In Assiniboine story-telling, both speech and gesture are an integral part of the narrative sense and gestures are not simply dramatic enhancement or a repeat of a spoken narrative (Farnell 1995). In addition both kinds of utterance are considered to be "talking" (hence the use in English of the term "sign talk"), and some use the English lexeme "word" to refer to either a vocal or a gestural utterance. Assiniboine people often use signs and speech simultaneously and do not privilege speech over gestural talking. On one occasion, for example, when I asked for the spoken equivalent of a gestural utterance by saying, "How would you say that in Nakota?" the reply was, "Like I just showed you." Obviously, there is a very different conception of "language" going on here, one that combines body and mind in ways that confound Cartesian dualistic thinking.

If this was a "lost" tradition, then I was led to ask, "Lost to whom?" The stereotypic silent but visible and stoic-faced Plains Indian so beloved by Hollywood, displaying his primitive grandeur by talking in signs had gone, and so, it was assumed, had the language. PST had become invisible to non-Indians, in part because of this change of contexts but also because that same Cartesian bias prohibits such gesturing with speech from being valued by the dominant culture. Waving one's hands around when talking is, for the most part, viewed as a sign of a deficiency—an inability to express oneself adequately in words, or a marker of lower class or undesirable ethnic origin. The French and Italians, for example, are stereotypically thought to be prone to such excesses of gesture in response to overly active passions, interpreted on the whole by those of Anglo-Saxon and derived cultures as evidence of less rational, more emotional and therefore uncontrolled (read "immoral") behavior.[6]

Nakota and the Embodiment of Mind

Examination of PST and Nakota reveals some fundamental distinctions between Assiniboine and Euro-American ways of thinking about language and the body. For example, when I asked how to say in Nakota that someone has a good mind, I was taught the phrase "*tʿawačį wašte* ." When I asked how to say this in signs, I was taught to move a pointed index finger from the heart away from the chest with the finger pointing straight forward, and then to add the sign GOOD, a flat hand with the palm down moving from the center of the chest diagonally to the right (Fig. 1 - p. 255).[7] Two things are important: first, in contrast to gestures used by speakers of English and ASL[8] there is no reference to head as a place where mind is located, and second, emphasis is on the movement not on a location. Later, I learned that in order to say "She thinks clearly," one would use the same word in the phrase "*taya t'awačį* " and the sign was almost the same. consistent with an apparent lack of distinction between verbs and nouns, well described by Siouan linguists (Boas and Deloria 1941), mind in Nakota acts more like a verb than a noun;—an action not an object. *Wačį* - "to think," seems to be a verb about thinking but one with a very wide semantic range. According to Lakota scholars it can be used in the sense of intention, willpower or one's will and unbounding consciousness.[9] Deloria (1940) defines the term for Lakota speakers as both a noun meaning mind and reason and as a prefix added to active verbs that indicates a willingness, desire, will, or disposition to do: an intention or plan. In Nakota also, *t'awačį mneha,* for example, means strong-willed, and *'awačįknuhana* undecided. *Wac`i* is one of four Nakota verbs relating to thinking and one in which remembering seems to be involved.

The phrase "*t'awačį wašte* " seems to indicate a general disposition: "It means they really like what you're doing" and "a good person in every way" were other meanings given to me. the Lakota Sioux use the phrase to mean a generous person (Raymond Bucko S.J., personal communication; also Buechel 1983). In other words, as the sign language emphasizes, mind is not a place but a disposition toward others: a capacity of a whole person, not a place in the head separate from a body.

Notions of personhood in Assiniboine and other Plains cultures involve the complex combination of a strong sense of agency (emphasizing personal autonomy in decision making for example) without resort to individualism because of the emphasis placed on kin relationships. People are defined and define themselves fundamentally in terms of social relationships, and so it is not surprising that the sign moves from the heart toward the space of relationship, linking the space between speaker and hearer.

The possessional prefix "*t'a*" is also involved in this social view of mind. It is a prefix denoting separable possession unlike those prefixes used with kinship terms, for example, which denote inseparable possession. Your mother and grandfather are always and inseparably yours, whereas your thinking and thoughts (*mit'awači*), while certainly yours, are separable from you in the sense that they can be shared.

Such data provide evidence of some fundamental philosophical differences in conceptions of mind/body between Nakota speakers and English speakers. This provides a basis from which to explore two spatial concepts that provide semantic and syntactic resources for both spoken Nakota and PST.

Sign Talk and Spatial Concepts

Many investigators of native North American peoples have noted the importance of two spatial concepts—the circle and the four cardinal directions. Though this idea has been discussed in the context of traditional religious symbolism (e.g. Neihardt 1972, Brown 1953 and Walker 1980), exactly how these concepts are formed and expressed with body movement as well as spoken language, and how they are used in the lived experience of cultural members has not been articulated. The Assiniboine both share in this widespread Plains symbolism and impress their own distinct variations upon it.

A brief glimpse into the lived experience of the shape of the circle in terms of human relationships and the sense of loss due to the altered shape of contemporary living spaces is possible through the following statement by one of my Nakota teachers, Mrs. Emma Lamebull:

> After the white people came they said, everything changed, you know, they're sitting there [the old-timers] telling stories, they said everything changed, they said. Long ago they said, everything we did in a circle, like in a tipi we always sat in a circle and looked at each other's faces. When we ate we sat in a circle. When we talked and visit each other, tell stories, we

sat in a circle, and when we looked at each other [we] could tell when this person was feeling bad, what his feelings were 'cause you could see their faces. and after the white people came, well then they took our kids to school and instead of looking at each other, they're looking at the back, at the back of heads—you don't see their face no more, you don't know if they're feeling bad or, if they don't feel good you can't comfort them because you can't see their faces. And then the teacher stands up there, teaching you, and instead of trying to make you learn lessons, they teach you your lessons but they learn you how to compete—they learn you to be higher than this one—you study harder and you get A's and they do things for you because they learn you how to compete. Even these animals, we learn to, they learn their children to kill them when they need it—when they need to eat. When the white people came they turn that into competing—they wanna see who killed the biggest elk or the biggest buffalo or the longest fish, you know, and ... they get recognized for doing the biggest things they killed you know. They don't think of the animal itself, what they're doing to them like that and they said it's sad the way some kids they don't even care now, or pay attention. It's hard to make them mind because now they went and bought homes like this one and they said, their brother's got TV and he's got his own room, sister's got TV and she's got her own room, parents got their own room—no more circle, they broke the circle.

Thus the circle was and still is, though perceived as diminished through architectural and social change, a powerful form for the organizing of social relations and interaction in a very practical sense. It symbolizes not only community and caring but also a face-to-face non-competitive ideal social world. In storytelling, for example, Mrs. Rose Weasel often begins with a large circular gesture saying:

Ž ei̯š   oyate ka   t'ipi   hu̯šta   kan.
That one, tribe   over there they live it is said over there.
So, the people were camped over yonder they say, over yonder

Or,

Wi ne eyaš kahạkeya t'ipi hụšta
Lodge this just over there they camped, it is said.
There was a lodge; just over there they lived, it is said.

In both cases Mrs. Weasel literally describes the camp circle (Fig. 2 gives a transcribed example - p. 256), but moreover the metaphor of the circle creates the social space within which the characters will interact and the story will unfold. The circle also circumscribes the limits of the signing space: clearing or setting the spatial stage.

Deixis in Nakota and PST

In the two Nakota sentences used as examples there are three different ways of saying "there" and two other indexicals (*ne* and *ze*, "this" and "that") all of which contribute to the fairly complex deictical system that organizes space/time in both the spoken language and the gestural system.[10]

Linguists have drawn attention to the ways in which spoken languages use such deictical devices, but on the whole they have neglected to pay attention to the embodiment that accompanies the use of these terms (Hanks 1990).[11] Yet the zero point of the deictical coordinates can be viewed not merely as the here and now of a speaker but as the body of the person. Time/space is measured from the here and now of the embodied person as mover and speaker in a space that is simultaneously physical and social. deictical terms refer to such embodied notions of time/space *at the same time* as they relate the speaker to the speech situation.

The Nakota deictic space falls readily into three horizontal zones (Fig. 3 - p. 257). Demonstrative pronouns, for example, express proximal, distal and extra distal areas, or "here, there, and there visible so that it can be pointed at" (Boas and Deloria 1941: 2). If we set aside standard spoken language classifications into categories such as demonstratives, pronouns and adverbials and categorize according to spatial criteria, we see that in Nakota deictic space these three zones are remarkably consistent. Proximal space is marked by a series of words all of which begin with *ne* and all terms dealing with near space use this root. Likewise all gestures referring to near space either with or without vocal accompaniment are performed closest to the body itself. Distal or "there" space consistently uses terms beginning with *ze,* and PST signs correspondingly refer to and reach into a space farther from the body than the *ne* space. The extradistal, or far but visible, space uses *ka,* although PST signs relating to this group do not necessarily reach out of the comfortable "signing space" in front of the torso during performance, because this is a relative rather than an actual positioning. Figure 4 (p. 258) shows the consistency of this arrangement in spoken language terms when applied to demonstratives and adverbials of space/time. Given this consistency it is not surprising to find that these three zones of horizontal space are maintained in the gestural system, although it would be a mistake to assume that this implies a naive realism in the deictic system, that is, that "here" and "there" only refer to zones of relative proximity in physical space (cf. Hanks 1990).

The Nakota spoken language, like English, often combines space and time, and this too is paralleled in gesture. Thus, *étu* or "close," refers to both near space and near time, and the sign is performed in near space and moves towards this zero point of the deictical coordinates—the here and now of the body itself. The same gesture is used with the word *ésten* meaning "soon/right away." Likewise the word *t'éhą,* "far away," refers to a long time or far distance and there is one gesture that can apply to both. In this case, however, the *ka,* or far space, is not used, perhaps because *t'éhą* refers to invisible rather than to visible distance. The same gesture is also used with the word *wąŋkaš* meaning "a long time ago," and in story-telling this often functions in a similar manner to the way "once upon a time" is used to begin European stories.

A shortened version of this gesture is often used as a past time or completed action marker. Nakota is a language that does not use verb tense and verbs mark only two categories of time: present or completed action and potential action. Thus we do not find any equivalent to the time line in ASL, wherein past time signs use the space behind the line of the body, present time signs are located at the body, and future time signs are in front, consistent with the way in which the English language locates time spatially (Baker and Cokely 1980).

This deictic organization extends to involve the four cardinal directions. They are referredto in Nakota as *t'atetopa* the "four winds" or *t'ateoyétópa*, "the four tracks of the winds." In Assiniboine religious thought it is from the four winds that various kinds of spiritual assistance or power comes. Each term would appear to connote a general direction *from* which certain things *come toward* a person in contrast to the Euro-American conventional picture of the four directions as lines moving *outward* from a given point, as shown by the pointing arrows on most geographic maps (Fig. 5 - p. 259). An additional difference lies in the conception of the cardinal directions as four quarters—that is as a circle sectioned into four quarters. Each direction therefore comprises an area in contrast to the single line of Euro-American convention.

Wíhinąp'e, "east," refers to the sunrise, literally "sun comes up," and is the direction from which the grandfather spirits come. In the prereservation era, when extended family groups were scattered to hunt, it was the direction in which the tipi would often be faced, so as to greet the morning sun with prayer. *Wiyota(hǫ)* is translated as "south" but refers literally to the "sun in the middle" and also means "noon." South is a particularly salient direction for the Assiniboine: the door of ceremonial structures such as the sundance lodge and sweat lodges face the south, for example. *Wiyohpe*, "west," refers to "sun going down." It is the home of the eagle who "lifts prayers to heaven" and the "thunderbirds" responsible for lightning and thunder and much more. It is also the direction in which departing souls are said to go when they leave this home on earth. *Wazíyata*, "north" refers to "where the snow comes from," the home of the old man who, some Assiniboine say, "lives in the cold and makes the cold and rarely takes pity on anyone."

Like the deictic terms discussed earlier, spatial concepts also coincide with notions of time passing as reckoned by the movement of the sun across the sky (Fig. 6 - p. 260). A day is marked by the circular passage of the sun from E-S-W, and the passage of the year is marked by "winters" with their northern connection.

What is particularly interesting about Assiniboine use of the cardinal directions is that, although these terms as described above exist in the spoken language, they are rarely if ever used in everyday contexts. Consultants who were fluent speakers of Nakota had to search their memories for the names of the directions, conceiving of these words being appropriate in only three contexts: religious concepts involving the four winds; the four seasons and passing time; and far distant places and peoples. Another term for "south," for example, was *maštamak'oče*, literally, "hot country," which might be used of someone traveling to Arizona, but not for someone traveling south within the reservation or the state of Montana. Two variant terms for "north"—*waziyam* and *wiyoħapa*—refer to places where other Assiniboine people live, on the Red Pheasant reserve and the Santaluta/Regina area, both in Canada. To ask, "Did you come from the North?" *Wiyoħapa etahąyahi?* refers to coming from Canada. The spoken language terms theselves therefore do not seem to involve either local geographical space or immediate orientation space. How is it then that information about such local space is organized?

I found that despite this lack of vocal reference in everyday contexts, the cardinal points nevertheless provide a constant frame of reference that all use, whether they speak Nakota or English only and regardless of whether they know the sign language or not. It is through indexical spoken expressions and gestures that this frame of reference is utilized. Today, even though few people are fluent in the sign language proper, there remains a use of gesture that is coincident with it and that undoubtedly stems from a very different view of language from that held by Euro-American people. For example, I found that both speech and gesture have become equally important when giving route directions, whether spoken Nakota or spoken English is used.

In asking how to get from the agency buildings on the Fort Belknap reservation to the nearby town of Harlem, I received the following reply in English from an Assinboine person: "You go out of here this way, then this way again and you'll come to the highway. Go this way again, over the river and you're gonna go that way into town." Obviously if one were to take notice of only the spoken component involved in this utterance, the information is somewhat ambiguous. Of equal importance in understanding these directions, however, is the accompanying gestures of the arms and hands, as shown in the movement text in Figure 7 (p. 261).

This is in marked contrast to a non-Indian Montana resident who said, "Well, go out of these doors to the parking lot, then take a left past the Headstart building till you get to the road, and take a left again. You'll get to Highway 2. Go west on 2 about three miles and Harlem's right there on your right. There's a sign right there says Harlem." The only gestures accompanying this were a hand directed towards the

doors in question and a raised hand at the end

indicating the road sign, as if placed in front of the speaker.

In contrast to the Assiniboine case, the Euro-American example encodes directions by making reference to landmarks such as doors and signposts, buildings, and a numbered highway, as well as directional terms such as left and right. In the route directions given by an Assiniboine person, indexical expressions such as "here," "this way," and "that way" are accompanied by gestures that point to the actual geographical directions involved. In this manner, the indexicals and gestures provide information just as accurate as that encoded in the Euro-American case, but in a different manner.

Assiniboine people always seem to know where the actual cardinal directions lie, even if they are deep inside a multi-roomed building and in a room without windows (which was the case when these directions were given). Consequently, when Assiniboine people give directions, the cardinal points provide a constant frame of reference, which everyone uses, even though the actual words "north," "south," "east," and "west" are not used. This implicit awareness of geographical direction means that people draw upon a map that is constant, regardless of which direction the speaker happens to be facing at the time. In this way, spoken indexical expressions plus the gestures of hands that point to actual geographical directions are sufficient, and no one (except perhaps the anthropologist) gets confused.

Even in situations when visual field is restricted, such as driving in a car, I found that an Assiniboine passenger will gesture and say "go this way" or "go that way" rather than use American English alternatives that do not require a gesture such as "take a right here" or "go east until you get to the highway," or British English alternatives such as "turn right at the Red Lion," and "take the Scarborough road." The intimate social space of a reservation community permits the use of indexicals and gesture well beyond this kind of general spatial orientation and extends into the frequent use of pronouns and demonstratives so that proper names of places and people are avoided whenever possible.

In the context of storytelling, this geographical frame of reference is frequently retained. When working with Mrs. Weasel on one occasion on the sign vocabulary in one of her stories I was puzzled as to why signs for "morning" and "afternoon" were performed as in Figure 8a (p. 262) when on another occasion they had been performed as in Figure 8b (p. 262). Although the hand shape (first finger and thumb create the shape of a circle, other fingers curled) and arm action (a curving arc of the whole arm, upward or downward, the whole sign being an iconic representation of the sun's rising in the sky and then lowering) remained the same, the space in which the rising arc was traced by the arm varied. On the first occasion Mrs. Weasel raised her arm on her right side and lowered it on her left side; on the second occasion the sun rose directly in front of her and set behind her. The puzzle was solved by realizing that in the first instance Mrs. Weasel had been sitting in a room and facing northwest, so east was on her right side and west to her left, whereas on the second occasion she had been facing east. This spatial orientation makes a difference in the transcription of those signs if they are to reflect accurately the ethnographic context; what is constituent to the signs is not the forward-middle or side-middle direction of the arm in relation to the torso. The arm goes toward geographical east (Figure 8c - p. 262).

Conclusion

The theoretical value of these observations lies in the exposure of a deeply rooted Cartesianism in our definition of language as traditionally constituted, reflected by the view that there are two separate systems involved in the human organization of space, time, and the body, one having to do with the movement of the body, a physical realm of sensory-motor organization and doing in the world; the other having to do with sound and speech and a mental realm of thought and reflection on the world. Such a conception may indeed be an accurate picture of the Western folk model of the person, but it is surely no longer acceptable as a cross-cultural analytic model. It creates dualities between mind and body, speech and action, reason and emotion, conception and experience, verbal and nonverbal, symbolic and instrumental, and a host of others, all of which may be misleading or irrelevant to understanding of the organizational principles in the knowledge systems of other people.

Mead (1933), Wittgenstein (1958), Goodman (1984) and others involved in a social constructivist view of mind have argued that mind is best conceived of as the sum total of ways in which knowledge can be organized through language and other semiotic practices. Such a definition, it seems, would accommodate Assiniboine conceptions of language and mind much better than the Cartesian legacy. The Assiniboine data on spatial orientation also shows that although such knowledge is usually tacit—that is, not normally expressed in words—it is nevertheless organized. Such cultural resources illustrate some of the integral connections between gestural and spoken languages such that we could reasonably posit a core of deictic features of this kind that will be common to both speech and action in any language community. Through these "semantic primitives" ... we can perhaps gain entrée into our own and other cultural epistemologies and metaphysics through a view of language as inseparably constituted *with* action and not independently *by* action.

[B.F.]

PRECIS 3

¹One of the criticisms some Native Americans have of the ²anthropological record is that it consistently tells them that ³they and their traditions are dying out; "Why does no one ⁴talk about the changes in the white man's culture that way?" ⁵they ask. "You don't live like your great-grandparents did ⁶either." Their complaint is justified and insightful. When ⁷American ethnologists began to document the ways of life ⁸of Native American peoples during the nineteenth and early ⁹twentieth centuries, the general assumption was that those ¹⁰cultures were doomed to extinction or assimilation given ¹¹the inevitable onslaught of "progress."

¹²Whether ethnologists aligned themselves with ¹³assimilationists or actively engaged in assisting Indian ¹⁴peoples to retain their lands and way of life, an understand- ¹⁵ably pessimistic outlook prevailed. The drastic economic,

[16]political, and social changes that were being imposed on [17]indigenous peoples a century ago (and since) created a [18]rhetoric that was predominantly one of loss and regret, [19]among Indians and ethnologists alike. In that climate, docu-[20]mentation of precontact and prereservation culture be-[21]came a priority, and these writings often presented an ide-[22]alized and normative view of pre-contact aboriginal cul-[23]tures, frozen in time. When current conditions were in-[24]cluded, the focus tended to be on the Indian as victim, and [25]little attention was paid to the remarkable flexibility of in-[26]digenous peoples and their accommodation to ongoing cul-[27]tural change that had, in fact, long been a feature of Plains [28]Indian life. Unwittingly perhaps, ethnologists contributed [29]to the anti-Indian political rhetoric of their own society: if [30]the only good Indian was not a dead Indian, then the next [31]best thing in terms of a more comfortable political accom-[32]modation to racist government policies was at least a dy-[33]ing Indian culture. The Indian-as-victim metaphor left out [34]of the record the strategies of resistance, the imaginative [35]assimilations of new ideas with older practices, and ways [36]that traditional symbols and practices were being actively [37]reinterpreted to accommodate new meanings. ...

[38]Ironically, however, the assumption that customs were "dy-[39]ing out" has, in unexpected ways, provided some distinct [40]advantages for later scholars. For example, Gen. Hugh L. [41]Scott, retired army veteran of the Plains wars and amateur [42]ethnologist, became convinced that PST—that unique ges-[43]tural *lingua franca* of the Plains—was dying out. So in 1930 [44]he persuaded the U.S. Congress to authorize the making [45]of a film record as soon as possible, thereby providing one [46]of the earliest and the most extensive film records of Plains [47]sign talk in use.

[48]In the film, General Scott is not wearing the uniform of the [49]army but that of the Boy Scouts of America. Although fas-[50]cinated by, and knowledgeable about PST, Scott neverthe-[51]less believed that its ultimate value and only hope of sur-

[52]vival lay in its potential application as an international com-
[53]munication system for that most Anglo-Saxon of boys' in-
[54]stitutions—the Boy Scouts of the world—who, of course,
[55]appropriated and romanticized many elements of a sup-
[56]posedly Indian forest lore and brotherhood. Had it not been
[57]for this odd combination of preservationist, political, and
[58]altruistic motivations, the film of the sign council and its
[59]accompanying film dictionary of signs would never have
[60]been produced.

[61]Twenty years later, in the 1950s, it was anthropologist Alfred
[62]Kroeber who noted that PST was falling into disuse, and
[63]he urged Carl Voegelin to find a student who could under-
[64]take a linguistic study of it before it was too late. ...Conse-
[65]quently, La Mont West Jr. embarked on a pioneering study
[66]of the language from the perspective of descriptive linguis-
[67]tics. West moved around the Northern Plains at a rapid
[68]pace during the fall of 1956, collecting data from twenty-
[69]five reservations and ninety-seven sign talkers in only fifty
[70]days, including travel time. Many of West's informants
[71]were elderly, and certainly the sign language as a *lingua*
[72]*franca* was in decline by the 1950s because English was
[73]gradually taking over the inter-tribal function. But it can-
[74]not have been dying out quite as rapidly as was assumed
[75]to be the case, for it is otherwise doubtful that West could
[76]have accomplished his project with such ease and speed. I
[77]suspect that the impression of impending extinction came
[78]from the fact that the contexts in which PST was still used
[79]were no longer quite so visible to outsiders. As a public
[80]inter-tribal language it had been clearly visible at events
[81]where non-Indians were present: at treaty councils, in trad-
[82]ing contexts, for public oratory, and among Indian army
[83]scouts who were often drawn from tribes speaking several
[84]different languages. ... The historical record focuses on
[85]those contexts and the impression is given that quite sepa-
[86]rate languages are involved—as if speech switches off as
[87]the sign language switches on. Ignored were contexts in

[88]which signs continued to be used among people who *did*
[89]speak the same language and for whom the sign talk was
[90]an integral part of their linguistic repertoire.

[91]West's work was pioneering because sign languages were
[92]not considered by linguists and educators at that time to
[93]be real languages—a battle that is still going on in the edu-
[94]cation of the Deaf today. In conjunction with a long-stand-
[95]ing cultural bias against the body generally, sign languages
[96]were considered to be simple codes, probable precursors
[97]to spoken language in the evolutionary scheme of things.
[98]Indeed considerable interest had been shown in PST by
[99]nineteenth-century anthropologists such as E.B. Tylor, pre-
[100]cisely because they seemed to provide indisputable evi-
[101]dence of a primitive state. The predominance of iconic or
[102]representational gestures in sign languages was viewed
[103]by some as evidence of an earlier stage of development
[104]when language was a direct representation of nature prior
[105]to the development of arbitrariness in the spoken language
[106]sign. The possibility that the so-called "savages" might
[107]be more sophisticated than Europeans because of their sys-
[108]tematic skill in the linguistic use of both movement and
[109]sound, was certainly ignored.

[110]In 1984, when I explored the possibility of turning my li-
[111]brary study of PST into field research, the general opinion
[112]among Plains scholars was that this long-standing and dis-
[113]tinctive language was now dead—a "lost" tradition, along
[114]with the buffalo hunting economy and buckskin dress of
[115]bygone days. Fortunately, I was encouraged (and stub-
[116]born enough) to go and see for myself, and I started with
[117]a visit to an elderly Assiniboine woman from Fort Belknap,
[118]Montana, who apparently "waved her hands around a lot"
[119]when she was telling stories. I was delighted to recognize
[120]from the nineteenth-century documentation that she was
[121]indeed using the sign language as she talked, and we later
[122]began to work together making video recordings of her

[123]stories and other vocabulary in both signs and spoken
Nakota.

[124]I thought I must have found the only remaining sign talker
[125]on the Plains, but I began to notice that other Nakota
[126]speakers in the community also frequently accompanied
[127]their speech with gestures belonging to that system. Upon
[128]mentioning this observation, I was told, "Of course, it's
[129]part of the language," and my remark was considered to
[130]be rather obvious if not altogether stupid. This alerted me
[131]to the consideration that the conception of a "Plains sign
[132]language" as a distinct and primarily intertribal language,
[133]is grossly misleading. It may be a product of what Roy
[134]Harris ... called "the language myth": the
[135]artifactualization of languages as "fixed codes." Instead,
[136]there exists, in the Assiniboine case at least, a continuum,
[137]moving from an informal use of gestures that accompany
[138]or replace speech in everyday interactions, to more for-
[139]malized contexts such as storytelling performances (and
[140]sign songs and hymns).

[141]In former times, and where deafness exists today, the con-
[142]tinuum extends to the use of a widely conventionalized
[143]intertribal system that can exclude speech altogether.
[144]People draw on an available repertoire of gestures that
[145]can be used with or without spoken language according
[146]to individual knowledge, personal preference, skill, and
[147]context. In Assiniboine story-telling, both speech and ges-
[148]ture are an integral part of the narrative sense and ges-
[149]tures are not simply dramatic enhancement or a repeat of
[150]a spoken narrative. ... In addition both kinds of utterance
[151]are considered to be "talking" (hence the use in English
[152]of the term "sign talk"), and some use the English lexeme
[153]"word" to refer to either a vocal or a gestural utterance.
[154]Assiniboine people often use signs and speech simulta-
[155]neously and do not privilege speech over gestural talk-
[156]ing. On one occasion, for example, when I asked for the

[157]spoken equivalent of a gestural utterance by saying, "How [158]would you say that in Nakota?" the reply was, "Like I [159]just showed you." Obviously, there is a very different con-[160]ception of "language" going on here, one that combines [161]body and mind in ways that confound Cartesian dualis-[162]tic thinking.

[163]If this was a 'lost' tradition, then I was led to ask, "Lost to [164]whom?" The stereotypic silent but visible and stoic-faced [165]Plains Indian so beloved by Hollywood, displaying his [166]primitive grandeur by talking in signs had gone, and so, [167]it was assumed, had the language. PST had become invis-[168]ible to non-Indians, in part because of this change of con-[169]texts but also because that same Cartesian bias prohibits [170]such gesturing with speech from being valued by the [171]dominant culture. Waving one's hands around when talk-[172]ing is, for the most part, viewed as a sign of a deficiency—[173]an inability to express oneself adequately in words, or a [174]marker of lower class or undesirable ethnic origin. The [175]French and Italians, for example, are stereotypically [176]thought to be prone to such excesses of gesture in response [177]to overly active passions, interpreted on the whole by those [178]of Anglo-Saxon and derived cultures as evidence of less [179]rational, more emotional and therefore uncontrolled (read [180]"immoral") behavior.

Find Definitions

• assimilation(-ist) [lines 10, 13, 35]; • lexeme [line 152]; • indigenous [lines 17, 26-7]; • norm(-ative) [line 22]; • rhetoric [lines 18, 29]; • romantic(-ized) [line 55]; • altruistic(-ism) [line 58]; • integral [line 148]; • precursor(s) [line 96]; • *lingua franca* [lines 43, 71]; • artifact(s, -ual, -ualization) [line 135]; • continuum [lines 136, 141-2]; • enhance(-ment) [line 149]; • bias [lines 95, 169]; • dual (-ist, -istic, -ism) [line 162]; • Cartesian [lines 161, 169].

Answer These Questions

I. To what "battle" does Farnell refer? [lines 91-94].

a. How is this battle connected with Baynton's essay?

II. Do you think Farnell's subject is connected with Glasser's essay? If so, how? If not, why?

III. In lines 106-109, what possibility was ignored?

IV. What did Farnell notice that was considered "obvious if not...stupid" by her native consultant? [lines 124-130].

V. How is "waving one's hands around" viewed? [lines 171-180].

VI. What two stereotypes are mentioned in lines 164-167?

VII. "[There is] a deeply rooted Cartesianism in our definition of language as traditionally constituted, reflected by the view that there are two separate systems involved in the human organization of space, time, and the body, one having to do with the movement of the body, a physical realm of sensory-motor organization and doing in the world; the other having to do with sound and speech and a mental realm of thought and reflection on the world. Such a conception may indeed be an accurate picture of the Western folk model of the person, but it is surely no longer acceptable as a cross-cultural analytic model. It creates dualities between mind and body, speech and action, reason and emotion, conception and experience, verbal and nonverbal, symbolic and instrumental, and a host of others" ... (p. 92 in Conclusion).

Question:
Why is a western folk model of the 'person' not suitable cross-culturally?

VIII. What's wrong with having a "deeply rooted Cartesianism in an English-speaker's definition of language" as traditionally constituted? Use your own insights as well as the author's in your answer.

IV. Write a précis of the entire 180 line passage using *no more* than 300 and *not less* than 150 words.

SECTION I
ESSAYS

CHAPTER 4

Theresa Buckland: Traditional Dance: English Ceremonial and Social Forms

SHORT BIOGRAPHICAL NOTE

Theresa Buckland is currently Head of the Department of Dance studies, University of Surrey, England where she directs two Master's degree programs. After initial dance training in ballet, she attended the Benesh Institute of Choreology, London (Intermediate Diploma) and went on to the University of Leeds to take a first class honors degree in English Language and Literature, followed by a PH.D. in Folk Life Studies. Now responsible for developing undergraduate and postgraduate courses in the anthropology of dance and popular culture at the University of Surrey, her previous institutional position was as Head of the Department of Arts, Design and Performance at Manchester Metropolitan University. She is an editorial board member of *Folk Music Journal*, *Folklore* and *Dance Research*, and Honorary Secretary of the International Council for the Traditional Music Study Group on Ethnochoreology.

Her research interests lie in the areas of popular dance culture, history, ethnography, and the anthropology of dance and human movement studies. She has published a number of papers on English traditional dancing and on video-dances; among them is 'Dance and Music Video: Some Preliminary Observations' in *Parallel Lines: Media Representations of Dance* [Stephanie Jordan, Dave Allen, Eds.] John Libby, 1993. She is currently completing an edited international collection on dances and fieldwork entitled *Dance in the Field: Theory, Methods and Issues in Dance Ethnography* to be published by Macmillan.

The following text is a reproduction, using British spelling and punctuation, of **Buckland, Theresa. 1994.** *Dance History: An Introduction* (Janet Adshead-Lansdale and June Layson, Eds.), London and New York: Routledge, pp. 45-58. The text is reprinted by permission of the author.

•• [N.B. For complete bibliography of magazines, etc. please consult original publication].

TRADITIONAL DANCE: ENGLISH CEREMONIAL
AND SOCIAL FORMS

Introduction

What constitutes traditional dance, or folk dance as it is frequently termed, has been the subject of recent debate in the United Kingdom (see Buckland 1983). Yet whatever the specific historical, cultural and socio-economic factors which have contributed towards its construction, a repertoire of English traditional dance has been recognised and practised as such since the early 1900s.

This canon of English traditional dance was primarily defined by Cecil Sharp (1859-1924) and consists of Morris, Sword and Country Dances. During the twentieth century, the repertoire has been extended, yet the criteria established by Sharp have been principally operative in the inclusion of any new dances.

A loose definition which might identify this repertoire is that its dances may be distinguished from other forms of dance by the fact that they have been handed down from generation to generation without close reference to national or international standards.

Traditional dances may begin their existence in the fashionable ballroom or, indeed, in the theatre. In many cases their origin cannot be discovered. However, the task of the student of the history of traditional dance is not to concentrate solely on origins but to extend present knowledge of the nature of the form, its context and transmission in the past.

Following Sharp's categorisation, the traditional dances of England can be broadly classified into two major groups: those dances which are executed at particular times of the year in a performer/audience context, and those which are not tied to the calendar and are performed mainly for recreational purposes. The former group are referred to here as ceremonial dances and the latter as social dances.

Ceremonial dancing in England at the time of Sharp was traditionally most frequently performed by men, although there were notable exceptions, especially in the north-west region. Morris and Sword dancing (see Cawte *et al.* 1960) constitute the two most common forms of English ceremonial dancing. Social dancing in England usually involves simultaneous participation by both sexes. The majority of these types of dances, however, have their origin in the fashionable ballroom or, if derived from other sources, at least existed in this context at some time. The characteristics of the two groups described above are not totally distinct as there are several dances which at any one time may display both ceremonial and social features.

A late-twentieth-century addition to Sharp's canon of English traditional dance is step dancing. Known as clog dancing when performed in such footwear, it is open to men, women and children and, although more usually seen as a display, it can be danced as a social form.

Previous Scholarship

Perhaps the most famous date in the history of English traditional dance scholarship is Boxing Day 1899. It was on this day that Cecil Sharp, then Principal of the Hampstead Conservatoire of Music, London, first witnessed the performance of a Morris team.

Although he noted down tunes which accompanied the dances, Sharp did not attempt to collect the choreography until 1905. In this year, Mary Neal, who organised an association for underprivileged girls in East London known as the 'Esperance Working Girls' Club', approached Sharp with a request for traditional English dances for the girls to perform (see Judge 1989). Thus began the attempt to collect folk dances before, as was feared, urbanisation and industrialisation destroyed the rural setting where the traditional dance culture appeared to flourish.

Many dances were undoubtedly either in a dead or moribund state and it cannot be disputed that, had Sharp and his fellow collectors delayed in their task, knowledge of English traditional dancing in the second half of the nineteenth century would be infinitely poorer. In 1911 Sharp founded the English Folk Dance Society with the purpose of fostering the revival of English traditional dance. The collections of traditional dances published by Sharp and his associates form the main corpus of material employed in the national revival and set out the 'pagan origin' theory of traditional dance which, until recently, remained unchallenged in English publications.

In his theoretical writing on traditional dance Sharp concentrated on origins. This orientation he shared with nineteenth-century folklorists from whom, albeit indirectly at first, he drew his interpretation of folk custom.

The theory of cultural survival, formulated by the anthropologist E.B. Tylor and popularised by Sir James Frazer (1890) in *The Golden Bough*, stated that all traditional customs had their origin in primitive rituals which still lingered in the countryside. Although there was no sound historical evidence to support this theory, it gained wide credence and remains today in many populist writings on traditional dance.

The effect of this theory was to channel the collecting activities of those interested in traditional dance into searching the countryside for any vestiges of a primitive dance culture. The towns and cities were ignored. Consequently, traditional dance types such as the Morris dancing of the north-west and the widespread traditions of solo step dancing often found in urban areas were not systematically collected.

An examination of the notes of early collectors such as Sharp, Maud Karpeles and Clive Carey reveal what today would be regarded as unmethodical collection, lack of social and historical data, insufficient detail on the context of documentation and a restricting belief that the purest form of traditional dance never alters its choreography except for the worse.

This latter point is again a feature of nineteenth-century folklorist theory: change and variation are thought to be indicative of degeneration from the primitive and pure archetype. Such an attitude demonstrates a misunderstanding of the practice of such dance forms.

However, with no historical records of the choreography available to the collectors, it was impossible for them to gain a historical perspective based on factual evidence. Furthermore social class differences between collector and informant supported the misleading notion of the uneducated, unreflective 'tradition-bearer' who had little of real significance to offer other than the dance itself. Instead of concentrating upon the obtainable facts from informants, the collector preferred to speculate upon the origins of dance in inaccessible antiquity.

The majority of past scholarship has tended to reflect the concerns of the national revival movement. Distinction between what might be designated as authentic tradition and as twentieth-century revival lies behind much of the literature. However, since the 1970s at least, these divisive categories of 'the tradition' and 'the revival' have been challenged (see, in particular, Sughrue 1988).

In general, the term 'traditional' or 'the tradition' has been used of dance forms and associated behaviour which have been practised largely outside influence from the national folk revival. This led to value judgements being made as to which dance activities were to be considered worthy of serious scholarly attention. Today, such distinctions cannot be supported as legitimate scholarly categories, although, as terms in common parlance within the folk scene, 'the tradition' and 'the revival' are still often employed to signify particular historical relationships and lineages.

Unless indicated otherwise, this chapter embraces both 'the tradition' and 'the revival' under the general heading of English traditional dance.

Written Source Materials

It must be stressed that, as a first port of call, the Vaughan Williams Memorial Library, housed at Cecil Sharp House, London, is essential to any student of the historical practice of traditional dancing in England.

There is in fact no general written introduction to English traditional dance to be recommended which does not suffer from inaccuracies or speculations. Hugh Rippon's *Discovering English Folk Dance* (1993) is perhaps the best and most concise introduction to date and is particularly illuminating on the interplay between 'the tradition' and 'the revival'.

Standard manuals on the performance of traditional dance are those produced in the early decades of this century chiefly by Sharp. Cawte has compiled a very useful index to Sharp's five volumes of *The Morris Book* (1983). *A Handbook of Morris Dances* by Lionel Bacon (1974) is a more comprehensive 'aide-memoire' with regard to ceremonial dance, and an invaluable bibliographic tool is Heaney's listing of articles on Morris dancing (1985) which is obtainable from the Vaughan Williams Memorial Library. The *Community Dance Manuals* published by the English Folk Dance and Song Society (EFDSS) between 1947 and 1967 have made available in written form a larger repertoire of social dances than that published by Sharp. A helpful guide to writings on sword dancing is Corrsin (1990) and, for step dancing, Metherell's introductory bibliography (1993) brings together essential references concerning this new and expanding area of traditional dance research.

More specialised articles can be found in the *Folk Music Journal*, formerly known as the *Journal of the English Folk Dance and Song Society*. The magazine *English Dance and Song*, now published four times a year, contains relevant material and is also held in the Vaughan Williams Memorial Library. There is a published catalogue of the library's holding which is the largest collection of information on English traditional dance and includes archival film, photographs and sound recordings, in addition to manuscript and published material.

Other organisations in England which produce periodicals on traditional dance are the Morris Ring, an association of men's ceremonial dance teams founded by revival groups in 1934, and the Morris Federation, originally the female equivalent, established in 1975. Their respective publications are *The Morris Dancer* and *Morris Matters* (both currently twice a year), the latter published in association with Windsor Morris. These organizations can provide address lists of member teams and hold archives of film, video, books, photographs and manuscript material, access to which is possible for bona fide researchers.

A number of conference proceedings since the 1980s provide insight into the methodologies and interests of traditional dance scholars, many of whom have shifted focus on to more recent history, particularly that of ceremonial dance teams (see Buckland 1982-8, Sughrue 1987, The Morris Federation and The Morris Ring 1991).

With regard to indices of source materials, a preliminary checklist of traditional social dances as practised in England does not exist and reference has to be made to the footnotes and bibliographies, where given, in various publications. Researchers of ceremonial dance have a better resource in the indices of the geographical distribution of these dances compiled respectively by Needham (1936) and Cawte *et al* (1960). The 1936 index lists all located references known at that time to ceremonial dance since 1800. The 1960 index extends its historical references to all known located records. There are inaccuracies and substantial omissions from this index (now in need of revision) but it does identify the chief characteristics of the regional forms and provides a ready checklist of sources. An exemplary listing is Heaney and Forrest's *Annals of Early Morris* (1991), which concentrates on sources for the three centuries prior to 1750 and refers to the whole of the British Isles. Such research aids should lead to more scholarly in-depth interpretations than hitherto.

Selection of an Area of Study

Detailed work on the history of traditional dancing in England has gathered pace (see, for example, the series of short monographs by various authors produced as *Morris Dancing in the South Midlands*, 1983-7), but there remains a wide field for investigation. The student may select a particular geographical area, for example, and discover the various types of traditional dancing practised there within a given span of time. Alternatively, one type of traditional dance could be chosen and the various contexts in which this type appeared investigated (see, for example, Chandler 1993a for a definitive study of morris dancing in the south Midlands 1660-1900).

The study of the history of traditional dancing can be divided into: dances beyond living memory, and dances within living memory. Sources for the first group are to be found mainly in written form, whereas the second group may consist of both written and oral sources.

Some students may know of traditional dance forms either through their own active involvement or possibly through that of their family and friends. Such first-hand knowledge of an area presents an ideal starting point for study.

Clearly new traditions have arisen since the last century, particularly those prompted by the impact of the revival movement. These traditions of perhaps only two or three generations, or, indeed years, present exciting new material to study. Since the early years of this century, new ceremonial dance teams, in particular, have sprung up all over the country, and numerous events take place at which revived traditional social dance can be seen. Teams and solo performers of step dancing would also repay close examination. These new developments need to be studied through both written and oral sources in addition to witnessing actual performances.

Revivals prior to those begun by the English Folk Dance and Song Society also require investigation. For example, the church and/or school within a community may have acted as patrons or even instigators of dancing. Very often introductions to ceremonial events such as May Day festivals or Jubilee celebrations were made which contained dance performances. Sometimes these introductions transformed already existing local customs into occasions for children who took on the main participants' role instead of adults.

It is clear that any attempt to account for the form of traditional dance must take social and historical contexts into account.

Dances Beyond Living Memory

The primary sources which make reference to traditional dance are classified in chronological order in the following sections, although some types of material may occur in more than one historical period. Since the student is likely to be dealing with local history material, the guides by Rogers (1977), Richardson (1977) and Riden (1989) would be invaluable in understanding the techniques normally used in this area.

Churchwardens' accounts

These records were generally kept at the parish churches or the local and diocesan record offices, but copies are now often available at county record offices. They can be particularly valuable for details of costume and properties used in traditional ceremonial dances and for information on the payment of the performers, for example:

1521-2 Eight yerds of fustyan for the Mores-daunsars coats 0.16.0
(Kingston-upon-Thames Churchwardens'
Accounts, quoted in Burton 1891: 106).

The church was responsible in varying degrees for organising the celebrations of holy days. Some of the dancing activities watched over by the church were utilised to raise money for charitable purposes as at Abbots Bromley, Staffordshire. Heaney and Forrest's *Annals of Early Morris* (1991) provides a useful starting point for examining such material.

Dance manuals

These exist in both manuscript and published form and are held chiefly in public and university libraries. In particular the collections at the Vaughan Williams Memorial Library should be consulted. Much of the published material does not deal with contemporary traditional dance but with popular and fashionable forms which may later become part of the traditional repertoire. There are no known British manuals of ceremonial dance predating the twentieth-century revival.

Diaries, journals, topographies, gazetteers

Many personal diaries such as that by Nicholas Blundell (1712), which contains a reference to an eighteenth-century performance of a Sword Dance near Liverpool, have been published. However, it is likely that many diaries and journals held in local libraries have not yet been consulted for references to traditional forms of dance. Most early diaries were written by people with leisure and education and thus tend to reflect upper- or middle-class attitudes towards traditional dancing. Therefore knowledge of the social status of the writer is vital to the interpretation of the record. Upper-class society is not necessarily adverse to traditional customs, nor are those of more humble origins equally well disposed.

A type of publication which sometimes contains references to traditional dancing is the topography, a description of an area's natural and artificial features. Topographies were popular from the seventeenth to the early nineteenth centuries and, since they were often written on a county basis, are most useful for discovering references to local instances of ceremonial dancing. Thus Robert Plot's *Natural History of Staffordshire* of 1686 contains the earliest known description of the Abbots Bromley Horn Dance (p. 434). Similarly, gazetteers may also include details of dance customs performed at particular feast or market days in the year although they are generally not the best sources for reference to social forms of traditional dancing.

Newspapers and periodicals

From the second half of the nineteenth century (and earlier in cities and some large towns) the student's task is enormously eased by the growth in local newspapers. Most local libraries hold back copies or issues can be consulted at the newspaper section of the British Library.

Reports of ceremonial dance are again easier to locate than those of social dance. With the former's appearance at certain times of the year the potential field is clearly narrowed. However, it is necessary to be alert to changing patterns of ceremonial behaviour in the locality. For example, Morris dances were performed at the traditional time of the local wakes (that is, the major annual holiday) in north-west England, some time between June and September. But reports of these occurrences became increasingly rare at the turn of the century and searches through the newspaper are more rewarding thereafter if references to May festivals, rose queen fetes and carnivals held in the spring and summer months are found. Advance notices of ceremonial dancing were by no means uncommon in the local press of that area. In addition to advertisements there are occasional accounts of Morris dancers practising in the streets before the commencement of the wakes holiday. Sometimes newspaper references to Morris dancers after their performance date can be found when their names and activities are recorded in the list of court appearances together with charges of drunkenness or trespassing.

Accounts of social dancing in traditional contexts tend to be rare except in brief references to competitive step dancing in the advertisements placed by publicans to attract patrons to their houses during festive periods. It is also possible to find the occasional article of reminiscences about past local life which may include a description of the local social dance gatherings.

As with all dance material, the student must investigate the political, proprietary and religious sympathies, in this case, of the newspaper. In the northern county of Lancashire during the early 1860s, the Oldham press was extremely sympathetic towards local customs whereas, in the very same period, the Rochdale papers, anxious to advertise the town as being at the forefront of Victorian progress and rationalism, supported the campaign against traditional celebrations. In Oldham Morris dancing continued to flourish at the end of the nineteenth century but it appears to have died out during this period in Rochdale.

Folklore and local history collections

In the second half of the nineteenth century, references to ceremonial dancing increased with the development of local history and folklore studies. Where these contain eye-witness accounts of traditional dancing such sources can be classified as primary. A related source is the autobiography which may include information on traditional dancing either witnessed or practised in the author's youth.

Historical novels

Historical novels often contain reference to traditional dances but these cannot be regarded as primary sources for the particular period in which the novel is placed unless the author is recalling a personal experience and setting it in the appropriate time-span. Examples of writers who use this device are Thomas Hardy (1872), referred to in this respect in Chapter 2, and the Lancashire author Ben Brierley (1844a, b) who described Morris dancing at the wakes. Nevertheless, such sources need to be checked against contemporary accounts since the novelist is not necessarily concerned to present a faithful record of remembered events.

Costume, regalia, photographs, film/video

Occasionally actual dance items such as dancing clogs are donated to museums. Unfortunately, the Cecil Sharp House collection of various artefacts of English traditional dancing was damaged by bombing in the 1939-45 war.

With the developing interest in the daily life of the past, many libraries are beginning to build up collections of old photographs depicting local life. These may include photographs of ceremonial dance teams. The North West Film archive of Manchester Metropolitan University possesses two interesting films of Morris dancers at Whalley, Lancashire, in 1913 and 1919. Such rare visual records provide numerous starting points for study including, in this case, the possibility of analysing changes over a short period of time. More recently the Vaughan Williams Memorial Library has produced video-tapes of step dancers.

Dances Within Living Memory

All the listings in the preceding section are also potential source material for the study of traditional dances within living memory. However, in the study of dances within living memory additional valuable information may be obtained from former participants.

Memories of former performers are best recorded on audio- or videotape to ensure accuracy and to communicate something of the character of the informant. Quotations from dancers help to illuminate the material from the human angle. Not only should students who are about to engage in collecting information from people familiarise themselves completely with operating their equipment, they should also practise interviewing techniques before starting fieldwork in order to achieve the maximum of freely-given information from their interviewees with the minimum number of questions. Of particular help in preparing to conduct interviews are Goldstein's publication (1964) and those of Ives (1980) and Agar (1980).

The performers

In the past very little emphasis was placed on the individuals who were involved in traditional dancing. Modern folklore study, however, insists that details such as the participants' age, sex, occupation and social status are collected in order to gain some understanding of the nature of traditional dancing.

Dancing styles are often transmitted through families, particularly in solo forms such as step dancing, although in the south Midlands kinship also played a vital role in the composition of Morris teams. Sometimes dance styles are the property of particular occupations such as the modified form of Lancashire step dancing performed by the lifeboat-men of Cromer, Norfolk.

It is important to ascertain how and why dancers become involved in their chosen style and also to discover how much or how little they had been exposed to it before participating. Dancers within revival groups may have joined after witnessing a public performance of a local team or through participation in some other aspect of the folk revival movement, such as being a member of a folk song club.

Distinctive modes of learning and rehearsing also need to be closely investigated. In Bampton, Oxfordshire, one traditional Morris team meets only a few weeks before their traditional day of Spring Bank Holiday Monday to practise whereas at Bacup, Lancashire, the 'coconut' dancers used to aim to rehearse once a week throughout the year. Practice nights are often social occasions as well as periods set aside to learn or maintain the performance of particular movements.

Occasions of performance

Most of the literature, following Sharp's example, has tended to refer to the annual traditional times of performance as if these were the only occasions on which ceremonial dance teams appeared. It is a partial assessment of the dancers' role in their society and fails to reflect adequately the response of dancers to their diverse and changing cultural contexts. Much information on the times of performance with regard to ceremonial dance can be gleaned from written records, particularly newspapers, and from former participants.

Informants should be questioned about all types of performance and about the existence and type of other activities taking place on the same occasion. Seemingly contradictory information on the performance routes undertaken by teams may be explained by changes introduced from year to year on the grounds of available time, personal choice and economics. The collection of money and hospitality shown by patrons to the dancers in the form of food and drink have a particular effect upon the choice of route. Ceremonial dancers in the past needed at least to cover their own expenditure and preferably earn some money from their exertions.

The dance

The chief rules in the collection of dance notations are to let the former participant provide the terminology and for the researcher to avoid any demonstration of steps since this might itself distort and bias the response.

In the case of revival teams detailed enquiries should be made with regard to the source of the dance notation. If this is a written source, it should be checked carefully against the notations offered by former dancers and, where relevant, against the dance as it is currently performed. Variations may have occurred over the years and it is important to note them. It is also useful to realise that individual variations within a group dance may, in some instances, have been desirable. This may account for apparent discrepancies between notations collected from different dancers. Such apparent discrepancies may also derive from differences in choreography and performance over time. The whole repertoire of dances should always be collected.

The music

Dancers and musicians have different perceptions of the performance and, accordingly, should be interviewed both separately and jointly if possible. This is especially valuable in determining timing and phrasing. All musicians with any connection to the dance should be recorded both playing and reminiscing. The provenance of music, how the musician came to be involved in the dance tradition, the process of learning the music, and her/his attitude towards it should all be investigated.

Costume and regalia

Queries regarding the dress for traditional dancing are as relevant to studies of social dancing as they are to considerations of the more obvious special attire of ceremonial dancers. Types of dress alter to suit the occasion, and footwear, in particular, has a marked effect upon the dance style.

Many of England's ceremonial dancers use properties such as sticks, swords and handkerchiefs, and the acquisition of those must be investigated. Information should also be acquired on the properties of the supernumeraries, such as hobbyhorses, fools and man/woman figures, which sometimes accompany traditional ceremonial dance teams.

Conclusion

Even if the student wishes to concentrate on one aspect of traditional dancing, for example the costume or the occasion of performance, the other components of the dance event must not be ignored. Characteristic relationships between particular types of dance and the environment, between costume and local industries, between the choice of musical instruments and the form of the dance, etc. may have existed and require discussion.

The number and quality of articles and monographs on English traditional dancing have significantly improved since the 1970s. Notable gaps remain in the history of social dancing, especially in the twentieth century, and opportunities for original research into dance practices at weddings, parties, barn dances, folk dance clubs and *ceilidhs* are abundant. Exploration of such practices will further illustrate the construct of 'folk' as the result of specific ideological and Eurocentric circumstances. There exists a wide range of primary sources, both written and oral, which, when explored, will not only deepen and broaden understanding of the form, transmission and context of traditional popular dancing in the past, but will also considerably illuminate the role of dance [forms] in society today.

[T.B.]

PRECIS 4

[1]Perhaps the most famous date in the history of English tra-
[2]ditional dance scholarship is Boxing Day 1899. It was on
[3]this day that Cecil Sharp, then Principal of the Hampstead
[4]Conservatoire of Music, London, first witnessed the perfor-
[5]mance of a Morris team.

[6]Although he noted down tunes which accompanied the
[7]dances, Sharp did not attempt to collect the choreography
[8]until 1905. In this year, Mary Neal, who organised an asso-
[9]ciation for underprivileged girls in East London known as
[10]the 'Esperance Working Girls' Club', approached Sharp
[11]with a request for traditional English dances for the girls
[12]to perform ... Thus began the attempt to collect folk dances
[13]before, as was feared, urbanisation and industrialisation
[14]destroyed the rural setting where the traditional dance
[15]culture appeared to flourish.

[16]Many dances were undoubtedly either in a dead or mori-
[17]bund state and it cannot be disputed that, had Sharp and
[18]his fellow collectors delayed in their task, knowledge of
[19]English traditional dancing in the second half of the nine-
[20]teenth century would be infinitely poorer. In 1911 Sharp
[21]founded the English Folk Dance Society with the purpose
[22]of fostering the revival of English traditional dance. The
[23]collections of traditional dances published by Sharp and
[24]his associates form the main corpus of material employed
[25]in the national revival and set out the 'pagan origin' theory
[26]of traditional dance which, until recently, remained unchal-
[27]lenged in English publications.

[28]In his theoretical writing on traditional dance Sharp con-
[29]centrated on origins. This orientation he shared with nine-
[30]teenth-century folklorists from whom, albeit indirectly at
[31]first, he drew his interpretation of folk custom.

[32]The theory of cultural survival, formulated by the anthro-
[33]pologist E.B. Tylor and popularised by Sir James Frazer ...
[34]in *The Golden Bough*, stated that all traditional customs had

[35]their origin in primitive rituals which still lingered in the [36]countryside. Although there was no sound historical evi-[37]dence to support this theory, it gained wide credence and [38]remains today in many populist writings on traditional dance.

[39]The effect of this theory was to channel the collecting ac-[40]tivities of those interested in traditional dance into search-[41]ing the countryside for any vestiges of a primitive dance [40]culture. The towns and cities were ignored. Consequently, [41]traditional dance types such as the Morris dancing of the [42]north-west and the widespread traditions of solo step danc-[43]ing often found in urban areas were not systematically col-lected.

[44]An examination of the notes of early collectors such as [45]Sharp, Maud Karpeles and Clive Carey reveal what today [46]would be regarded as unmethodical collection, lack of so-[47]cial and historical data, insufficient detail on the context of [48]documentation and a restricting belief that the purest form [49]of traditional dance never alters its choreography except for the worse.

[50]This latter point is again a feature of nineteenth-century [51]folklorist theory: change and variation are thought to be [52]indicative of degeneration from the primitive and pure ar-[53]chetype. Such an attitude demonstrates a misunder-[54]standing of the practice of such dance forms.

[55]However, with no historical records of the choreography [56]available to the collectors, it was impossible for them to [57]gain a historical perspective based on factual evidence. Fur-[58]thermore social class differences between collector and in-[59]formant supported the misleading notion of the unedu-[60]cated, unreflective 'tradition-bearer' who had little of real [61]significance to offer other than the dance itself. Instead of [62]concentrating upon the obtainable facts from informants, [63]the collector preferred to speculate upon the origins of [64]dance in inaccessible antiquity.

[65]The majority of past scholarship has tended to reflect the [66]concerns of the national revival movement. Distinction be-[67]tween what might be designated as authentic tradition and [68]as twentieth-century revival lies behind much of the lit-[69]erature. However, since the 1970s at least, these divisive [70]categories of 'the tradition' and 'the revival' have been challenged.

[71]In general, the term 'traditional' or 'the tradition' has been [72]used of dance forms and associated behaviour which have [73]been practised largely outside influence from the national [74]folk revival. This led to value judgements being made as [75]to which dance activities were to be considered worthy of [76]serious scholarly attention. Today, such distinctions can-[77]not be supported as legitimate scholarly categories, al-[78]though, as terms in common parlance within the folk [79]scene, 'the tradition' and 'the revival' are still often em-[80]ployed to signify particular historical relationships and lineages.

Find Definitions:

•moribund [lines 16-7]; •vestige(s) [line 41]; •divisive [line 69]; •(un)methodical [line 46]; •archetype [line 52-3]; •parlance [line 78]; •Boxing Day [line 2]; •populist [line 38].

Answer These Questions

I. "Although there was no sound historical evidence to support this theory [i.e. that of 'pagan origin'], it gained wide credence and remains today in many populist writings ..." [lines 36-8]. Discuss.
II. What does an examination of the notes of early collectors reveal? [lines 44-49].
III. Why couldn't early collectors gain an historical perspective? [lines 55-57].
IV. To what did the distinction between 'traditional' and 'revival' lead? [lines 71-80].
V. Finally, write a précis of the 80-line passage using between 100 and 150 words.

SECTION II
PREDISPOSITIONS OF THOUGHT

CHAPTER 5

Records and References

CHAPTER 5

Records and References

Classifications and Categories

In a booklet entitled *How Do You Talk About People?* published by New York City's Anti-Defamation League, the author illustrated 'people classification' thus:

> I knew a man who had lost the use of both eyes. He was called a "blind man." He could also be called an expert typist, a conscientious worker, a good student, a careful listener, a man who wanted a job. But he couldn't get a job in the department store order room where employees sat and typed orders which came over the telephone. The personnel man was impatient to get the interview over. "But you're a blind man," he kept saying, and one could almost feel his silent assumption that somehow the incapacity in one aspect made the man incapable in every other. So blinded by the label was the interviewer that he could not be persuaded to look beyond it (Lee 1950: 15).

The example is instructive: any label identifies one (and only one) feature of the person thus identified. Readers are left with the impression that the job interviewer was more blind than the interviewee.

Naming, labeling and classifying people can be injurious in practical ways. In this case, because of labeling a blind man was unjustifiably eliminated from competition for a job. However, *that doesn't mean that naming and labeling are themselves damaging*. It isn't the English language or the labels that are at fault. The fault lies in the ways that people *use* classifications and categories.

Classification and Dances

Since we cannot do without the abstracting process of which names, labels, classifications and categories consist, we must deal with them. It is especially important to anthropologists of human movement because sign language and sign-talkers, dances and dancers, are consistently surrounded by classificatory issues, as we saw in the previous section — some more obvious than others.

Consider the fact that Glasser's essay begins with "some terminological questions [which] need clarification." She identifies the word 'art' as a problem because people tend to associate it with a domain of experience that "exists on a separate level of reality" (p. 21). If she permits her readers to think of the dances she discusses as 'art', and if they associate 'art' with a separate reality, she will fail to bring home her point: dances are as much a part of 'reality' as any other cultural phenomenon.

Writers cannot avoid dealing with commonly used words about dancing and dances because they must establish their point of view, otherwise their arguments are open to any and all interpretation. Glasser wants her position on the political nature of the dance in South Africa to be understood. She must therefore explain the terminology she uses.

On the other hand, Georgina Gore is blunt regarding commonly used terminology for dances in West Africa. She draws attention to a criticism that sociocultural anthropologists often make about writers who have no anthropological training. She suggests using indigenous classifications and categories when describing dances from other cultures:

> To speak of West African dance is in fact a misnomer. ...[T]he ethnocentricly European term 'dance' is not applicable to systems of structured human body movement of non-European peoples, *who have their own terms of reference for conceiving of such activities* (p. 22 - italics added).

We frequently talk about other peoples as if they had no terms of reference for what they do, think or feel.

Why Movement Is Thought To Be Inferior

Baynton nails the fundamental classificatory problem for sign languages and dances in his section, 'The Stigma of Inferiority', where he says,

> The languages of early humans could not be directly studied, of course. No fossils are left recording speech, gesture or expressions of the face. [Physical] anthropologists, however, began in the latter decades of the nineteenth century to see the so-called "savage races" as examples

> of earlier stages of evolution. Assuming a model of linear evolutionary progress, they depicted them - Africans, American Indians, Australian Aborigines and others — as "living fossils" left behind by the more rapidly progressing cultures ... (p. 48).

The idea that movement is inferior to speech is a deeply embedded prejudice that is not easily overcome.

Farnell's essay extends the range of this notion by locating the classificatory problem with sign languages in American anthropological history; i.e.,

> West's work was pioneering because sign languages were not considered by linguists and educators at that time to be real languages— a battle that is still going on in the education of the Deaf today. ... [S]ign languages were considered to be simple codes, probabler precursors to spoken language in the evolutionary scheme of things. ... [C]onsiderable interest had been shown in PST by nineteenth-century anthropologists such as E. B. Tylor, precisely because they seemed to provide indisputable evidence of a primitive state (p. 80).

Nor has the language problem been solved. Consider this passage from the introduction to the 1994 edition of Clark, Escholz and Rosa's textbook, *Language: Introductory Readings*, in a section headed 'Non-Languages':

> Other kinds of human communication [besides speech] are sometimes called language: body language, or kinesics, is one example. The way we use our bodies in sitting, standing, walking, is said to be expressive of things we do not say. It probably is but that does not make it language. Body language lacks duality, in that it is not symbolic but rather a direct representation of feeling; discreteness in that there is no alphabet of distinctive movements or postures; and productivity, in that "original" expressions are likely not to be understood. Moreover it appears to be only partly arbitrary, for the movement or posture is often selected by its "meaning" as representational, not arbitrary; "barrier signs" such as crossing one's arms or legs need no dictionary (Bolton, in Clark, Escholz and Rosa (Eds.) 1994: 6-7, cited in Farnell 1995b: 136).

There are authoritative writers who have proved beyond any doubt that "body languages" are representational. There is evidence to show that their elements (i.e., movement images plus concepts) possess duality. Furthermore, there are clear equivalents to alphabets and vocabularies of distinctive movements for sign languages and dances.

Some Labels Are More Powerful

As we have seen, the job interviewer couldn't get past labeling a blind person. To the interviewer, the classification 'blindness' dominates every other characteristic of the applicant. The job he offered required typists who could take telephone orders. *There was nothing wrong with the blind man's hearing.* Had the blind man applied for a job requiring keen eyesight, the interviewer's attitude would have been justified. In the situation Lee describes, the interviewer's attitude is not justifiable. Because he couldn't get beyond the job-applicant's blindness, the interviewer proved to be prejudiced. Some labels, like that of "blind man,"seem especially powerful: those of "savage races," "Native American," "primitive dance" and others, operate the same way as "blind man." The labels are problems because *they tend to prevent alternative classification.*

We might, for example, say that a certain person is a *humanist*, an *artist*, a *dancer*, a *Native American* and a *scholar*. Someone might be all of these, but chances are that 'Native-American' and/or 'dancer' will stand out, although neither of these labels refers to the whole nature of the individual. *No single word sums up the whole nature of an individual* — only his or her proper name is meant to do that. An additional problem has to do with labels that are attached to whole groups of people (i.e., dancers, "savage" races, deaf-people, etc.)

Given a list of characteristics (humanist, artist, dancer, native American and scholar), one or two tend to project over others. For example, 'Native American dancer' almost always activates the association, 'primitive dancer' or 'ethnic dancer', but what if the person to whom the label is attached is Maria Tallchief or her sister, Marjorie?[1]

Unless one has devoted considerable time and energy studying the relevant subject matters, one is likely to evaluate dancers, dance forms and sign languages with considerable lopsidedness. People are likely to assume that 'native-Americans' perform 'primitive dances', or they are likely to assume that there is direct continuity between African or

Australian Aboriginal dances and the dance forms of today, regardless of the facts of their ethno-historical backgrounds. They might assume (as Curt Sachs did - see Preface, p. 5) that there is a direct line of continuity between birds and/or apes and human dancing.

Writing About Dances and Sign Languages

Strange though it may seem, it isn't helpful to try to define what the word 'dance' means, for, as the Vicar of St. Albans in England pointed out long ago,

> As soon as one attempts to define what dancing is in its essence one realizes the difficulty of doing so. It can be defined in such a number of ways, all of which contain elements of truth. ... The recording of a number of definitions would be wearisome, Voss[2] alone gives dozens by different people ... [T]hey show that the term dancing connotes a great deal more than is attached to it nowadays (Oesterley 1923: 5).

Oesterley was right: the recording of a number of definitions of dancing would be wearisome, not only because it distracts readers from the purposes of this book, it perpetuates the myth that there is a single interpretation of 'dance' out there somewhere that captures its 'essence' across time/space and cultures. If there were such a definition, it would solve many classificatory problems once and for all. Unfortunately, there is no such thing (see Best 1996).

Like the single words to which they are attached, categories and classifications become problems for students at any level who try to write about dancing and sign languages — and, let's face it, writing is a major component of university students' lives. While it is true that graduates may not pay much attention to commonly used reference books for their sources of information, beginning students and the general public do. For many people, encyclopedias constitute their first encounter with a field of study. On the whole, encyclopedias are dependable reference sources, but there are some areas that are not as well-handled as others. The dance is one of these, although writing about dances and dancing has improved over the past two centuries.[3]

Anthropologists of the dance who have criticized Sachs and others[4] seem to have failed to convince dance scholars and the general public once and for all of the basic inconsistencies and the unsoundness of cross-cultural usages of the category 'dance' — far less its usual accompaniments, 'primitive', 'tribal' and 'ethnic'. These words are still widely used, mainly because such classifications are found in authoritative books of reference. To illustrate, we will examine two columns headed TRIBAL AND ETHNIC DANCE in the *Encyclopædia Britannica*, where the author points out that

> Ballet, modern dance, and Indian classical dance are forms of theatre dance, the dancers usually being highly trained professionals performing for audiences in particular venues and on special occasions. Tribal and ethnic dance, on the other hand, may be characterized by a number of almost opposite features. They are not necessarily the province of trained specialists (although they may be); such dances may be participatory (i.e. with no real distinction between dancer and spectator); and while they may take place in special venues or on special occasions, these are often intimately related to the everyday life of the community (*Macropædia*, Volume 16: 954).

What are some of the problems with that passage? For a start, ballet and modern dancing have always been "forms of theatre dance," but Indian classical dancing has not.

Classical Indian Dance and the Theater

> 'Bharatanatyam' is the contemporary name for an idiom of dance (from the Madras State - formerly Tamilnadu - in south India) which is the most popular and well-known of the classical dance forms[5] performed in India today. Until the early nineteen-thirties it was referred as *Sadir Nac* or *Dasi Attam*, the dance of the *devadasis* (literally, 'servants of god') of the temples of Tanjore ... [T]he *devadasis* were women who were dedicated to temple service and who performed dances as part of the many rituals connected with a temple. Their dedication included the performance of a marriage ceremony with the deity of a particular temple and incorporation into temple society. Apart from their temple services, on special occasions such as weddings, they would be invited to perform at the houses of leading citizens. Some were also attached to the courts of *rajas* (hereditary rulers) and were expected to dance at the palace, for which they received a salary.

To the British colonizers, many of whom were entertained by these dancers when they visited a local ruler, the name *devadasi* became synonymous with 'dancing girls'. They disapproved of the custom, and in the nineteenth century an anti-nautch (anti-dance) movement was launched by a group of social reformers who sought to prohibit the institution (Puri 1983: 14).[6]

As a result of the anti-nautch movement, royal patronage was withdrawn and the *devadasis* fell into disfavor. It was not until the growth of Indian national consciousness at the beginning of the twentieth century that urban Indian *literati* sought to revive the *Sadir Nac* tradition outside of the temples. In the early 1930s, a group of dance and music scholars in Madras attempted to demonstrate that "far from being immoral the dance was an intrinsic part of Indian aesthetic, philosophical and religious beliefs and practices" (Puri 1983: 15). Although there was some resistance at the beginning of their efforts, by the 1950s, young girls from respected families began to study *Sadir Nac* and present it to audiences in Madras in theaters.

'Ethnic' Dancing

As it is commonly used inside (and outside) the dance world, 'ethnic dance' means any dance form that is not ballet or modern dancing.Typically, "our" dance forms are not called 'ethnic'. Only "their" dance forms are thus labelled. The following passage doesn't help to clarify:

> In describing many dances, reference is often made to their ethnic, rather than their tribal, origins. An ethnic dance is simply a dance that is characteristic of a particular cultural group. Under this definition even the polka, which is almost always considered a social dance, may be called ethnic, as it began in a culturally distinct region of Europe. Flamenco, which began as an improvised dance among Andalusian gypsies, combines toe and heel clicking with body movements similar to Indian dance. Indian dances may be regarded as a general ethnic type, but there are numerous forms and traditions within the type: some are classical (see above Indian classical dance), while others are popular, being danced by nonspecialists for communal festivities and for recreation (*Macropædia*, Volume 16: 955, col. 1).

As far as it goes, the author's definition of 'ethnic' is correct, but why single out the polka (usually classified as 'social' or 'folk' dancing) that is 'ethnic'.[7] How is 'ethnic' actually defined?

Any dance form anywhere in the world is ethnic, including the ballet and modern dancing because all dance forms have been generated by some ethnic group somewhere in the world. That, of course, is the main point of Keali'inohomoku's criticism of the 'ethnic dance' category (1997).

An Indigenous Classification from India

It is hard to imagine what the author sees in Flamenco dancing that is similar to Indian dancing. That Flamenco dancing "combines toe and heel clicking with body movements," reminding the writer of Indian dancing is hardly enough, as the Bharatanatyam and Kathak dancer's technique of using their bare feet in order to activate the bells worn on their ankles is completely unlike the Flamenco dancer's footwork, the sounds of which are amplified by specially constructed shoes. Moreover, the concepts conveyed by the two dance forms are different. Apart from that, readers should be told about the *Indian* categorical definitions of *Margi* (classical) and *Desi* (popular) which have an important historical and linguistic basis:

> *Margi* means 'of the proper way' and refers to a 'high' style of acting, dancing or singing. *Desi* means 'of a region' and commonly refers to the 'vulgar' or 'popular' style of acting, dancing or singing. *Margi* traditions are those which most closely adhere to the precepts of the ancient texts, thus to the highest form of Vedic culture.[8] *Desi* traditions are those which develop naturally — from the people. They are tied to local cultures and evolve without conscious reference to the contraints of the classical cultural tradition (Puri 1997: 180).[9]

'Tribal Dance'

How the Britannica author deals with 'tribal' dancing is as confusing as the passages we have read so far:

> A tribal society is essentially a self-contained system. While it may possess sophisticated cultural and social structures, its technological

and economic structures are generally primitive. Consequently, by the late 20th century such societies had become increasingly rare, and many tribal dances had either died or become transformed.

Some tribal dances have been preserved, however, even in cases where tribes have been absorbed into other social structures, as a means of preserving cultural identity and a sense of historical continuity. This is quite common in many African states. A frequently cited case is that of King Sobhuza II, the Ngwenyama ("Lion") of Swaziland, who in 1966 joined his people in a six-day *Incwala*, or ritual ceremony. Dressed in animal skins and elaborate plumage, Sobhuza performed dances that would ensure the renewal of the land, the king and the people.

In extant tribal societies, such as the Hopi Indians of northeastern Arizona, dance retains most of its traditional form and significance. The Hopi still dance as a form of worship, with specific dances for different ceremonies. Such dances, however, as in any other tradition, have undergone inevitable change and development throughout history, and they cannot be used as accurate evidence of what the tribal dances of early man were like. Generalizing about tribal dance is made difficult not only by the lack of evidence concerning its origins and the rapid dying of extant forms but also by the fact that the term tribal covers so many different kinds of dance (*Macropædia*, Volume 16: 954, col. 2).

If it is true that "generalizing about tribal dance is made difficult" by the lack of evidence concerning origins (and much else), then *why generalize in this way*? Why continue to use a label that, by the writer's own admission, no longer exists?[10]

Getting to the 'Tribal Dances' of Early Man

There are many who see the study of movement systems (dances, sign languages or whatever) as being *about* physical actions, consequently, they look for what appear to be 'similar' physical movements in two or more systems. They isolate one movement (or set of moves) in two or more contexts that superficially seem to be the same. Having done that, instead of talking about the dances or sign languages and their systemic characteristics, they talk about the moves they have extracted, *as if the moves are not spatially orientated and, as if they exist without their larger socio-cultural frameworks of meaning*. Probably the clearest example of such analytical movement-isolation is to be found in Alan Lomax's attempts to identify "work movements" in order to show that a "dance style varies in a regular way in terms of the level of complexity and the type of subsistence activity of the culture which supports it" (1968: *xv*).

Lomax suggests correlations between the level of complexity to be found in a dance and the level of agricultural or technological complexity in a society. We are thus led to believe that we will find 'simple' dances among hunting and gathering peoples, and 'more complex' dances among agricultural peoples. Dancing of peoples who till their fields with plows and hoes will be 'simpler' than the dancing of people who till their fields with tractors. Lomax believed that a "more productive complex technology [using tractors instead of hoes] makes further demands on the body for control," but that is simply not true (see Williams 1991: 142-143).

Lomax assumes that 'work movements' were a constant factor in African dances, because he wanted to establish *a causal relation* between dances and human activities connected with securing food because he wanted to substantiate one interpretation of evolutionary theory. He combined two independent activities: dancing and working with a simple-to-complex continuum of agricultural technology. *He could only do this by separating physical movements from their cultural settings and from the complex of social relationships in which they exist.* If Lomax's theory were true, then we might expect Bharatanatyam, Kathakali or Kathak to be 'simple' — but they are not, even though much farming in India is still done using simple technology.

In fact, Choreometrics possesses no mediating theory of culture, nor does it have any systematic frameworks within which 'dancers' and 'workers' find their their actions, their relationships and their cultural practices meaningful.

Theory

In her conclusion, Glasser emphasizes the importance of dances to peoples whose "criticisms would have been unacceptable in verbal forms" (p. 34), although she doesn't want the dance to be *reduced to* "political movement" for this, or any other reason. However, "In South Africa, *where* you dance, *with whom* you dance, *what kind* of dances you do and *your attitudes toward dancing* will say something about you as a political being, as well as saying something about you as a performer/artist" (p. 34) Glasser advocates developing a theory of dance-culture that includes politics because political interests are significant elements of cultural practices in southern Africa and, very likely, elsewhere.

Baynton concludes by reminding us of on-going questions: Are structured systems of human movement nothing but evidence of "subhuman characteristics" of human beings? Should we look at speech as "the greatest of all objects" at the expense of the medium of movement? If these questions are "an unfortunate by-product of evolutionary theory" (p. 68), then we must re-examine the theory. Over the past three decades, evidence has been produced in the field of human movement studies that shows how limited and inadequate evolutionary theory is. We must be able to talk about dancers, deaf people and others in more enlightened ways.

Farnell's conclusion points to concepts that belong to a "Western folk model of the person," remarking that this folk model is "surely no longer acceptable as a cross-cultural analytic model" for sign languages and dances. If western concepts cannot be universally used for all cultures because they are no longer acceptable, then we must set about discovering those features of our concepts that prevent "understanding of the organizational principles in the knowledge systems of other people" (Farnell, p. 92). Buckland's conclusion advises students that "the other components of the dance event must not be ignored" (see p. 117), after pointing out that "pagan origins theory" is outdated and unsupported by historical evidence.

The Old Record

A distinguished Australian anthropologist, William Stanner, begins his superb monograph entitled 'Religion, Totemism and Symbolism' by saying: "Sir Edward Tylor's observation that "a once-established opinion, however delusive, can hold its own from age to age" has no better illustration than the early judgments made by Europeans of Aboriginal religion" (1979[1962]: 106).

The still-existing old record about the dances of non-European peoples provides evidence of "the early judgments made by Europeans" about 'tribal', 'primitive' and 'savage' dancing. Sir James Frazer's wife, under the pen-name Lilly Grove wrote:

> Mr. J.G. Frazer, the author of the *Golden Bough*, tells me he believes that the more closely savage dances are looked into, the more prominent will appear their magical character. He thinks that a great many are pantomimes, intended to produce by 'sympathetic magic' the events which they imitate. What the savage mostly cares about are love, success in the chase, and prowess in war, and all these he thinks procurable by mimetic dancing. The representation of his wishes or of certain events will, in his belief, result in the realization of such wishes and events (Grove 1895: 27 - cited in Williams 1991: 27).

Lady Frazer spoke for most English-speaking *literati* of her day who, on the whole, were both educated and humanitarian. Nevertheless, her vision of "savage dances" faithfully records and/or reflects the efforts of early explorers to find the significance of "strange gesticulations," "outlandish" rites and danced movements, "quaint" dances, etc.[11]

Both the writer herself and the people from whom she received so much information (e.g. Haddon, Molina, Lang, Capt. Cook, Chateaubriand) were unable to see facts about human movement that seventy years later convinced anthropologists of human movement that the dances and sign languages of non-European peoples are worthy of study for reasons other than the establishment of a universal science of evolutionary development based on human custom.

Anthropologists of human movement are obliged to learn how to talk about people differently — to examine their individual predispositions of thought. This means they will be able to write about dances and sign languages in new, more enlightened, ways.

[The Editor]

PRECIS 5

[1]In a booklet entitled *How Do You Talk About People?* pub-[2]lished by New York City's Anti-Defamation League, the [3]author illustrated 'people classification' thus:

> [4]I knew a man who had lost the use of both eyes. He was called [5]a "blind man." He could also be called an expert typist, a con-[6]scientious worker, a good student, a careful listener, a man [7]who wanted a job. But he couldn't get a job in the department [8]store order room where employees sat and typed orders which [9]came over the telephone. The personnel man was impatient to [10]get the interview over. "But you're a blind man," he kept say-[11]ing, and one could almost feel his silent assumption that some-[12]how the incapacity in one aspect made the man incapable in [13]every other. So blinded by the label was the interviewer that [14]he could not be persuaded to look beyond it ....

[15]The example is instructive: any label identifies one (and [16]only one) feature of the person thus identified. Readers [17]are left with the impression that the job interviewer was [18]more blind than the interviewee.

[19]Naming, labeling and classifying people can be injurious [20]in practical ways. In this case, because of labeling, a blind [21]man was unjustifiably eliminated from competition for a [22]job. However, that doesn't mean that naming and label-[23]ing are themselves damaging. It isn't the English language [24]or the labels that are at fault. The fault lies in the ways [25]that people *use* classifications and categories.

[26]Since we cannot do without the abstracting process of [27]which names, labels, classifications and categories con-[28]sist, we must deal with them. ...Consider the fact that [29]Glasser's essay begins with "some terminological ques-[29]tions [which] need clarification." She identifies the word [30]'art' as a problem because people tend to associate it with [31]a doman of experience that "exists on a separate level of [32]reality"... If she permits her readers to think of the dances [33]she discusses as 'art', and if they associate 'art' with a sepa-[34]rate reality, she will have failed to bring home her point:

35dances are as much a part of 'reality' as any other cultural phenomenon.

36Few (if any) writers can avoid dealing with words that are 37commonly used about dancing and dances. Among other 38things, they are obliged to establish their point of view, 39otherwise their arguments are open to any and all inter- 40pretation. Glasser wants her position on the political na- 41ture of the dance in southern Africa to be understood. 42She must therefore explain the terminology she uses.

43On the other hand, Georgina Gore is blunt regarding com- 44monly used terminology for dances in West Africa. She 45draws attention to a criticism sociocultural anthropolo- 46gists often make about writers who have no anthropo- 47logical training. She suggests using indigenous classifica- 48tions and categories when describing dances from other cultures:

> 49To speak of West African dance is in fact a misnomer. ...[T]he 50ethnocentricly European term 'dance' is not applicable to sys- 51tems of structured human body movement of non-European 52peoples, *who have their own terms of reference for conceiving of* 53*such activities* ...

54We frequently talk about other peoples as if they had no 55terms of reference for what they do, think or feel: we as- 56sume that their terms of reference will be the same as ours.

57Baynton nails the fundamental classificatory problem for 58sign languages and dances ...

> 59The languages of early humans could not be directly studied, of 60course. No fossils are left recording speech, gesture or expressions 61of the face. [Physical] anthropologists, however, began in the latter 62decades of the nineteenth century to see the so-called "savage races" 63as examples of earlier stages of evolution. Assuming a model of 64linear evolutionary progress, they depicted them - Africans, Ameri- 65can Indians, Australian Aborigines and others — as "living fossils" 66left behind by the more rapidly progressing cultures.

67The idea that movement is inferior to speech is a deeply 68embedded prejudice that is not easily overcome.

Find Definitions:

•abstract(-ing) [line 26]; •category(-ies, -ize) [lines 25, 27, 48]•de-fame(-ation) [line 2]; •classify (-ication, -icatory) [lines 3, 19, 25, 27, 47-8, 57]; •terms of reference [lines 52, 56].

Questions and Thought Exercises:

I. *Why* do you think some people see 'art' as a 'separate real-ity'? [lines 29-32].

II. Write a précis of the editor's passage, using no *more* than seventy-five words and no *less* than fifty.

III. How would you answer this question: "I'm here to learn about the origins of dance. Why do I have to know all that stuff about 'dualisms', 'Cartesianism', 'theory', etc.?"

IV. On p. 124, we encountered a passage from a textbook entitled *Language: Introductory Readings*, in which there is a sub-section headed "Non-Languages." In the passage, the author classifies 'body language' as NON-language.

 a. What reasons does the author give for his contention that bodily action is 'non-language'? Do you think these reasons are valid?

 b. Where do *you* stand regarding this issue? Do you agree with the author's arguments in the passage above or do you disagree with them? In either case, why?

 c. Briefly state the *grounds* for your agreement or dis-agreement.

SECTION II
PREDISPOSITIONS OF THOUGHT

CHAPTER 6

Objectivity and Subjectivity

CHAPTER 6

Objectivity and Subjectivity

Is Art Subjective?

Farnell makes the valuable point that the "deeply rooted Cartesianism in our definition of language as traditionally constituted" created several dualisms pertaining to Euro-American concepts of human beings. All of these are stumbling-blocks on the path towards understanding structured systems of human movement. "[The Western folk model of the person] creates dualities between mind and body, speech and action, reason and emotion, conception and experience, verbal and nonverbal, symbolic and instrumental, and a host of others" (p. 92). The "host of others" includes objectivity and subjectivity, which leads to a strong division between 'science' and 'art' and the natural sciences and social sciences.

In the first eight paragraphs of an essay about aesthetic and artistic response (1996).[1] David Best skillfully summarizes the problem of subjectivity and objectivity in the field of art education:[2]

[1].[2] A principal reason for the pervasive scepticism about the educational values of the arts is the persistent assumption that artistic experience lacks genuine intellectual content. It is assumed that, unlike, for instance, the sciences, learning in any substantial educational sense is not possible in and through the arts, since, it is believed, the arts are concerned with feeling, rather than with cognition or understanding which is a necessary condition for any legitimately educational activity. That is, the arts are taken to be unquestionably subjective, by contrast with the undoubted objectivity and rationality of the sciences, mathematics and other such disciplines. As an editorial in the [London] *Times Higher Educational Supplement* expressed the point some years ago:

It is thought that such subjects do not need to be taken seriously, since it is stated quite explicitly that creativity is an inspirational

... activity rather than a cognitive and disciplined process. As a result, the arts are often regarded as of low academic content, and hopelessly subjective.

[2]. As this editorial intimates, the most damaging aspect of such educationally fatal subjectivist assumptions is that they are asserted not primarily by the detractors of the arts, but as doctrinaire articles of faith by the supporters of the arts, who persistently fail to recognise that to deny the objective, rational, cognitive content of artistic experience is to deny any legitimate place for the arts in education. Thus these "supporters" defeat their own case. For it makes no sense to suppose that there could be learning in an educational sense if there can be no place for understanding, and rationality. On the subjectivist, non-cognitive basis the only learning possible would be of the causal, stimulus-response kind of which an animal is capable.

Cognition - normal or supernatural?

[3]. It seems to me that what largely contributes to this syndrome of self-defeating conceptions is the continuing general influence of logical positivism or its heirs. By "logical positivism" I mean, to put it roughly, the unquestioned, axiomatic assumption that cognition, understanding, rationality and objectivity are the exclusive province of, to cite paradigmatic examples, the empirical sciences, and deductive logic. Thus genuine objective reasoning is supposed to be limited to the deductive, and to the inductive, as characteristically exemplified in the reasons citing evidence in support of scientific conclusions. Such kinds of reasons also apply, of course, to disciplines such as geography and history. The deeply seductive belief is that the only propositions which make any sense, are those which can be supported by such reasons. This may be a rather oversimplified outline, since logical positivism has been modified in some versions, but these do

not concern me; it is the broad general position which is important ...

[4]. I said above that this is an unquestioned assumption, but "assumption" is an understatment, since the notion is more of a *foundation*, which is in practice beyond question: its deep and pernicious influence can hardly be exaggerated. Although it is well past its heyday in philosophy, its pervasive effects continue to influence many areas of life, and perhaps most importantly educational policy, not only in the arts, but generally, including the sciences. But that is beyond my present brief.[3]

[5]. A profoundly significant consequence of this conception is that the arts, like morality and religious belief, are assumed to be non-cognitive, non-rational, and thus, as the *Higher* puts it, hopelessly subjective.

[6]. Instead of exposing the deep and seductive fallacies of this conception most arts theorists implicitly accept it, and "support" the arts in terms which either repudiate cognition and rationality as characteristic of artistic experience, or, what is equally disastrous, posit supposed kinds of reason and cognition which refer to the occult or supernatural metaphysics. In both cases such proponents of the arts often do not recognise their implicit acceptance of the positivist foundation-assumption which holds that, for instance, whereas scientific propositions are supportable by normally intelligible reasons, the arts are outside the province of normal rationality. Hence the common cliché, which is a banner of educationally self-defeating subjectivism, that the arts are a matter of feeling not of reason.

[7]. I am certainly not saying that the arts can be supported by scientific methodology, although there are some deeply misguided attempts of this kind, which again implicitly concede underlying positivism. What I am arguing is (a) that although there are obvious differ-

ences between the sciences and the arts, there are also very important similarities which are widely overlooked,[4] (for example, creativity is as important in science as in art); and (b) that the rationality, objectivity and cognition characteristic of the arts, even in the respects which differ from the sciences, are still intelligible in a perfectly normal sense. It is the common failure to recognise that (b), at least, is a crucial necessary condition for any attempt to provide a sound rationale for the arts as genuinely and importantly educational which has led to some of the prevalent excesses of wild subjectivism, whether explicit or implicit.

[8]. *The arts will never be taken seriously while their proponents assert that, unlike the sciences, the arts are concerned with mysterious, unintelligible realms and/or are answerable solely to occult "inner" feelings which give access to a transcendental Aesthetic universal.* It is this kind of woolly, supernatural mystery-mongering which understandably gives the arts the dismissive reputation as airy fairy and educationally irrelevant. Small wonder that one philosopher referred to the aesthetic, as "the natural home of rapturous and soporific effusion." What is urgently required is to bring the arts out of the supernatural metaphysical clouds, and show clearly that their feet are as much on the normal, intelligible objective ground as any other subject (Best 1996: 1-3 - italics added in paragraph eight).

In conclusion, Best calls for further research, needed because it could provide sound reasons to show that the arts are "as fully and intelligibly cognitive, objective and rational" as any other subject, including science.

Positivism and the Performing Arts

Logical positivism created an intellectual horizon that limited the available knowledge about the performing arts within the confines of:

1. concepts of objectivity and subjectivity and
2. the supremacy of spoken language over any other medium of human expression.

Although Susanne Langer challenged this positivist position as early as 1942 in a brave attempt to elevate 'gesture' from its lowly position of subservience to a position of equal status to spoken language, her ideas didn't appreciably affect mainstream thought about these matters (see Williams 1991: 19-21 and 200-202 for further discussion).

Entrenched assumptions about subjectivity and objectivity formed (and still form) the framework through which Western performing arts are understood, both by audiences and performers. Conceptualizing aesthetic and artistic experience by opposing the subjective and the objective became a 'natural' way of thinking about the arts in general and dancing in particular.

Then, too, there is a damaging tendency to polarize 'subjective' and 'objective' into two mutually exclusive spheres to which Best refers elsewere as "a disease of the dichotomous mind" (1993: 203). Polarizing these concepts produces caricatures of the arts by classifying them as experiences suitable for people only interested in their feelings. It produces equally distorted caricatures of the sciences by classifying them as suitable for people who deny or suppress their feelings. It may be that 'true subjectivists' (like 'true objectivists') also misunderstand the nature of human feelings and knowledge.

Against this background, one can appreciate why it is that so much modern writing about dancing is flawed by these kinds of predispositions of thought. For example, Sklar asserts, "Dance ethnography is ... grounded in the body and the body's experience rather than in texts, artifacts, or abstractions" (1991: 6). Her statement clearly illustrates two dualistic concepts: speech vs. action and the verbal vs. the alleged "nonverbal."

In the same publication, Sklar characterizes her remarks about dance ethnography as having "a phenomenological foundation" by which one presumes she refers to the phenomenologists revolt against positivism, which to Sklar and many American post-modernists, depends upon the ideas of the French phenomenologist Merleau-Ponty,[5] about whom we shall hear more later.

It requires uncommon effort for graduate or undergraduate students who are new to the study of dances and human movement to free themselves from inherited predispositions of thought. A few, of course, choose to study the performing arts because they hold a secret belief that studying dances will be "easier." Hoping to be released from the demand for disciplined thinking, they often find themselves doing more work than students who choose disciplines where rigorous thinking is a known requirement. They may also be surprised to discover that their subject is not the only one saddled with the objective/subjective distinction.

Is Social Science Subjective?

In a book entitled *The Counter-Revolution of Science* (1952), Freidrich von Hayek (an Austrian-born British economist) remarked, "There are no better terms available to describe [the] difference between the approach of the natural and the social sciences than to call the former 'objective' and the latter 'subjective'." There are many who would agree with him today, however,

> between 1958 and 1962, with the publication of Polanyi's *Personal Knowledge* (1958) and Kuhn's *The Structure of Scientific Revolutions* (1962), objectivity came to be recognized as a problem of fundamental, not to say, ultimate, importance. The problem is of ultimate importance for the pursuit of all forms of knowledge and of fundamental importance to the natural and social sciences. ...
> It has been understood for some time now that Polanyi and Kuhn represented the revolt against positivism as a conception of the way science is and should be practiced. Within the framework of the positivist conception was a special view of the nature of scientific objectivity. This special view is essentially this: to attain knowledge and to be certain that the attainment *is* knowledge, one is to confine oneself to the methodological conduct of mind prescribed by science for scientists. ... (Varela 1994: 43).

The conduct of mind required of scientists (which in general tried to control irrationality), kept religion, art, politics and everyday life strictly separate from science. Scientific thinking occupied a kind of "sacred space" in its attempts to preserve certain forms of intellectual purity from the myriad dangerous impurities of the rest of the world. Varela says that in this context, the problem of objectivity is the problem of *the positivist view of objectivity*,[6] and, "That view is now rejected as inadequate and a new view of objectivity is required" (1994: 43). The inadequate views of objectivity and subjectivity are summarized in Fig. 1.

DECARTES	MERLEAU-PONTY
"I think"	"I can [experience]"
Talk *about* the body	Talk *of* the body
3rd person objectivist	1st person subjectivist
Body as 'it' (not 'me')	"I" feel, experience
"I can *see* it"	"I *can* feel my ...".
A reduction of the body to a biological organism or to a social object	A conflation of the body with "organism"
Model of Causality	Model of Causality
= a substance and its qualities	= substanceless qualities
A ghost *and* the machine.	A ghost *in* the machine.
Talk *about* actions using word glosses	Talk *of* actions using word glosses.

Figure 1. The "objectivist/subjectivist pendulum-swing" (after Farnell 1994: 934).

What we are dealing with boils down to a question of knowledge. *What* will be accepted as 'knowledge' in the anthropology of human movement? *Who* is identified as a 'knower'? What is required to *become* someone who knows?

Decartes' *Cogito* ("I think, therefore I am") led to a mind-body split — to the human body as an "it" that in the end had nothing to do with "me." It included *impersonal* knowledge only. The phenomenologists rejection of that idea was valuable: they turned the tables from "third person objectivist" into "first person subjectivist" terms. Many saw this change as a shift from impersonal (therefore objective) knowledge to *personal* (therefore subjective) knowledge, but, valuable though their ideas were, they didn't solve the problem of a dualistic mind/body split. Phenomenology simply provided the opposite side of the same coin. Much more was needed — and it was supplied. The "new view of objectivity that is required" is summarized in Fig. 2.[7]

REALIST/SEMASIOLOGICAL PERSPECTIVE

"I act"

"I can act as a person"

1st person agency ("agentic")

resulting in talk *from* the body.

Through causal powers and capacities,

an agentic entitlement of the body as a

cultural entity enacted by the person who is

socially entitled to be a certain kind of actor.

<u>Model of Causality</u>

= dynamical substance and

immaterial structures of powers

Talk *from* the bodies of the investigator and

his or her informants recorded in movement 'scores' or texts.

Figure 2. A dynamic concept of space/time and the body
(from Farnell 1994: 935).

The new realist perspective that emerged from Polanyi's idea of personal knowledge meant that there was a shift from impersonal to *personal, but not subjective,* knowledge (Varela 1994: 61).

At the heart of these changes was a new understanding of the human knower. A person knows and does so from a commitment to a tacit ground of assumptions and world view. The implication of this understanding was a new role of the knower; the discovery of the central importance of the tacit ground for objectivity and the control of prejudice meant that *reflection* is not enough. The knower is now required also to be reflexive, meta-theoretical, introspective and evaluative. ... [That is] *Knowing who one is when one is knowing others puts one in a better position to control for distortion* (Varela 1994: 61).

David Pocock provides an essential approach for sociocultural anthropologists, enabling them to deal with the shift from "impersonal to personal, but not subjective, knowledge" in *The Idea of a Personal Anthropology* (1994[1973]: 11-42). David Best provides an approach for artists and educators whereby they can avoid the pitfalls of subjectivism and a positivistic standpoint, and Varela tackled the problem of objectivity in general.

Although none of these authors deal directly with the history or the prehistory of dances and sign languages, their insights can be applied to the many vexed questions that constantly arise about the origins of dancing, sign languages or any structured system of human actions. I am convinced, however, that the finest applications of Pocock's, Best's and Varela's ideas can occur if students have first attempted to deal with (a) received concepts of time and (b) different kinds of evidence, and it is to these questions that we shall now turn.

Bushman Dancing to Ballet

The earliest reliable evidence of a prehistorical dance form that we presently possess comes to us through the work of David Lewis-Williams (1990), whose studies of Bushman rock art established the continuous existence of San forms of trance-dancing from twenty-six thousand years ago.[8] The evidence upon which Lewis-Williams's work is based is discussed in detail in Chapter 9 (pp. 198-201).

For now, carefully consider the diagram in Fig. 3 (p. 147) which establishes a time relation between (a) Bushman trance-dancing, (b) the forms of Indian dancing that arose from the Natyashastra and (c) the beginnings of the ballet. Notice that the beginnings of Western recorded history occur between the time the Christian millenia began and the vast stretch of pre-recorded history in which not only Bushman rock art, but other archæological artifacts exist.[9]

Consider, too, that the underlying rule of western science is that "one must be there to see for oneself." Western science is based upon objective empirical fact. That is, science is "based upon perception, experience, sensations — everything that contributes to direct, immediate observations" (Charles Varela - private communication, 2/23/98). But, *science operates in many more realms than the simply observable.*

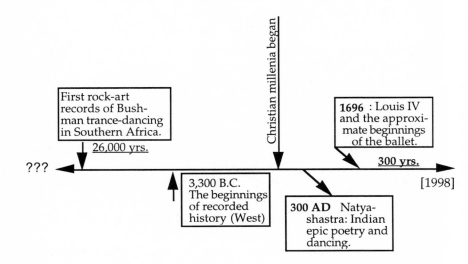

Figure 3. Prehistory, The Beginnings of Recorded History and 'The Present'.

Archæology and cosmology are sciences that provide impressive examples of exceptions to the rule of direct observation, and they are not the only ones. Cosmologists were not there during the first few minutes of the 'Big Bang' theory of the beginning of the universe — if that is how the universe began. Nevertheless, cosmologists declare knowledge of the beginnings and the endings of the universe. Like cosmologists, archæologists declare knowledge of the lives and practices of prehistorical peoples although they *never have recourse to the actual people* who in fact created, lived and knew about their own artifacts, settlement patterns, etc.

> Although we knew about certain planetary phenomena, bacteria, viruses, molecules and such before telescopes, radio-telescopes and electron microscopes were invented, one of the things science does is to make what was inobservable observable. Still, there are things in the world which are not now, and never will be, observable, for example, 'quarks', 'neutrinos', 'social structures', and such (Varela, private communication, 2/23/98).

Generally, even historians do not deal with the directly observable in the ways that social and cultural anthropologists do. Historians work with *records of* empirical observations — the written documents of people who were living, observing and experiencing different times from the present.

Most of what we know about the macro-history of the human race comes to us through the work of archæologists and cosmologists. Except for pictographs (considered by some to be a form of writing), archæology does not deal with written records. The evidence archæologists work with consists of artifacts, structures of community living, skeletons, land stratification, etc. From a strict empiricist's standpoint, archæology (like cosmology) is solely based upon *indirect* observation.

Unless, like Baynton, historians have living populations with which to compare, they are not concerned with direct observation. Of the types of science implied in Fig. 3, it is social and cultural anthropologists working with living populations of people, using the method of participant-observation, who are the only investigators among the three who use direct observation. In spite of this, however,

> [T]here is no doubt that ... the moving human body ... has remained virtually invisible to the vast majority of sociocultural anthropolo-

gists until recently. This is largely due to a long-standing bias against the body in the western philosophical tradition, which in turn has led to few social theorists taking the embodiment of persons seriously. ... This absence of the body in social theory has meant that most sociocultural anthropologists (although they are by no means alone in this) literally do not see movement empirically. When they do, it is most often viewed as "behavior" and not as "action." Many find it hard to imagine how movement might "mean" at all, far less contribute anything to our understanding of social and cultural practices (Farnell 1995a: 4).

Farnell asserts that "the visible — the *observable* human movement — is only a starting point for investigation. Although necessary, it can never be sufficient as an explanation of that movement" (1995a: 4 - italics added).

In fact, students have a decision to make: they can choose to be 'objective' in the old positivistic sense of the word, thus treating human movement as 'behavior' that has no meaning, or, they can choose to treat human movement as 'actions' which means re-assessing most of their received ideas about the subject of human movement.

Unless empirical observation is informed by more recent knowledge of embodiment and the semiotic practices involved in human socio-cultural practices (including language-use, cultural conceptions of the body and of what 'persons' consist), the field of study will continue to languish in the grip of outdated positivistic thinking.

[The Editor]

PRECIS 6

[1]Farnell makes the valuable point that the "deeply rooted [2]Cartesianism in our definition of language as traditionally [3]constituted" created several dualisms pertaining to Euro-[4]American concepts of human beings. All of these are stum-[5]bling-blocks on the path toward understanding structured [6]systems of human movement. "[The Western folk model of [7]the person] creates dualities between mind and body, speech

[8]and action, reason and emotion, conception and experience, [9]verbal and nonverbal, symbolic and instrumental, and a host [10]of others." The "host of others" includes objectivity and [11]subjectivity, which led to a strong division between 'sci-[12]ence' and 'art' and between the natural sciences and social sciences.

[13]In the first eight paragraphs of an essay about aesthetic [14]and artistic response ... David Best skillfully summarizes [15]the problem of subjectivity and objectivity for artists:

[16]A principal reason for the pervasive scepticism about the [17]educational values of the arts is the persistent assumption [18]that artistic experience lacks genuine intellectual content. [19]It is assumed that, unlike, for instance, the sciences, learn-[20]ing in any substantial educational sense is not possible in [21]and through the arts, since, it is believed, the arts are con-[22]cerned with feeling, rather than with cognition or under-[23]standing which is a necessary condition for any legitimately [24]educational activity. That is, the arts are taken to be un-[25]questionably subjective, by contrast with the undoubted [26]objectivity and rationality of the sciences, mathematics and [27]other such disciplines. As an editorial in the [London] *Times* [28]*Higher Educational Supplement* expressed the point some years ago:

[29]It is thought that such subjects do not need to be taken seri-[30]ously, since it is stated quite explicitly that creativity is an [31]inspirational ... activity rather than a cognitive and disci-[32]plined process. As a result, the arts are often regarded as of [33]low academic content, and hopelessly subjective.

[34]As this editorial intimates, the most damaging aspect of [35]such educationally fatal subjectivist assumptions is that [36]they are asserted not primarily by the detractors of the arts, [37]but as doctrinaire articles of faith by the supporters of the [38]arts, who persistently fail to recognise that to deny the ob-[39]jective, rational, cognitive content of artistic experience is [40]to deny any legitimate place for the arts in education. Thus

⁴¹these "supporters" defeat their own case. For it makes no
⁴²sense to suppose that there could be learning in an educa-
⁴³tional sense if there can be no place for understanding, and
⁴⁴rationality. On the subjectivist, non-cognitive basis the only
⁴⁵learning possible would be of the causal, stimulus-response
⁴⁶kind of which an animal is capable.

⁴⁷It seems to me that what largely contributes to this syn-
⁴⁸drome of self-defeating conceptions is the continuing gen-
⁴⁹eral influence of logical positivism or its heirs. By "logical
⁵⁰positivism" I mean, to put it roughly, the unquestioned,
⁵¹axiomatic assumption that cognition, understanding, ra-
⁵²tionality and objectivity are the excusive province of, to
⁵³cite paradigmatic examples, the empirical sciences, and de-
⁵⁴ductive logic. Thus genuine objective reasoning is supposed
⁵⁵to be limited to the deductive, and to the inductive, as char-
⁵⁶acteristically exemplified in the reasons citing evidence in
⁵⁷support of scientific conclusions. Such kinds of reasons also
⁵⁸apply, of course, to disciplines such as geography and his-
⁵⁹tory. The deeply seductive belief is that the only proposi-
⁶⁰tions which make any sense, are those which can be sup-
⁶¹ported by such reasons. This may be a rather oversimpli-
⁶²fied outline, since logical positivism has been modified in
⁶³some versions, but these do not concern me; it is the broad
⁶⁴general position which is important.

⁶⁵I said above that this is an unquestioned assumption, but
⁶⁶"assumption" is an understatment, since the notion is more
⁶⁷of a *foundation*, which is in practice beyond question: its
⁶⁸deep and pernicious influence can hardly be exaggerated.
⁶⁹Although it is well past its heyday in philosophy, its per-
⁷⁰vasive effects continue to influence many areas of life, and
⁷¹perhaps most importantly educational policy, not only in
⁷²the arts, but generally, including the sciences. But that is
⁷³beyond my present brief.

⁷⁴A profoundly significant consequence of this conception
⁷⁵is that the arts, like morality and religious belief, are as-

[76]sumed to be non-cognitive, non-rational, and thus, as the
[77]*Higher* puts it, hopelessly subjective.

[78]Instead of exposing the deep and seductive fallacies of this
[79]conception most arts theorists implicitly accept it, and "sup-
[80]port" the arts in terms which either repudiate cognition
[81]and rationality as characteristic of artistic experience, or,
[82]what is equally disastrous, posit supposed kinds of reason
[83]and cognition which refer to the occult or supernatural
[84]metaphysics. In both cases such proponents of the arts of-
[85]ten do not recognise their implicit acceptance of the posi-
[86]tivist foundation-assumption which holds that, for instance,
[87]whereas scientific propositions are supportable by normally
[88]intelligible reasons, the arts are outside the province of nor-
[89]mal rationality. Hence the common cliché, which is a ban-
[90]ner of educationally self-defeating subjectivism, that the
[91]arts are a matter of feeling not of reason.

[92]I am certainly not saying that the arts can be supported by
[93]scientific methodology, although there are some deeply
[94]misguided attempts of this kind, which again implicitly
[95]concede underlying positivism. What I am arguing is (a)
[96]that although there are obvious differences between the
[97]sciences and the arts, there are also very important simi-
[98]larities which are widely overlooked, (for example, creativ-
[99]ity is as important in science as in art); and (b) that the
[100]rationality, objectivity and cognition characteristic of the
[101]arts, even in the respects which differ from the sciences,
[102]are still intelligible in a perfectly normal sense. It is the
[103]common failure to recognise that (b), at least, is a crucial
[104]necessary condition for any attempt to provide a sound
[105]rationale for the arts as genuinely and importantly edu-
[106]cational which has led to some of the prevalent excesses
[107]of wild subjectivism, whether explicit or implicit.

[108]The arts will never be taken seriously while their propo-
[109]nents assert that, unlike the sciences, the arts are concerned
[110]with mysterious, unintelligible realms and/or are answer-

[112]able solely to occult "inner" feelings which give access to [113]a transcendental Aesthetic universal. It is this kind of [114]woolly, supernatural mystery-monging which under-[115]standably gives the arts the dismissive reputation as airy [116]fairy and educationally irrelevant. Small wonder that one [117]philosopher referred to the aesthetic, as "the natural home [118]of rapturous and soporific effusion." What is urgently re-[119]quired is to bring the arts out of the supernatural meta-[120]physical clouds, and show clearly that their feet are as [121]much on the normal, intelligible objective ground as any other subject.

[122]In conclusion, Best calls for further research, needed be-[123]cause it could provide sound reasons to show that the arts [124]are "as fully and intelligibly cognitive, objective and ra-[125]tional" as any other subject, including science.

Find Definitions

•pervasive [lines 16, 69-70]; •rational (-ality) [lines 26, 39, 44, 51-2, 76, 81, 89, 100, 124-5]; •dual (-alities, -ism) [lines 3, 7]; •transcendental (-dence) [line 113]; •metaphysical [line 119-20]; •pernicious [line 68]; •paradigmatic [line 53].

Answer These Questions

I. What are some of the dualities that Cartesianism creates? [lines 6-12]. Why are dualisms of the kind Farnell lists detrimental to human movement study?

II. In lines 34-35, Best talks about "the most damaging aspect of educationally fatal subjectivist assumptions." Specifically, what *is* the most damaging aspect? [lines 36-40].

III. What does this author mean by "logical positivism"? [lines 49-57].

IV. What is the cliché written on the "banner of educationally self-defeating subjectivism"? [lines 89-91].

V. In lines 78-89, just what *is* Best arguing?

VI. What does the author tell us that is "urgently required"? [lines 118-121].

VII. Write a précis of the 125 lines of text above using no *more* than 100 words.

SECTION II
PREDISPOSITIONS OF THOUGHT

CHAPTER 7

Universality

CHAPTER 7

Universality

Is Art Universal?

Western art has traditonally been considered to be the production of forms of expression and communication capable of crossing cultural and linguistic barriers. Most people believe that if anything is universal or suited to being universally understood in this world, it is the arts — especially the performing arts. Of those, dancing often heads the list because (being a so-called "nonverbal" art form) language barriers are held to be minor problems. Sklar expressed the position very well; i.e., "Dance ethnography is ... grounded in the body and the body's experience rather than in texts, artifacts, or abstractions" (1991: 6). She easily dismisses "texts" (language) and "abstractions" (theory; concepts) by exhibiting extraordinary faith in the body (material) and personal experiences (subjectivities) as the primary factors necessary to ethnography. Her dualistic concepts of speech vs. action and the verbal vs. the so-called nonverbal are plain. She is not the only movement specialist whose thoughts are grounded in phenomenological ideas (see Fig. 1, p. 144, under 'Merleau-Ponty').

Removing the connection between movement and spoken language however does not resolve a major problem: spoken languages are known to require translation across cultures, but the popularly held belief among many peoples of the world is that *body languages do not require translation*. Malcolm Chapman puts the matter succinctly and well:

> It will be clear that the possibility for misjudgement and misinterpretation of the kind that I have described is very great in "non-verbal" matters. Character, emotional states, and changes of mood, are judged and expressed according to a great diversity of non-verbal "semantic" phenomena, including bodily posture, gesture, stress or rapidity of pitch in speech, frequency or rapidity of movement of the body, avoidance or seeking of bodily contact, and so on. All these things are semantically loaded, rule governed, and category based, and vary

greatly from culture to culture. *There is not, however, any serious popular conception that such things require "translation" from one culture to another. Most people, when faced with an unintelligible foreign language, will recognize the need for "translation;" non-verbal "language" gestures, and generally semantic use of the body, of the person, or of groups of people, are not usually granted the same status as language in this respect. Translation will not be thought necessary* (Chapman 1982: 133-34 - italics added).

Chapman remarks that English-speakers tend to interpret the body language, gestures and facial expressions of others according to an entirely English set of rules. He concentrated on "nonverbal" category systems in his study of Celtic peoples because he wanted to "emphasize ... that such categories are as "semantic" as language." (1982: 139). He also makes the valuable point that

It was, and remains, imaginatively difficult to accord to alien category systems their own autonomy, their own right to be considered, from their own point of view, fundamental and normal, and not extended or metaphorical or demented ... Our language and conceptual system have their own way of dealing with meaning in English, and of dividing "real" meanings from meanings that are secondary, fictional, expressive, metaphorical, symbolic and so on. While we can assume that all languages and cultures have ways of distributing relevance and trenchancy to, say, the various different usages of the same word, we discover nothing about these simply by applying our own criteria, and assuming "symbolic" significance ... wherever the categories of English literality are disturbed (1982: 140-41).

Chapman criticizes the lack of general perceptions about (1) the unequal status that exists between "verbal" and "nonverbal" expression; (2) the necessity for translating one body language into another; (3) the difficulty of comprehending an alien categorical system and (4) the general practice of applying the criteria of our own language — bodily or spoken — to the languages of others.

Spoken Language and Taxonomies of the Body

On the whole, popular ideas of the universality of art in the United States are based upon the belief that Eurocentric — especially American — views of the world are translatable into any language in any social space anywhere in the world. "The question of translation of other people is, then, already much complicated. The observer of others must be aware that his'observations of others are, in subtle ways, made for him in advance" (Ardener 1989[1977]: 176). Reflecting on Ardener's work in West Africa, Farnell comments:

> Like the Ibo taxonomy of the body, the Assiniboine (Nakota language) taxonomy does not coincide with English. Whereas 'arm' in English usually includes the hand, in Nakota, the 'arm' (*istó*) extends from the shoulder to the wrist only, the 'hand (*napé*) is a different body part. As we have seen, for Ibo and Assiniboine people, a 'handshake' can involve neither the hand (as bounded by the English term) nor a shaking action (1994: 954).

Everyone performs and observes ordinary human actions such as hand-shaking and other common gestures everyday. On the whole, they do so without considering their connections with spoken language, nor do they question whether or not such actions are intertranslatable. Because all human beings possess bodies, a kind of universality of meaning is presumed that does not exist. Moreover, subjects like 'taxonomies of the body' are considered by many to be of interest only to anthropologists, but we suggest this is not the case. Steiner's work on Polynesian *taboo* provides an excellent example of why it is that concepts of the body (including taxonomic features) permeate all aspects of social life:

> To understand [the restricting power of personal *taboos*], we must realize that in Polynesian belief the parts of the body formed a fixed hierarchy which had some analogy with the ranking system of society. Although it need not be stressed in a sociological context, it cannot be accident that the human skeleton was here made to play a peculiar part in this ascetic principle of *mana-taboo*.

> Now the backbone was the most important part of the body, and the limbs that could be regarded as continuations of the backbone derived importance from it. Above the body was ... the head, and it was the seat of *mana*. When we say this, we must realize that by *mana* is meant three things: the soul aspect, the life-force, and a man's ritual status.

This grading of the limbs concerned people of all ranks and both sexes. It could, for example, be so important to avoid stepping over peoples' heads that the very architecture was involved: the arrangement of the sleeping-room show such an adaptation in the Marquesas. The commoner's back or head is thus not without its importance in certain contexts. But the real significance of this grading seems to have been in the possibilities it provided for cumulative effects in association with the rank system. The head of a chief was the most concentrated *mana*-object of Polynesian society, and was hedged around with the most terrifying *taboos* which operated when things were to to enter the head or when the head was being diminished; in other words, when the chief ate or had his hair cut. Hair-cutting involved the same behavior as actual killing, and the hands of a person who had cut a chief's hair were for some time useless for important activities, particularly for eating. Such a person had to be fed. This often happened to chief's wives or to chiefs themselves, and among the Maori these feeding difficulties were more than anything else indicative of exalted position. The hands of some great chiefs were so dangerous that they could not be put close to the head (Steiner 1956: 45-6, cited in Williams 1980: 5-6).

Any Polynesian, Maori or Marquesan action-sign system, including dances and sign languages, would obviously be affected in profound ways by such concepts of the body.

The Universality of *Hamlet*

The best account of a failed ecumenism and the arts in anthropological literature however, originated from Laura Bohannan. She wrote about how radically she had to change her mind regarding the universality of drama in a short essay entitled 'Miching Mallecho: That Means Witchcraft' (1967):

Three days before I once again left Oxford for West Africa, conversation turned to the season at Stratford. "You Americans," said a friend, "often have difficulty with Shakespeare; he was, after all, a very English poet, and one can easily misinterpret the universal by misunderstanding the particular."

I protested that human nature is pretty much the same the whole world over; the general plot and motivation of the greater tragedies at least would always be clear—everywhere—though some details of custom might have to be explained and difficulties of translation might produce other slight changes ... [M]y friend gave me a copy of

Hamlet to study in the African bush ... It was my second field trip to
that African tribe ... (Bohannan 1967: 43).

Bohannan wanted to study Tiv[1] ceremonies and rituals, but
because of bad weather, found herself with ample time on
her hands. "Before the end of the second month, grace de-
scended on me. I was quite sure that *Hamlet* had only one
possible interpretation, and that one obvious universally"
(1967: 44).

She found herself in a situation where the Tiv elders (from
whom she wanted information) demanded that she tell them
a story. In fact, "They threatened to tell me no more stories
until I told them one of mine ... Suddenly realizing that here
was my chance to prove Hamlet universally intelligible, I
agreed" (1967: 45).

I began in the proper [Tiv] style, "Not yesterday, not yesterday, but
long ago, a thing occurred. One night three men were keeping watch
outside the homestead of the great chief, when suddenly they saw
the former chief approach them."

"Why was he no longer their chief?"

"He was dead," I explained. "That is why they were troubled
and afraid when they saw him."

"Impossible," began one of the elders, handing his pipe on to his
neighbour, who interrupted. "Of course it wasn't the dead chief; it
was an omen sent by a witch. Go on."

Slightly shaken, I continued. "One of these three was a man who
knew things'—the closest translation for scholar, but unfortunately it
also meant witch [in the Tiv language]. The second elder looked tri-
umphantly at the first. "So he spoke to the dead chief saying, "tell us
what we must do so you may rest in your grave," but the dead chief
did not answer. He vanished, and they could see him no more. Then
the man who knew things—his name was Horatio—said this event
was the affair of the dead chief's son, Hamlet (1967: 45-6).

Already, Bohannan was in deep trouble. Where she thought
of Hamlet's dead father as a ghost, i.e. "someone who is dead
but who walks around and can talk and people can hear him
and see him but not touch him" (1967: 48) — she forgot that
her listeners didn't believe in ghosts. *The concept was
untranslatable.* They interpreted her 'ghost' as 'zombie' or
'omen'. She continued:

The old men muttered: such omens were matters for chiefs and elders, not for youngsters; no good could come of going behind a chief's back; obviously this Horatio was not a man who knew things.

"Yes, he was," I insisted, shooing a chicken away from my beer. "In our country the son is next to the father. The dead chief's younger brother had become the great chief. He had also married his elder brother's widow only about a month after the funeral."

"He did well," the old man beamed and announced to the others, "I told you that if we knew more about Europeans, we would find they really were like us. In our country also," he added to me, "the younger brother marries the elder brother's widow and becomes the father of his children. Now, if your uncle, who married your widowed mother, is your father's full brother, then he will be a real father to you. Did Hamlet's father and uncle have one mother?" (1967: 45).

At the outset, Bohannan was up against a people who are not monogamous. Moreover, she was talking to people to whom a *sororate* made perfect sense.[2] In Tiv understanding, Hamlet's uncle had done the right thing to marry Gertrude, thus one of the major motifs of Shakespeare's play (and one of Hamlet's deepest moral concerns) was erased from the picture. Bohannan's informative tale closes thus:

"That was a very good story," added the old man, "and you told it with very few mistakes. There was just one more error, at the very end. The poison Hamlet's mother drank was obviously meant for the survivor of the fight, whichever it was. If Laertes had won, the great chief would have poisoned him, for no one would know that he arranged Hamlet's death; then, too, he need not fear Laertes's witchcraft: it takes a strong heart to kill one's only sister by witchcraft.

Sometime," concluded the old man ... "you must tell us some more stories of your country. We, who are elders, will instruct you in their true meaning, so that when you return to your own land your elders will see that you have not been sitting in the bush, but among those who know things and who have taught you wisdom." (Bohannan 1967: 54).

The Tiv elders were no less sure that *their* cultural concepts and practice would provide the true meanings of *Hamlet* than Bohannan was that *her* cultural concepts and practice were universally understandable.

No matter who we are or where we hail from, we see the world through classifications and categories that are obviously "true" because they are so much a part of social usage that they have long since ceased to be questioned. Nor must we forget that the average person who hears talk about "primitive people" and "primitive dances" regards any attempt to doubt the universal applications of such terminology "just semantics" — possibly not even worthy of serious discussion. On the whole, people simply want to be entertained. Problems of accuracy, accountability and translation, or theoretical insights about the origins of dancing aren't relevant to the pursuit of entertainment: it doesn't matter what terminology is used or what effect will result through translation into another spatial idiom. Nor does it matter what indigenous peoples may think about how their life forms are used.

Translation

Students of human movement are, however, essentially concerned with the *accuracy* of reports about the action systems of other peoples. Glasser's preoccupation with "terminological questions" is painfully real, expressing a dilemma common to all anthropological endeavor. She says,

> It is difficult, for example, to discuss dancing or dances in isolation because they are often associated with other forms of the performance arts, i.e. opera, drama and story-telling. Not only that, the word, 'art' is problematic as it tends to suggest a domain of experience that exists on a separate level of reality (p. 13).

In her essay entitled 'The Non-Art of the Dance' Keali'i-nohomoku observed:

> There can be powerful and dissonant side-effects from the insistence of including art as an interface to dance. The manipulative attitudes of superordinate peoples can force adaptation by subordinate peoples that is not the same as an internally developed evolution. We may, for example, eventually force the Hopi *kachinas* onto the proscenium stage and Hopi "dance" may become an art. If this happens, the world will lose at least as much as it gains (1980: 83).

Georgina Gore denies the validity of using any words other than indigenous terminology for dances (see p. 123).

Apart from obvious problems of definition, these authors draw attention to matters of translation — not just the mere translation of words, but the translation of sociocultural facts. These are not the same as 'facts' as we ordinarily think of them.

In general, a 'fact' is a thing that is known to have occurred, to exist, or to be true. It is a fact, for example, that water boils at 212° (Fahrenheit) at sea-level. A 'fact' is a datum of experience; e.g., "fire burns," "it is raining," etc. Sociocultural facts are not that simple.

Cultural facts are *complexes of language, thought and action* in shared cultural contexts. Social anthropologists study what Wittgenstein called "forms of life" (Crick 1976: 80). "Forms of life" not only include practical knowledge, they include formal and informal theories, concepts, language, action, moral values — *everything that is part of the life of the society under investigation.*

Social Semantics

The meanings that arise from the study of cultural facts *do not produce the same kind of meanings* that arise from the study of facts in the physical and natural sciences. It is for this reason that the language of biology (and bare biological fact) does not provide an adequate framework for sociocultural anthropology. For instance, the 'facts of life' for a biologist begin and end with information about sexual intercourse and the 'mating behaviors' of various species. The facts of life for sociocultural anthropologists include marriage, marriage ceremonies, kinship rules, divorce, the customs involving separation, and the society's notions about role/rule relationships between men and women -- possibly much more. *It is impossible to arrive at the social semantics of 'marriage' in any human society considering biological facts alone.*

In the citations above, notice that Glasser singles out the word 'art', but it is not with the word by itself that she is concerned: it is the *domain of experience* that the word implies (or might imply to some readers) that is the problem.

Keali'inohomoku draws attention to a possible mistranslation of contextual spaces when she speaks of what will happen if Hopi *kachinas* are forced into Western theatrical contexts.

Gore argues for indigenous definitions and explanations, telling us that we are not the only people who "have their own terms of reference for conceiving of such activities." All three authors stress the differences between indigenous forms of dancing and those from Euro-centered societies.

Cultural Diversity and Meaning

As students gain familiarity with anthropological literature, they will find that cultural diversity is accentuated over and over again. This is because social meanings are generally unique — peculiar to the people who generated them. *The semantic powers of human beings create multi-dimensional realities in which they live, move and have their beings.* There is never anything 'simple' about multi-dimensional realities, but, does the complexity hide an undesirable consequence? Is it the case that the anthropology of human movement leads to a form of extreme relativism — to a thesis of untranslatability?

If the boundaries separating different forms of life are immutable, therefore untranslatable, then communication itself is impossible — but everyone knows that communication *is* possible and that human beings *do* communicate with one another. They engage in translation all the time, even though the tendency is to privilege their own form of life (its definitions, concepts and ideas) over all others.

It is, however, unacceptable for an anthropologist of human movement to privilege his or her forms of life over others, however acceptable such privilege may be in other contexts. Furthermore, we know there are features of human life that overlap — that are common to all human groups everywhere in the world. Deeper, more universal structures of human movement have been discovered and explained (see Williams 1976a and 1976b).

Because of this, no area of human experience is accepted as generally incommunicable through some system of human body language, in spite of the great cultural variety in the systems that exist. Human body languages also provide opportunities for change and adaptation to new fashions, new concepts and new modes of thought. The conceptual structures which cause any given system (whether sign languages, dances, rituals, martial arts, ceremonies or everyday movements) to hang together — to be coherant as a system — are capable of including innovation and change, which is one of the features that make body languages equal to spoken languages. They are parallel with conventional language in their potential for expression and communication.

Body languages interact with every other aspect of cultural life in human societies, but they do more than merely 'interact'. As David Best puts it: "Human movement does not symbolize reality, *it is reality*" (1978: 87 - italics added). While it is true that human action signs can be devised which "symbolize reality," most are themselves the reality.

Structural Universals vs. Semantic Diversity

In terms of translation, there is considerable tension between the ideas of semantics and social meaning (containing the diversities of forms of life) on the one hand, and 'structures', which contain the universals of human movement on the other hand. Structural universals have two fundamental aspects: 1. those pertaining to space and 2. those pertaining to the bodies that move in space.

Spatial universals are commonly expressed in terms of the dimensions of up/down [U/D], right/left [R/L], front/back [F/B] and inside/outside [I/O]. Bodily universals are not so easily expressed — or thought about, as they consist of the degrees of freedom of the jointing parts of all human bodies. That is, all human elbows and knees, for example, only have one degree of freedom. Other joints have more — shoulder and hip joints have three; wrists and ankles have two, etc.

However, spatial and bodily universals by themselves have no semantic content. The semantics are 'supplied' so to speak, by specific societal usage and application. Thus, we say that the dimension, U/D, is universal, but the semantics of the dimension are not. Likewise, the degrees of freedom that comprise the bodily members 'arms' and 'hands' are universal, but the gestures and actions made by these body members have different semantic content in different social contexts. Even taxonomic features of what appear to be 'the same' body members will vary (as we saw in the case of Ibo and Assiniboine gestures of 'shaking hands' - p. 91). In an excerpt from an essay, 'Metaphors We Move By'. Farnell (1996a) provides a paradigm example of how it is that the distinction between structural universals and semantic diversity holds.

She examines "concepts about the vertical dimension [that] are entirely the reverse of those held by English speakers" (Farnell 1996a: 324).

> Martin's description of a Haitian *Vodou* ceremony describes how the open space of the ritual ground (*peristil*) is covered by a sheltering roof supported by poles. The center-post (*potomitan*) represents the center of the universe and the four peripheral supporting posts represent the cardinal points of the universe.[3] Together, they define the conceptual space of the Vodouisants' metaphysical world:
>
> > [T]he floor of the *peristil* symbolizes the profane world, while the vertical pole (*potomitan*) in the center of the *peristil* represents the *axis mundi*, the avenue of communication between the two worlds. Although the downward reach of the *potomitan* appears to be limited by the *peristil's* floor, mythologically its foot is conceived to plunge into *Vilokan*, the cosmic mirror. The point at which the *potomitan* enters the *peristil's* floor symbolizes the zero point. During the ceremonies, the *potomitan* becomes charged with or "polluted" by the power of the *lwas* (ancestral spirits; Demangles 1992: 105, cited in Martin 1995: 104; italics added).

In this belief system, then, 'down' rather than 'up' signifies the sacred domain. Martin goes on to explain that:

> The *potomitan* signifies a vertical/horizontal cross (and intersection) of axes. The horizontal axis (the floor or ground out of which it arises) is the visible, moral world, while the vertical axis (signified by the *potomitan* itself) is the invisible, immortal world of

the spirits (the *lwa*). The metaphor of a mirror, reflecting human and spiritual space, which includes past, present and future time, is applied at the point of intersection of these two imaginary axes. At certain times during a ceremony, *Vodouisants* may touch the *potomitan* or kiss the ground in recognition of these concepts (Martin 1995: 106).

Demangles adds, "A possessed devotee becomes a medium whose feet are planted in the sacred mirror and whose body is the vertical line whereby the revitalizing forces of the universe flow to the community" (cited in Martin 1995: 106).

This being understood, it is not surprising to learn that the opening of a ceremony begins with the pouring of libations on the ground, and complex, intricate designs in ritual sand paintings depicting aspects of the spirits may be drawn on the ground before, during or after the salutations. In addition, the substances that make up an individual's physical body are considered to be part of the earth (as sacred), which reclaims its elemental contributions through recurring cycles of life and death. In this ritual context at least, the systematicity found in an English speaker's metaphorical uses of the up/down dimension no longer apply (e.g. GOOD IS UP; MORE IS UP; HAVING CONTROL IS UP; CONSCIOUS IS UP; HIGH STATUS IS UP;[4] etc.) They are, in fact, reversed (Farnell 1996a: 324-325).

It is hardly possible to be clearer about the universality of structure (in this case the dimension of up/down), and the diversity of semantic content (the reversal of values assigned to 'up' and 'down' in Voudou rituals). In the interests of promoting further certainty about what it is we mean, however, we shall continue:

In this Voudou ritual context there arises a metaphorical relationship between a Haitian dancer's use of the downward pull of gravity and the mythological downward pull of the spirit world. ... The complexity of potential meanings to be found in the "natural" experience of gravity, and the associated difficulties of translation across cultural boundaries, are made especially clear in the following two statements:

1. Theoretically if a dancer fully experiences gravity's downward pull, he or she will also discover the equal and opposite upwards thrust that provides buoyancy—a quality also evident in [other] Haitain dances. However, it is said that the possessed person becomes "heavy" with the spirit. This weightiness is particularly evident in movements of the head, which is often pulled off-balance during possession (Martin 1995: 107).

2. Those of us whose understanding and practice of Haitian dances and body language has "an American accent," so to speak, *often find it hard to achieve such an experience of gravity.* This may be because of cultural conditioning towards standards of airborne flight, so highly prized in our indigenous forms of ballet and modern dancing. Or, it may be connected to our tendency to believe that if an application of physical force doesn't seem to work, more force is the way to go (Martin 1995: 113, note 16- italics added, cited in Farnell 1996a: 325-26).

But, these metaphors generate problems: if 'GOOD IS UP' then 'BAD IS DOWN'. If we *spatialize* these values, then "good" is up and "evil" is down. For many, the problem is best expressed in terms of 'right' and 'wrong'. How can 'heaviness', 'weightiness' and the like be spiritually *beneficial*? These values are the reverse of an upwards pull toward 'heaven', therefore they must be wrong. How can the "downward pull of the spirit world" connote a *sacred* domain? The drive to make the whole world and everyone in it conform to a set of personally held customs and beliefs is strong. If it is not resisted, the investigator invites the possibility of misinterpretation, mistranslation and distortion in the descriptions of the ceremonies, dances and belief systems of others.

In his discussion of Bushman rock art, David Lewis-Williams emphasizes such points when he says,

Adopting a foreign perspective is, of course, no easy matter. It is very difficult to think oneself into other people's minds and, inevitably, our reponse will be inadequate. Even though we now know a great deal, we do not respond to all the nuances intended by the creators of Bushman art. Perhaps this is particularly so with depictions of animals. A representation of, for instance, an eland says to us little more than 'This is an eland', and we could easily conclude, as some rock art writers have done, that the artist was merely painting or engraving something he or she saw in the veld and wanted to 're-see' at home (Lewis-Williams and Dowson 1989: 25).

[The Editor]

PRECIS 7

[1]Removing the connection between movement and spoken [2]language, however does not resolve a major problem: spo-[3]ken languages are known to require translation across cul-[4]tures, but the popularly held belief among many peoples [5]of the world is that *body languages do not require translation.* [6]Malcolm Chapman puts the matter succinctly and well:

> [7] It will be clear that the possibility for misjudgment and mis-[8]interpretation of the kind that I have described is very great [9]in "non-verbal" matters. Character, emotional states, and [10]changes of mood, are judged and expressed according to a [11]great diversity of non-verbal "semantic" phenomena, includ-[12]ing bodily posture, gesture, stress or rapidity of pitch in [13]speech, frequency or rapidity of movement of the body, avoid-[14]ance or seeking of bodily contact, and so on. All these things [15]are semantically loaded, rule governed, and category based, [16]and vary greatly from culture to culture. There is not, nowever, [17]any serious popular conception that such things require [18]"translation" from one culture to another. Most people, when [19]faced with an unintelligible foreign language, will recog-[20]nize the need for "translation;" non-verbal "language" ges-[21]tures, and generally semantic use of the body, of the person, [22]or of groups of people, are not usually granted the same sta-[23]tus as language in this respect. Translation will not be thought
> necessary ...

[24]Chapman remarks that English-speakers tend to interpret [25]the body language, gestures and facial expressions of oth-[26]ers according to an entirely English set of rules. He con-[27]centrated on so-called "non-verbal" category systems in [28]his study of Celtic peoples because he wanted to "empha-[29]size ... that such categories are as "semantic" as language." [30]He also makes the valuable point that

> [31]It was, and remains, imaginatively difficult to accord to alien [32]category systems their own autonomy, their own right to be [33]considered, from their own point of view, fundamental and [34]normal, and not extended or metaphorical or demented ... [35]Our language and conceptual system have their own way of

[36]dealing with meaning in English, and of dividing "real"
[37]meanings from meanings that are secondary, fictional, ex-
[38]pressive, metaphorical, symbolic and so on. While we can
[39]assume that all languages and cultures have ways of distrib-
[40]uting relevance and trenchancy to, say, the various different
[41]usages of the same word, we discover nothing about these
[42]simply by applying our own criteria, and assuming "sym-
[43]bolic" significance ... wherever the categories of English lit-
[44]erality are disturbed (1982: 140-41).

[45]Chapman criticizes the lack of general perceptions about
[46](1) the unequal status that exists between "verbal" and
[47]"non-verbal" expression; (2) the necessity for translating
[48]one body language into another; (3) the difficulty of com-
[49]prehending an alien categorical system and (4) the general
[50]practice of applying the criteria of our own language —
[51]bodily or spoken — to the languages of others.

[52]On the whole, popular ideas of the universality of art in
[53]the United States are based upon the belief that Eurocentric
[54]— especially American — views of the world are translat-
[55]able into any language in any social space anywhere in the
[56]world. "The question of translation of other 'people' is,
[57]then, already much complicated. The 'observer' of others
[58]must be aware that his 'observations' of others are, in
[59]subtle ways, made for him in advance ... Reflecting upon
[60]Ardener's work in West Africa, Farnell comments:

> [61]Like the Ibo taxonomy of the body, the Assiniboine (Nakota
> [62]language) taxonomy does not coincide with English. Whereas
> [63]'arm' in English usually includes the hand, in Nakota, the
> [64]'arm' (*istó*) extends from the shoulder to the wrist only, the
> [65]'hand (*napé*) is a different body part. As we have seen, for
> [66]Ibo and Assiniboine people, a 'handshake' can involve nei-
> [67]ther the hand (as bounded by the English term) nor a shak-
> ing action ...

[68]Everyone performs and observes ordinary human actions
[69]such as hand-shaking and other common gestures every-
[70]day. On the whole, they do so without considering their

[71]connections with spoken language, nor do they question [72]whether or not such actions are inter-translatable. Because [73]all human beings possess bodies, a kind of universality is [74]assumed that simply does not exist. Moreover, subjects like [75]'taxonomies of the body' are considered by many to be of [76]interest only to anthropologists, but I suggest that this is [77]not the case. Steiner's work on Polynesian *taboo* provides [78]an excellent example of why it is that concepts of the body [79](which include taxonomic features) permeate all aspects [80]of social life:

> [81]To underand [the restricting power of personal *taboos*], we [82]must realize that in Polynesian belief the parts of the body [83]formed a fixed hierarchy which had some analogy with the [84]rank system of society. Although it need not be stressed in a [85]sociological context, it cannot be accident that the human [86]skeleton was here made to play a peculiar part in this ascetic [87]principle of *mana-taboo*. . . .

> [88]Now the backbone was the most important part of the body, [89]and the limbs that could be regarded as continuations of the [90]backbone derived importance from it. Above the body was [91]. . . the head, and it was the seat of *mana*. When we say this, [92]we must realize that by *mana* are meant both the soul as-[93]pect, the life-force, and a man's ritual status.

> [94]This grading of the limbs concerned people of all ranks and [95]both sexes. It could, for example, be so important to avoid [96]stepping over peoples' heads that the very architecture was [97]involved: the arrangement of the sleeping-room show such [98]an adaptation in the Marquesas. The commoner's back or [99]head is thus not without its importance in certain contexts. [100]But the real significance of this grading seems to have been [101]in the possibilities it provided for cumulative effects in as-[102]sociation with the rank system. The head of a chief was the [103]most concentrated *mana*-object of Polynesian society, and [104]was hedged around with the most terrifying *taboos* which [105]operated when things were to to enter the head or when [106]the head was being diminished; in other words, when the [107]chief ate or had his hair cut. Hair-cutting involved the same [108]behavior as actual killing, and the hands of a person who

[109]had cut a chief's hair were for some time useless for impor-
[110]tant activities, particularly for eating. Such a person had to
[111]be fed. This often happened to chief's wives or to chiefs
[112]themselves, and among the Maori these feeding difficulties
[113]were more than anything else indicative of exalted posi-
[114]tion. The hands of some great chiefs were so dangerous that
[115]they could not be put close to the head ...

[116]Any Polynesian, Maori or Marquesan action-sign system,
[117]including dances and sign languages, would obviously
[118]be affected in profound ways by such concepts of *mana-taboo*.

Find Definitions
•[In the Précis Text]•

•autonomy (-mous) [line 32]; •criteria (-on) [lines 42, 50];
•taxonomy (-omies; -onomic) [lines 61, 62, 75, 79]; •Polynesia
(-ian) [lines 77, 82, 103, 116]; •taboo [lines 77, 87, 104, 118];
•Marquesas (-san) [lines 98, 116]; •mana [lines 87, 91, 103,
118]; •Maori [lines 112, 116].

•[In the Essay Text]•

•veld [p. 168]; kachina(s) [p. 162]; •potomitan [p. 166]; *N.B.
Find what the potomitan signifies*; •superordinate [p. 162];
•monogamous [p. 161]; •sororate [p. 161]; •Tiv [p. 160];
•ecumenism (-ical) [p. 159];

Answer These Questions

I. a. What do you think Malcolm Chapman means when he
says, "All these things are semantically loaded, rule gov-
erned, and category based ..." [lines 14-16].
  b. Explain what is he talking about and why it is important to movement study.
II. Upon what belief is the universality of art based in the
United States? [Lines 52-59].

III. What difference does it make — specifically in terms of gesture and movement — whether other people's taxonomies of the body differ from ours? [lines 61-67].

IV. Having read the passage from line 77 through line 93, how would you answer this question: "Who cares what the Ibo, the Assiniboine or the Polynesians think?"

V. Write a 100-word précis of the 118 lines of text above. Follow the précis with one or two paragraphs (no more than 300 words) of your own experience with the idea of the translation of movements/actions.

Thought Exercises

1. Choose an "alien category system" — one that is NOT mentioned in this chapter — and demonstrate the need for the translation of the movements/actions it involves. Below is an example of the kind of thing you might choose to discuss:

> [Martha] Graham often recounted the following anecdote to students, company members and audiences:
>
>> A woman came to me and asked me, with regard to *Deaths and Entrances*, why I fell down in an evening gown. I asked her, in return, "what would you do if, suddenly, at a ball, you saw someone whom at one time you had loved very much? You would fall inside!" And that is why she falls ... (paraphrased from Graham's communications in classes and lectures).
>
> It is this kind of externalization of inner emotion that is referred to in the word glosses above, i.e. "momentary overwhelming and recovery;" "inevitability and doom" and "awe and respect." One understands, of course, that the "falling inside" to which Graham refers in her statement is a metaphorical understanding of what such momentary emotional shocks might feel like (Hart-Johnson 1997: 198).

Use any category system involving movement that you know fairly well. Look at the system imagining what someone who knows nothing about it might think. Or, draw from your own experience, as Hart-Johnson did. We do not often think of modern concert dancing as "alien," yet, Graham often had to explain why she performed certain moves. All the woman who asked the question saw was a dancer who "fell down in an evening gown."

2. The subsection, 'Structural Universals vs. Semantic Diversity'(p. 165 *ff*) is an important section in this chapter. There are many ways of approaching the subject; but, using the outline provided by the section, each member of the class could write a short essay (1000 words) on the subject, then read these aloud and discuss them in a seminar.

3. The spatial dimensions are rich in examples of explanatory power and significant differences . There are several essays written on the dimension R/L (right/left) which a librarian could provide from anthropological literature, starting with Needham (1973).

SECTION II
PREDISPOSITIONS OF THOUGHT

CHAPTER 8

Time

CHAPTER 8

Time

Time and Measurement

There is a limited sense in which 'time' in human movement studies is a straightforward component of movement
analysis with regard to dances. In the great majority of dances,
time is the regular re-occurrence of accented beats. It is the rhythmic, metered structure of the form of musical accompaniment
that governs any specific dance-event. Because of this, we
understand the majority of dances to be "externally motivated" in the sense that their time-frames are dominated by
the music (the drums, or whatever form of accompaniment
is used) for the dance. In that context, time is defined as the
length of time it takes to complete a single move, several
moves, or the whole dance.

Equating time with length is not unusual. It is common
practice in Euro-centered societies to talk of the length of
time it takes to "do" a dance, tell a story, finish a ritual, have
a (signed) conversation, conclude a game, or complete a ceremony. These are expressions of *time as duration*.

However, signed conversations, many rites and ceremonies, and games are not externally motivated by musical accompaniment. Other factors determine the length of time
required to perform them. These systems are therefore seen
as internally motivated. This means that when an investigator composes a movement text, say, for signed story telling
(see Fig. 2 on p. 256 for example), a conventional size of
written symbol is used instead of numerically identified
'measures'.

The time taken to tell a story is determined by the person
telling it. Likewise, in many rites and ceremonies (see Fig. 3,
for example), a different kind of movement-writing staff is
used — a 'non-metered staff' — shown on the right side of
Fig. 1:

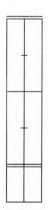

Externally motivated, metered staff   Internally motivated, unmetered staff

Figure 1. The beginning two measures of a metered staff
and an unmetered staff, both indicating places
for 'starting positions'.

Below, a *plié* is illustrated, using a metered staff similar to
the metered staff in Fig. 1, only in 4/4 time:

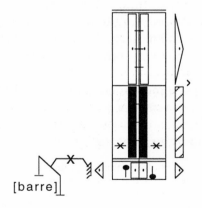

Figure 2. A plié in fifth position à la barre.

Here, the length of the symbols indicate how many 'beats'
are used for the gestures of each body part. In contrast to
Fig. 2 is Fig. 3, where the actions have no set time length:

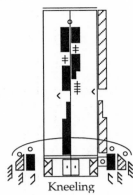
Kneeling

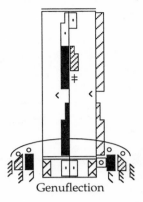
Genuflection

Figure 3. Two actions from the Tridentine Mass using an unmetered staff.

There is a sense in which the difference in the two kinds of movement-writing staff permits the same differences that exist between writing poetry and writing prose. In the latter, there are no explicit measured time constraints involved.

The measurement of time in Western music and dancing is arithmetical, corresponding to the kinds of measurement of length that are made in nearly all aspects of practical living. The predispositions of thought that arise from these concepts of measurement may blind the investigator to other characteristics of time in the movement systems (and lives) of other peoples and their own people, as we shall see.

Littlejohn forcefully demonstrates the point about distance measurement in in his explanation of a *Temne* house:[1]

> From the account of measurement in house-building it is apparent that unlike European space it is not "hodological," not articulated through geometry and arithmetic. This is more clearly seen in measurement of distance. The only unit here is *an-wula* which means both the stretch between one village and another and also wasteland, i.e. if you ask how far it is to X the answer is so many intervals between villages, or simply the number of villages between "here" and destination ... As villages are not evenly spaced over the ground this measure cannot be characterized mathematically, it is not in fact the application of a unit *to* distance but a meaning which arises *out of* the Temne landscape and human movement in it, just as the measure of

short length is a meaning inherent in the Temne body ... (Littlejohn 1967: 333).

The author tells us that

> The only unit of measure is *an-fatm* which is the outstretched arms of any adult man. It was *Pa Nes*, the spider, who showed men how to measure and older Temne say there is no other way. However, if need arise they will use the pace, the foot (actual human foot), the span and lengths between index finger knuckles. These measures have no names, are rarely used and do not form units in a system of measure. For the most part in housebuilding measuring is done by direct perception of "shorter/longer than" and "equal to," once a stick of the wanted length has been selected to serve as standard. There is no way whatsoever of measuring area. The area of a farm is the only one ever estimated and that is done by estimating the number of bags of rice it ought to yield (Littlejohn 1967: 332).

Both space and time are vulnerable to misunderstanding if other aspects of the life of a people are not taken into consideration, as Middleton points out:

> In general, anthropologists have approached mythology and cosmology from the point of view that they are cultural phenomena, or, in Durkheim's words, "collective representations" or "social facts." The underlying implication of this view is that myths and cosmological notions are not mere fairy tales, exotic and quaint expressions of a "primitive mentality." They are statements, made deliberately and consciously by the people who tell them. The popular notion that a "myth" is in some way "untrue" — indeed, that its untruth is its defining characteristic — is not only naive but shows misunderstanding of its very nature. Its "scientific truth" or otherwise is irrelevant. A myth is a statement about society and man's place in it and in the surrounding universe. Such a statement is, in general, a symbolic one, so that *an important anthropological problem becomes one of understanding the reality that the statement is used to symbolize* (Middleton 1967: x - italics added).

No clearer illustration exists of the importance of mythology and cosmology in the lives of a people than that of Bushman rock art. David Lewis-Williams set about understanding the realities of Bushman trance dances from the evidence he discovered while deciphering the meanings of the rock art.[2]

It is well-known that shamans in other parts of the world experience after-images and recollections of what they saw while in a trance state for months afterwards. It seems likely that shamans painted their pictures after the trance. This hypothesis was confirmed by an old Bushman woman, the last survivor of the southern Drakensberg Bushmen, in 1985. She identified paintings done by her father and insisted that all the paintings had been done by shamans (Lewis-Williams 1989: 36, cited in Glasser 1993: 192). *The potency of animals such as the eland was stored and kept in the paintings.* This potency could flow from the paintings to the shamans while in trance and give them more power to heal, make rain, or have successful hunting expeditions (1993: 192-93 - italics added).

Valuable though the concept of time-as-duration and typical quantitative measurements (either of space or of time) may be when constructing a text of a movement system, *time-as-duration* tells us nothing about the cosmology (hence the meanings), of the system.

Time-Reckoning

Pocock (1967[1964]) wisely distinguishes time-as-duration from 'time-reckoning', in several ways, drawing attention to systems of *continuous* and *discontinuous* time:

Much of the evidence which Nilsson used shows how selective different peoples are in relation to natural phenomena. ... Nilsson's major contribution is that systems of time-reckoning *are not necessarily continuous.* In his language, time-reckoning is preceded by time indications. By *continuous* time-reckoning Nilsson means the mathematical calendar systems with which we are familiar, in which units of time (seconds, minutes, days, etc.) accumulate and add up to the next larger unit. *Discontinuous time indications are exemplified from all over the world and are characterized by reference to events.* Thus: six moons, three harvests and so on. The moons or harvests are not units and are not interconnected by other units with which they are considered to be equal. *What is counted is the event.* This aoristic method Nilsson calls *punktuell* since the calculation is based upon a *punktum*—a particular point. Before going on it might be pointed out that Nilsson is incorrect in supposing that the use of [such] time indications is limited to primitive society, as will be recognised by anyone who recalls how often our continuous time-reckoning lets us down when we are trying to locate an event in the past and how often we are obliged to have recourse to some other event which occurred before, after or simultaneously with the event we are trying to place (Pocock 1967[1964]: 305 - italics added).

Many Americans more easily remember the date of some event in their own lives by placing it before, during or after the time that marked, for example, President Kennedy's death. There are many other such localized points in time around which people's memories of events are arranged. In these instances, Western societies are like the Nuer,[3] whose "concept of seasons is derived from social activities rather than from the climatic changes which determine them" (Evans-Pritchard 1940: 95).

The Nuer concept of "wet season" and "dry season" (like Australian concepts of "the wet" and "the dry" in northern Australia) is not based on abstract units of time: "The [Nuer] words *tot* and *mai* ... stand for the cluster of social activities characteristic of the height of the drought and height of the rains" (Evans-Pritchard 1940: 99).

Pocock's concern with time-*reckoning* (as against duration) is to examine the experience people have of change in cultural settings where they adhere to a set of values which seems to deny change. He thus vindicates Patidar denials of change in their social context by placing them in a larger context — their concepts of time-reckoning:

> The horror of duration and the human experience that things fall short of the ideal are made tolerable by being made understandable ... Thus not only are departures from the current ideals justified but changes in social practice can be recognised and justified by reference to the condition of the time (Pocock 1967[1964]: 311-312).

Two Concepts of Time

The reason why Pocock's essay on time-reckoning is so important for anthropologists of human movement is two-fold: 1. it stands as a constant reminder that all measurements of time as duration exist within a larger context of "time-reckoning" which provides a larger framework within which duration and measurement can be understood, and 2. it reminds us that *rites de passage*, are about "[T]he nature of society as a complex of meaning maintaining itself against forces that would devalue it [or] render it meaningless. Forces which are nevertheless conditions of its existence" (1967[1964]: 309).

In other words, while dealing with time measurement and duration in a dance, a ceremony, a sign language, etc., investigators must remember that *data of this kind never stands alone*. It is always connected with concepts of time-reckoning. Both time-reckoning and time-duration are always related to a uniquely distinct balance which each society tries to maintain between "mobility and fixity," between "the social and the individual" and between instances of particularity and concepts of "the eternal," even when such oppositions may superficially seem contradictory.

Time-as-Duration and the Micro-Histories of Dance Forms

At this stage of the discussion, it is important to remember the question that inspired this book: How are the micro-histories of dance forms (or sign languages) conceived, then fitted into, the macro-history of the human race? (Preface, p. 7). In broad terms, of what does the "micro-history" of the ballet consist?

Fig. 4 (p. 183) begins with a date, 1520, which marks the birth of a French man, Thoinot Arbeau, who wrote one of the most important books in the history of the ballet; *Orchesography*, first published in France in 1588. It was translated and published by Cyril Beaumont in England in 1925, and finally published by Dance Horizons, Inc., in the United States in 1968.

The reason why the book is so important is that Arbeau (whose original name was Jehan Tabourot) was one of the first known theoreticians and historians of western dancing. He was also one of the first to attempt a system of movement-writing . He was born March 17, 1519 (or 1520) in Dijon, France, and died in Langres in 1595.[4] The *Orchesography* contains carefully detailed, step-by-step descriptions of sixteenth century (and some earlier) dance forms.[5]

BY CENTURIES [1500 to 1996]

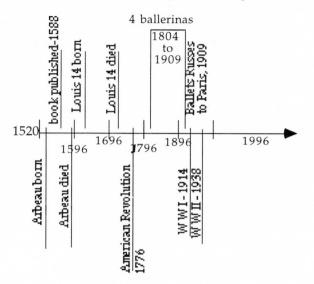

Figure 4. The Origins of Ballet-Dancing

About the book, a leading author/critic, Cyril Beaumont, says

> While French literature is rich in technical and historical works on dancing of all the great epochs, our own is singularly deficient in this respect. The present volume is the first of a contemplated series designed to provide British students with classical works on dancing which hitherto have not been available in an English translation, or which have become so rare as to be almost unobtainable and then only at a price prohibitive to the average pupil. ... The late Cecil Sharp has remarked that "it would be difficult to exaggerate the historical importance of his [Arbeau's] treatise, for it contains all the exact knowledge that we have of the dances of the fifteenth and sixteenth centuries." (Beaumont 1968: vii).

The *Orchesography* is written as a dialogue between a teacher (Arbeau) and a student (Capriol). Arbeau illustrates, then discusses the *Pavane, Gavotte, Allemande* and other sixteenth century dance forms,[6] most of which are now called *Pre-classical Dance Forms* (Horst 1937). This means, of course, pre-classical *ballet*.

Ballet dancing, in forms we would easily recognize, originated much later. But, in the late seventeenth century, Arbeau
outlined principles that provided the basis of the five fundamental positions of the feet in classical ballet, thus the origin
of the dance form is dated earlier.[7] Besides containing a
wealth of technical information about the dances of his time,
Arbeau's book provides a good account of late sixteenth century French social etiquette (always a good indication in any
society of customs and beliefs).

Beginning in the late nineteenth century, the distinguishing characteristic of ballet dancing is the use of *pointe* shoes
(sometimes called 'toe shoes'), which was an Italian invention. *Pointe* shoes were not worn until the end of the nineteenth century and it was an Italian-born ballerina, Marie
Taglioni (b. 1804; d. 1884) who was the first to wear them.[8]
Pointe shoes ushered in a new artistic period known as 'Romantic Ballet', which is the dance form that most people
would recognize as ballet today.[9]

Ballet as we know it today actually developed out of elaborate court spectacles of the Renaissance. The French *ballet de
cour* ('court ballet') in which social dances were performed
by royalty (and the aristocracy) were presented in harmony
with music, speech, verse, song, pageant, decor and costume.
It was Louis XIV (The 'Sun King') of France (b. 1638; d. 1715)
who, apart from being a devotee and performer of ballets
himself, established the *Academie Royale de Danse* in 1661.

The ballet emerged from the manners required of French
aristocracy during the fourteenth and fifteenth centuries.
Early dancing masters were mainly Italians, and they were
nearly all Jewish. They were usually men of humble origin,
who invented the art of choreography and who made themselves indispensable to European courts of the time. The
Russian rise in the history of ballet dancing began shortly
before the middle of the nineteenth century, *circa* 1836.

It was the early dancing masters who were responsible for
the transformation of ballet dancing from an aristocratic pas-
time into an art form that possessed a definitive technique.

It was owing to them that professional dancers first appeared *circa* 1630. The appearance of professional dancers meant that "the general public was permitted to observe theatrical presentations ... and the dancing masters began to choreograph for audiences whose ranks were no longer comprised solely of the nobility" (Durr 1985: 29-30).[10]

> Even when the aristocracy stopped performing in the courtly presentations, the values which suffused the rules and norms of their concepts of behavior were transferred to the theatrical events themselves. The aristocracy became [part of] the audience, taking an active role in sanctioning what they witnessed. . . . [It was thus that] an 'elitist' picture of the art [was formed] (Durr 1985: 32).

Time-as-Duration and the Category 'Primitive'

Curt Sachs's time-schematics (see Preface, p. 8) suggest that all dance forms in the world are more 'primitive' than ballet dancing. He also suggests that somehow, all dance forms, including ballet dancing originated in the alleged 'dances' of animals and birds. The historical facts outlined above do not support either contention. First, does 'primitive' with reference to dance forms means earlier in time? If so, we have a serious problem with the dance forms we have so far discussed.

Bushman trance-dancing, for example, undoubtedly preceded the ballet chronologically. According to Lewis-Williams, Bushman shamans were doing their dances at the same time that they produced their rock art, some of which is dated 24,000 to 26,000 B.P. Bushman trance-dancing precedes the ballet in time by many centuries, thus it is a 'primitive' dance form. However, classical Indian dances and theater also preceded the ballet chronologically. *According to the criteria of time succession, Bharatanatyam* (p. 69 above) *is also a primitive dance form.*

"But," you say, "we don't classify south Indian *Bharatanatyam* as a primitive dance form and most people would consider doing so nonsensical."

Why? Because *Bharatanatyam*, as well as *Kathak, Kathakali, Odissi* and *Manipuri* dancing are as intricate and complex as ballet dancing, and just about anyone who knows anything about these dance forms knows that. Surely the fact that these dance forms originated *circa* 300 A.D. doesn't justify labelling them 'primitive'.[11]

No, it doesn't. Nor does it help matters to learn that the term 'primitive' (as it is applied to whole societies) originated with economists who devised a way of distinguishing 'developed' nations with gross national products, cash economies and advanced technologies from those societies that didn't possess such things.

If, however, the criterion for a 'primitive' dance form is *the level of technological sophistication of the culture in which it exists*, then *Bharatanatyam* is a "primitive" dance form because India has not reached a level of technological sophistication equal to that of Europe and America. The same holds for Balinese dances, Javanese dances, many Japanese and Chinese dance forms, as well as many other dances throughout the world.

The *external criteria* of chronology and/or technological advancement doesn't help to explain anything about dancing of any kind, nor (as we shall discover in the next chapter) does chronology or technological expertise aid anyone's understanding of Bushman trance-dancing or ancient Greek dances which have never been categorized as 'primitive'.

Glasser documents two sets of meanings for the word 'primitive' as it has been commonly understood in South Africa and nearly all English-speaking countries in the recent past: "**1.** Savage, underdeveloped, uncivilized, unskilled, unsophisticated, simple, basic, and **2.** Natural, instinctive, spontaneous, exotic, romantic, colorful, unspoiled" (1993: 84).

The second set of meanings is somewhat less obnoxious than the first, but neither contains much to recommend it, even though the second group is more akin to the ways people describe 'primitive art'. I'm not prepared to argue that 'primitive art' has no meaning when used in connection with Picasso, Matisse or Modigliani's paintings, but I am prepared to argue that such words are meaningless when they are applied to dances and dancing.

Recalling Evans-Pritchard's comments about primitive religion where he makes an important connection between searching for origins and so-called "primitive"religions, we find that

> However some [anthropologists] may have protested that by 'origin' they did not mean earliest in time but simplest in structure, the implicit assumption in their arguments was that what was simplest in structure must have been that from which more developed forms evolved. ... (1965: 16 - see quotation on p. 2 of Preface).

Saying that 'primitive' means 'first' — not 'savage', 'underdeveloped', etc. doesn't solve the classificatory problem. Saying that it means 'simpler in structure' doesn't solve the problem unless we are willing to classify *Pavanes*, *Gavottes*, and other sixteenth-century court dances as 'primitive' in relation to modern forms of the ballet. Or, why not classify the ballet as 'primitive' in relation to modern concert dancing, which originated with Isadora Duncan in the early part of the twentieth century? Some have suggested that the word, 'primitive' simply be abolished, substituting the word 'ethnic' in its place, but that isn't a satisfactory solution because *all dance forms are ethnic, including the ballet*, as Keali'inohomoku so forcefully reminds us (1997[1969]: 15-16). Moreover, using the external criteria of technology as the measure (as Alan Lomax imprudently tried to do - see pp. 130-31, this volume) only further muddies the waters.

Time-as-Duration and Evidence

In Chapter 5, we learned that science operates in many more realms than the simply observable. We also learned that Western science is based upon objective empirical facts; upon perception, experience, sensations — everything that contributes to direct, immediate observation. Nevertheless, archæologists do not (because they cannot) have recourse to the actual people who created, lived and knew about their own day-to-day lives. Historians, on the other hand, mainly deal with documents written by people who, if not eye witnesses of the events they recorded, were located more closely to the event in time/space than is the historian. In contrast to both, the sociocultural anthropologists has recourse to methods of participant-observation, although he or she may use documents and/or archæological information to support field observations. It is useful to conceive of 'macro-history' and 'micro-history' in the anthropology of human movement studies in this way:

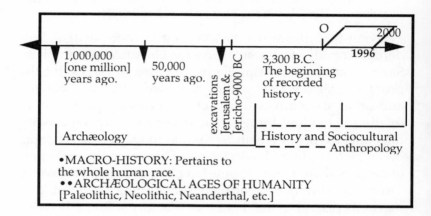

Figure 5. 'Time' in the Disciplines of Archæology, History and Sociocultural Anthropology

It is useful to think about Fig. 5 with the time diagram in Chapter 6, p. 147, since students can then begin to make relevant connections between concepts of time, field observations and the kinds of evidence used by archæologists, historians and sociocultural anthropologists (see pp. 148-49).[12] Consideration of these connections will prepare students for the next chapter, which contains meaningful insights regarding archæological evidence from southern Africa and, following that, from ancient Greece (Lawler 1964).

[The Editor]

PRECIS 8

[1]The measurement of time in Western music and dancing is [2]arithmetical, corresponding to the kinds of measurement [3]of length that are made in all aspects of practical living. The [4]predispositions of thought that arise from these concepts of [5]measurement may blind the investigator to other charac-[6]teristics of time in the movement systems (and lives) of other [7]peoples and their own people, as we shall see.

[8]Littlejohn forcefully demonstrates the point about distance [9]measurement in in his explanation of a *Temne* house:

[10]From the account of measurement in house-building it is ap-[11]parent that unlike European space it is not "hodological," [12]not articulated through geometry and arithmetic. This is more [13]clearly seen in measurement of distance. The only unit here [14]is *an-wula* which means both the stretch between one village [15]and another and also wasteland, i.e. if you ask how far it is [16]to X the answer is so many intervals between villages, or [17]simply the number of villages between "here" and destina-[18]tion ... As villages are not evenly spaced over the ground [19]this measure cannot be characterized mathematically, it is [20]not in fact the application of a unit *to* distance but a meaning [21]which arises *out of* the Temne landscape and human move-[22]ment in it, just as the measure of short length is a meaning [23]inherent in the Temne body ...

[24]The author tells us that

[25]The only unit of measure is *an-fatm* which is the outstretched [26]arms of any adult man. It was *Pa Nes*, the spider, who [27]showed men how to measure and older Temne say there is [28]no other way. However, if need arise they will use the pace, [29]the foot (actual human foot), the span and lengths between [30]index finger knuckles. These measures have no names, are [31]rarely used and do not form units in a system of measure. [32]For the most part in housebuilding measuring is done by [33]direct perception of "shorter/longer than" and "equal to," [34]once a stick of the wanted length has been selected to serve [35]as standard. There is no way whatsoever of measuring area. [36]The area of a farm is the only one ever estimated and that is

[37]done by estimating the number of bags of rice it ought to
yield ...

[38]Both space and time are vulnerable to misunderstanding
[39]if other aspects of the life of a people are not taken into
consideration:

> [40]In general, anthropologists have approached mythology and
> [41]cosmology from the point of view that they are cultural phe-
> [42]nomena, or, in Durkheim's words, "collective representa-
> [43]tions" or "social facts." The underlying implication of this
> [44]view is that myths and cosmological notions are not mere
> [45]fairy tales, exotic and quaint expressions of a "primitive men-
> [46]tality." They are statements, made deliberately and con-
> [47]sciously by the people who tell them. The popular notion
> [48]that a "myth" is in some way "untrue" — indeed, that its
> [49]untruth is its defining characteristic — is not only naive but
> [50]shows misunderstanding of its very nature. Its "scientific
> [51]truth" or otherwise is irrelevant. A myth is a statement about
> [52]society and man's place in it and in the surrounding uni-
> [53]verse. Such a statement is, in general, a symbolic one, so that
> [54]an important anthropological problem becomes one of un-
> [55]derstanding the reality that the statement is used to symbol-
> ize ...

[56]No clearer illustration exists of the importance of mythol-
[57]ogy and cosmology in the lives of a people than that of
[58]Bushman rock art. David Lewis-Williams set about under-
[59]standing the realities of Bushman trance dances from the
[60]evidence he discovered while deciphering the meanings
[61]of the rock art.

> [62]It is well-known that shamans in other parts of the world
> [63]experience after-images and recollections of what they saw
> [64]while in a trance state for months afterwards. It seems likely
> [65]that shamans painted their pictures after the trance. This hy-
> [66]pothesis was confirmed by an old Bushman woman, the last
> [67]survivor of the southern Drakensberg Bushmen, in 1985. She
> [68]identified paintings done by her father and insisted that all
> [69]the paintings had been done by shamans ... *The potency of*
> [70]*animals such as the eland was stored and kept in the paintings.*

71This potency could flow from the paintings to the shamans
72while in trance and give them more power to heal, make
73rain, or have successful hunting expeditions ...

74Glasser also observes,

75Anthropologists ... have revealed the high degree of skill
76and planning which Bushmen displayed in their daily lives.
77They also disclosed an egalitarian society with mechanisms
78for dealing with conflict that their "civilized" brothers could
79do well to emulate. They had a highly sophisticated belief
80system and world-view. It was the work of David Lewis-
81Williams, however, who connected the strands and inter-
82preted the rock art as part of Bushmen's religious beliefs and
83ritual practices, and connected trance-dancing with the rock-
art. . . .

84Valuable though the concept of time-as-duration and typi-
85cal quantitative measurements (either of space or of time)
86may be when constructing a text of a movement system,
87*time-as duration* tells us nothing about the cosmology, hence
88the meanings, of the system.

89Pocock wisely distinguishes time-as-duration from 'time-
90reckoning', in several ways, drawing attention to systems
91of *continuous* and *discontinuous* time:

92Much of the evidence which Nilsson used shows how selec-
93tive different peoples are in relation to natural phenomena.
94... Nilsson's major contribution is that systems of time-reck-
95oning *are not necessarily continuous*. In his language, time-
96reckoning is preceded by time indications. By *continuous*
97time-reckoning Nilsson means the mathematical calendar
98systems with which we are familiar, in which units of time
99(seconds, minutes, days, etc.) accumulate and add up to the
101next larger unit. *Discontinuous time indications are exempli-*
102*fied from all over the world and are characterized by reference to*
103*events.* Thus: six moons, three harvests and so on. The moons
104or harvests are not units and are not interconnected by other
105units with which they are considered to be equal. *What is*
106*counted is the event.* This aoristic method Nilsson calls
107*punktuell* since the calculation is based upon a *punktum*—a

[108]particular point. Before going on it might be pointed out [109]that Nilsson is incorrect in supposing that the use of [such] [111]time indications is limited to primitive society, as will be [112]recognised by anyone who recalls how often our continu-[113]ous time-reckoning lets us down when we are trying to lo-[114]cate an event in the past and how often we are obliged to [115]have recourse to some other event which occurred before, [116]after or simultaneously with the event we are trying to place.

[117]In other words, while dealing with time measurement and [118]duration in a dance, a ceremony, a sign language, etc., in-[119]vestigators must remember that *data of this kind never stands* [120]*alone*. It is always connected with concepts of time-reck-[121]oning. Both time-reckoning and time-duration are always [122]related to a uniquely distinct balance which each society [123]tries to maintain between mobility and fixity, between the [124]social and the individual and between instances of par-[125]ticularity and concepts of the eternal, even when such op-[126]positions may superficially seem contradictory.

Find Definitions

•hodological (-graph) [line 11]; •predisposition(s) [line 3-4]; •aoristic [line 106]; •*an-wula* [line 14]; •cosmology (-logies) [lines 37, 41, 44]; •*an-fatum* [line 25]; •hypothesis [line 65-6]; •egalitarian [line 77]; •symbol (-ic, -ize) [lines 53, 55].

Answer These Questions

I. What are the differences between [a] continuous and discontinuous time and [b] time-reckoning and time-duration? [c] Why are these distinctions important? [lines 92-116].

II. What are the underlying implications of the anthropologis's view that mythology and cosmology are cultural phenomena? [Lines 40-55]. (Your answer will be a précis of the relevant lines).

III. According to Glasser, what have anthropologists revealed about Bushmen's daily lives? [lines 75-83].

IV. Investigators would do well to remember *what* with reference to movement data? [lines 117-126].

Thought Exercises on Time

In a letter to a friend, *circa* 1810, the English essayist and critic, Charles Lamb, confessed, "Nothing puzzles me more than time and space; and yet, nothing troubles me less, for I never think about them." Undoubtedly, his attitude is shared by many, but students of human movement can ill afford to be among this group. Students need concepts of **1.** time-as-duration, **2.** time-reckoning, **3.** time as the recurrance of accented beats, and **4.** time spans in relation to anthropological, archæological and historical time. They need clear ideas about the types of evidence they may use that are crucial to the success of their future investigations.

On the whole, the only concept of time that has real significance to the majority of students at any level is a concept of time measured by single years.

1979	1981	1983	1985	1987	1989	1991	1993	1995
1980	1982	1984	1986	1988	1990	1992	1994	1996

ONE DECADE

The memory of things or events that occurred ten, fifteen or twenty years ago may, however, be vague, lacking in relationships to other things or events. Students often find that a series of related time diagrams assist them more effectively to organize concepts of time. That is, they start by locating their own birthdate and those of others on the 'decades' diagram below. Having done that, they may want to create a personalized history of the people, events and things that seem more important to them.

For example, one modern dance enthusiast developed an interesting picture of the history of her field by developing the 'decades diagram' in full, locating the personalities and events she considered most important and their relationships to each other and to her own life. Before completing this exercise, she had not realized how short the history of dance education in America is. It won't reach the century mark until 2018, as the first dance department was established at the University of Wisconsin, Madison, in 1918.

BY DECADES

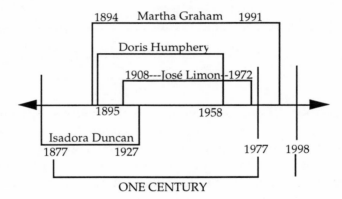

1900 1910 1920 1930 1940 1950 1960 1970 1980 1990 2000

1906 1916 1926 1936 1946 1956 1966 1976 1986 1996

One Century

Knowing when Isadora Duncan was born and the histories of the early pioneers provided her with an accurate 'map' of the territory of modern concert dancing in this country. She was able to locate the micro-historical origins of modern concert dancing in Duncan's rebellion against the ballet.

THE TITANS OF MODERN CONCERT DANCE

1894   Martha Graham   1991

Doris Humphery

1908---José Limon--1972

1895   1958

Isadora Duncan

1877   1927   1977   1998

ONE CENTURY

Thinking about the history of the ballet requires a considerable expansion of historical consciousness (see Fig. 4, p. 108).

BY CENTURIES

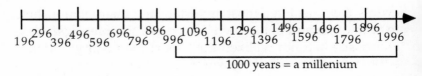

196 296 496 696 896 1096 1296 1496 1696 1896 1996
     396   596 796   996   1196 1396 1596 1796

1000 years = a millenium

The centuries diagram can be marked by the origins of classical Indian dancing *circa* 300 A.D., illustrating the considerable gap between that date and the origins of the ballet, whether the publication of Arbeau's book (1588) is chosen as the beginnings of ballet dancing, or the establishment of the *Academié* by Louis IV (1661).

The gap between the beginning of the Christian millenia (see below) to prehistory and the date of the rock art which documents Bushman trance-dancing is enormous. It is this gap, however, that marks the division between archæological and historical evidence (see pp. 148-49).

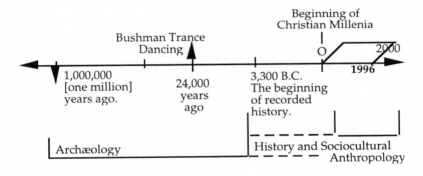

The Imponderables

The introduction to Hawking's book, *A Brief History of Time*, is amusingly instructive:

A well-known scientist (some say it was Bertrand Russell) once gave a public lecture on astronomy. He described how the earth orbits around the sun and how the sun, in turn, orbits around the center of a vast collection of stars called our galaxy. At the end of the lecture, a little old lady at the back of the room got up and said: "What you have told us is rubbish. The world is really a flat plate supported on the back of a giant tortoise." The scientist gave a superior smile before replying, "What is the tortoise standing on?" "You're very clever, young man, very clever," said the old lady. "But it's turtles all the way down!" Most people would find the picture of our universe as an infinite tower of tortoises rather ridiculous, but why do we think we know better? *What do we know about the universe, and how do we know it?* Where did the universe come from, and where is it going? Did the universe have a beginning, and if so, what happened before then? What is the nature of time? Will it ever come to an end? Recent breakthroughs in physics, made possible in part by fantastic new technologies, suggest answers to some of these long-standing questions. Someday these answers may seem as obvious to us as the earth orbiting the sun—or perhaps as ridiculous as a tower of tortoises. Only time (whatever that may be) will tell (Hawking 1989: 1-2).

The questions that students of the anthropology of human movement should address are these: **1.** What do we know about the *real* histories and origins of dance forms and sign languages? **2.** *How do we know what we know* about sign languages, dance forms, etc.? **3.** How much of what we *think* we know about the origins of dancing and signing amounts to conjecture, speculation and ill-founded interpretations?

Professionals grapple with these questions throughout their working lives. Such questions are 'imponderables' because they are questions that cannot be answered in ultimate ways. Answers are always provisional, because the answers must continually be *reassessed* as knowledge of human action-sign systems continues to increase.

[The Editor]

SECTION III
INTELLECTUAL RESOURCES
[Archaeological Insights]

CHAPTER 9

Ancient Dances

CHAPTER 9

Ancient Dances

Bushman Trance-Dancing

In the previous chapter, we learned that the Bushmen left a legacy of hundreds of thousands of paintings and engravings in southern Africa in rock caves and shelters. Unfortunately, many people still consider these 'primitive' in content as well as style. It takes a long time for attitudes rooted in ethnocentrism and cultural superiority to change.

> It was the work of David Lewis-Williams, however, who connected the strands [of evidence] and interpreted the rock art as part of Bushmen's religious beliefs and ritual practices ... [He] connected [present day] trance-dancing with the rock-art (Glasser 1993: 190).

Lewis-Williams began his career as a social anthropologist, turning to archæology when he became interested in the idea of possible connections between prehistoric paintings and engravings and some of the dances performed by Bushmen today. He says "some [Bushmen] still cling to their main religious ritual, the trance dance, [but] it will not save their traditional way of life. As one woman put it, 'Death is dancing with me'" (Lewis-Williams and Dowson 1989: 92).

It seems likely that shamans painted their pictures after their trances -- an hypothesis confirmed by an old Bushman woman (the last survivor of the southern Drakensberg Bushmen) in 1985. "She identified paintings done by her father and insisted that all the paintings had been done by shamans" (Lewis-Williams and Dowson 1989: 36). Lewis-Williams discovered that the potency of animals such as the eland was stored and kept in the paintings. "This potency could flow from the paintings to the shamans while in trance and give them more power to heal, make rain, or have successful hunting expeditions" (Glasser 1993: 192-93).

Archæological Evidence

The fact that Lewis-Williams incorporated both archæological and anthropological evidence is significant because it gives his work a sense of completeness and continuity that few other works on dancing possess. For students, it is of equal importance to understand the nature of the archæological evidence upon which Lewis-Williams relied to arrive at the date assigned to Bushman trance-dancing (see Fig. 5, p. 188):

> [T]he most recent paintings were done in the 1880s and 1890s, and perhaps even more recently by the few Bushmen who survived in the Drakensberg and Maluti mountains. Some of these paintings are easily dated because they depict white settlers and their horses. *The other end of the time scale is more difficult to define.*
>
> At present it is virtually impossible to date rock paintings by radiocarbon, the way organic finds are usually dated, but important work is being done on particles of carbon present in some black paints. These particles are so minute that an atomic accelerator has to be used to measure the amount of radioactive carbon present. Working with this sort of paint sample from the western cape, Nick van der Merwe and his fellow reseearchers obtained a date of approximately 500 B.P. (years before the present) for paint taken from a human figure that appears to have been drawn with a finger dipped in black paint (1989: 21 - italics added).

Notice that rock paintings are not all ancient. Moreover, the farther one travels backwards in time, the more difficult dating becomes:

> Until this dating technique has been more extensively applied, we shall have to rely on painted and engraved stones retrieved from deposits in cave sites. These stones vary from about the size of a hand to about 30cm. across. Some were placed in graves, but most were simply part of the accumulation of cave debris. Although neither the stone itself nor the paint on it can be dated, *carbon from the stratum in which they were found can be used.* Dates thus obtained show that painted mobile art, as these stones are called, was being made as long ago as 26,300 (+400) B.P. This astonishingly early date comes from Eric Wendt's excavation in the Apollo 11 shelter in southern Namibia. ... It means that at least some southern African rock art was contemporaneous with the Upper Palæolithic art of Western Europe. The most famous of the European painted caves, Lascaux, has been dated to about 17,000 B.P., ten thousand years later than the Apollo 11 art (Lewis-Williams and Dowson 1989: 21 - italics added).

There are six important points to be remembered in the above passage.[1]

1. Rock art paintings aren't all the same age;
2. some are easy to date because they include drawings of horses and white settlers;
3. it is extremely difficult to carbon-date rock paintings, but work on paint particles, using an atomic accelerator have dated some paintings at 500 B.P.
4. Until more of the kind of dating described in item 3 can be done, dates are obtained from the *stratum* in which the stones were found;
5. the 'stratum-dates' show that rock art was being made as long as 26,000 years ago (plus or minus 400 years) and that it was made by Bushmen.
6. Finally, Wendt's research in Namibia indicates that some southern African rock art was made 10,000 years earlier than the Lascaux cave-paintings in western Europe.

There is a seventh point as well: notice that the dating techniques pertain to paint, rocks and geological strata. There is no 'dating' of the actual movement or the action-signs involved.

Archæological evidence itself is constantly being re-evaluated. Because of new evidence and new technology, ideas are abandoned from time to time — for example, diffusionist theories about the spread of ideas:

> The great age of the Apollo 11 mobile art counts against the belief that the practice of painting on rocks spread by diffusion from Europe, through East Africa to southern Africa. Southern African rock art is more probably an independent tradition, and *today archæologists believe that there is little or no evidence for the diffusionist explanation.* Other painted stones, notably from Hilary and Janette Deacon's excavation at Boomplaas, near Oudtshoorn, have been dated to 6,400 B.P. and 2,000 B.P. Still others, from Ronald Singer and John Wymer's excavation at Klasies River Mouth, have been dated to 2,285 and 4,110 B.P. ... The paintings on the Apollo 11, Oudtshoorn and Klasies river stones show animals and geometric forms. Significantly, one of the Apollo 11 animals has been painted in two colours. *This calls in question the commonly held belief that the oldest art is monochrome* and that bichrome and polychrome paintings are much later developments. It

seems more likely that people used more than one colour from very early times (Lewis-Williams and Dowson 1989: 20-21 - italics added).

Powerful Outdated Theories

Diffusionism is a theory that focuses on the transmission of customs, ideas, practices, etc. These are thought to 'diffuse', spreading from a chosen central or original point to other areas and peoples. Extreme forms of diffusionism, notably the *Kulturkreis* school of Schmidt and Graebner, *ignored other factors* affecting culture-transmission. While it is true that every culture borrows from others, few (if any) anthropologists or archæologists today hold the theory of diffusionism. As Kaeppler (1978) points out, it has not yet been abandoned in other areas of study.[2]

Diffusionist claims aren't the only ones that have restricted understanding of ancient dances:

> Mistaken ideas about the mental capabilities of so-called 'primitive people' and a lack of close attention to the art itself are the basic ingredients of a recipe for misunderstanding. It was, in fact, this combination that led to one of the earliest interpretations of Bushman rock art - sympathetic magic.
>
> The sympathetic magic explanation proposes that people made depictions of animals prior to a hunt in the belief that the act of depiction or, of shooting arrows at the depictions, would ensure success. At the beginning of this century, sympathetic magic was considered to explain the Upper Palæolithic art in such European cave sites as Altamira and Font-de-Gaume. Researchers who had spent much of their lives studying the French and Spanish art brought the idea to southern Africa. This explanation was never as widely held in southern Africa as it was in Europe because there is no evidence that the Bushmen believed in sympathetic magic of that kind and because the art seems to be too diverse for so restricted an explanation (Lewis-Williams and Dowson 1989: 23-24).

Sir James Frazer's notions about sympathetic magic, used to explain many of the ideas held by alleged 'primitive peoples' have long been abandoned in social anthropology, especially with regard to dances and dancing (see Williams 1991: 64 and 69-70). Popular interpretations of such matters usually lag far behind:

Another explanation [for Bushman rock art] has achieved far more acceptance because it seems to accord better with the supposed diversity of the art. It is that the Bushmen painted whatever caught their fancy: hunting escapades, fights, dances, amusing incidents, meat-providing animals, an occasional 'mythical' figure, and so forth.

This view has been put forward in so many popular books and articles that it is deeply ingrained in many people's view of the art. They believe that, because the art is little more than a record of daily life, anyone can look at it and - without any knowledge of the Bushmen, their life and beliefs - tell what the pictures mean. Inevitably, the art is reduced to amusing vignettes and becomes a vehicle for a writer's ingenuity and a target for his jibes and drollery. There are numerous reasons why such comments distort Bushman rock art. Perhaps the most telling reason is that they result from viewing the art through Western eyes. Contrary to the adage that every picture tells a story, *it is not possible to get at the meaning of a work of art without some guidance from the artist, or at the very least, a thorough understanding of the culture from which it comes* (Lewis-Williams and Dowson 1989: 23-24 - italics added).

The achievement of alternative explanations of Bushman rock art have not been gained without struggles and "sometimes, a good deal of bitterness. From the start, controversy and debate have been the order of the day" (Lewis-Williams 1990: 69).

Politics, vested interests and personal aggrandisement are never very far from scholarly issues. Keen students quickly learn to choose reliable authorities with care!

A researcher who dominated rock art research for many decades was the French prehistorian, the Abbé Henri Breuil. He had achieved fame at the beginning of the twentieth century through his work on the Upper Palæolithic cave art of France and Spain, and his forceful personality soon made him an authority on rock art world-wide. ... [He] made many pronouncements on the rock art [of southern Africa]. Some of his views were resisted at the time, but they nevertheless had a lasting impact on people's ideas about the art, and some still live on in the popular imagination. *One of his most celebrated blunders was his claim that a painting in the Brandberg, Namibia, depicted a woman of Mediterranean origin.* Today people still speak of the White Lady of the Brandberg ... even though the painting depicts a male and is an ordinary, if quite striking, San painting (Lewis-Williams 1990: 69 - italics added).

In sum, many fictions regarding Bushman rock art and the prehistory of cave paintings all over the world for whatever reasons were propagated. They unfortunately continue to flourish. Because authoritative statements are often the sum total of what we possess regarding ancient dances in nonliterate cultures, students are well-advised to check and re-check the legitimacy of sources.

Cultural Translation

There is a positive side of the issue of cultural comprehension. An excellent example is the work of Sylvia Glasser, who painstakingly acquired a thorough understanding of Bushman culture that resulted in a recent choreography, *Tranceformations*, an admirable example of cultural translation that really works. She tells us,

> I had wanted to choreograph a dance based on a collection of Bushman stories in a book by Dorothea Bleek, *Mantis and Friends* (1924). I had a vague idea about choreographing a dance using a Bushman theme, but discovered I couldn't understand the stories in the Bleek volume, where people or animals changed into other animals or strange creatures without any apparent reason (1996: 288).

Her research, (involving three years of social anthropological study from 1987 to 1990), came about because she was honest enough to admit to herself and others that *she didn't understand Bushman stories*.

Colleagues in the dance world suggested that she choreograph a 'surrealistic' work based upon her own impressions, but, unsatisfied with this solution, she found herself in a meeting with Lewis-Williams, where

> I became aware of the complex issues surrounding what I wanted to do, and of the many problems about which I hadn't been sufficiently aware. Lewis-Williams asked questions which forced me to think of the choreographic project in a totally different way. Did I realise that I was dealing with the religious beliefs and sacred symbols of the Bushmen? Did I realise that rock art was part of the religious symbols of these people? How would Christians or Jews feel if their sacred religious symbols were translated into a dance, perhaps by people

who were not themselves religious? ... I decided that I wasn't ready
to tackle either the Bleek stories or a dance based on rock art (Glasser
1996: 288).

Today's students are fortunate in having a full account available of *Tranceformations* and the many discoveries that Glasser and her company members made while the work was in progress during the years 1991-92. These make a vital contribution to a possible better understanding of the relationship between art, artists, archæology and anthropology.

They are also fortunate in having Lillian Lawler's excellent book, *The Dance in Ancient Greece* (1964) to use for guidelines should any of them want to pursue research in that area of human movement study.

Ancient Greek and Roman Dances

When his student, Capriol, asks his master (Arbeau) to teach him the actual movements of ancient Greek and Roman dances, Arbeau (see p. 183-84) tells him that the dances — for whatever reason — *have been lost*. All he can do is talk about the writings of a few Greek- and Latin-language philosophers in which dances and dancing are mentioned (Arbeau 1925[1588]: 20-29). Capriol was doomed to disappointment because he assumed his teacher would know ancient Greek and Roman dancing. Students who ask the same questions today are as bound to disappointment as Capriol.

We don't know exactly how ancient Greeks and Romans danced. We only know *that* they danced because of the writings of Athenæus, Lucian and other philosophers. From these writings, we know something about the reasons the philosophers gave for *why* ancient Greeks and Romans danced, but we know nothing about indivdual Greek or Roman dancers' *motivations* for dancing. Likewise, we know nothing about prehistoric humanity's motivations for dancing. Nor do we know what steps, moves and choreographic patterns they used. What we *can* know (and perhaps in future, discover) about ancient Greek dancing is admirably spelled out in a lively and interesting manner by Lillian Lawler:

In 1964 Lillian B. Lawler, Visiting Professor of Classics at the University of Iowa, had published in Iowa and in London respectively, two books which appear to have been the culmination of her major writings on dance. They are *The Dance of the Ancient Greek Theatre* (1964a) and *The Dance in Ancient Greece* (1964b). ... In these two works and in Lawler's other two major writings on ancient Greek dance, i.e. 'The Dance in Ancient Crete' and 'Terpsichore' — she refers to many of her journal articles.[3] ... These, along with her major writings, constitute a corpus of research on ancient Greek dance which is invaluable (Rovik 1991: 159-168).

Especially is *The Dance in Ancient Greece* a treasure-house for students of ancient Greek dances, not only because it provides bibliographic references and explanations of other kinds of available source materials, but because the author's commentary on existing material evidence is invariably illuminating. Lawler was not only a remarkably well-read and intelligent woman, she was a thorough scholar. She lists seven types of sources for study, starting with the music that was played:

[M]etrical sources can furnish information on the tempo and mood of a large number of dances, and even, now and then, give a clue to the actual step used in a given situation. Further, through such features as recurring refrains, balanced stophes, sudden metrical shifts, etc., they can afford some idea of the pattern, or choreography, of the dance in question. Metrical sources are primary sources; and, especially where they corroborate information obtained elsewhere, they cannot be ignored (Lawler 1964: 16).

About archæolgical sources, she observes:

Archæological sources include tangible objects which have survived from antiquity and which furnish representations of dancing and dancers and objects used by dancers. They include statues, figurines, reliefs, mosaic floors and stuccoed ceilings, gold and silver jewellery, carvings on gems and ivory, an occasional votive object, and paintings on both walls and pottery (Lawler 1964b: 17).

Although Lawler considers archæological sources to be of primary importance, she points out that *no sources are so capable of serious misinterpretation* because artistic conventions and cultural concepts are not the same as those which followed them. That is,

In the first place, they usually have come down in a more or less damaged condition. In the second place, the student must never forget for a moment that Greek art is often deliberately unrealistic, and is concerned with ideal beauty, design, balance, rhythm, linear schemes, and stylization, rather than with an exact portrayal of what the artist saw in life. In the third place, the observer must understand and allow for technical limitations, especially in the work of primitive artists, and for artistic conventions found in each of the arts, throughout the whole span of Greek civilization. *These are not easy facts for the amateur to grasp,* and a great many amazing errors have been made by writers on the dance who have tried to interpret representations in Greek art without knowing how to do so.[4] The results are sometimes as absurd as would be similar attempts to interpret modern art realistically (Lawler 1964b: 17 - italics added).

Lewis-Williams pointed out that concepts of Bushman rock art are often distorted because of "viewing the art through Western eyes." The same holds for ancient Greek art when viewers have not taken the trouble to gain "a thorough understanding of the culture from which [the art] comes" (Lewis-Williams and Dowson 1989: 23, and p. 168 this volume). Clearly, cultural understanding is required whether the society is 'foreign' or one which we consider to be a direct forerunner of our own civilization. In particular, Lawler speaks of

The Greek vase painter [who] often draws figures without a 'floor line' — a convention which has led some modern interpreters to insert an imaginary 'floor line' of their own in a given scene, and then to deduce from its position all sorts of untenable conclusions, e.g. that the ancient Greeks engaged in something like ballet, and even toe-dancing. Naturally the observer must use great caution, and avoid all such fantastic interpretations (Lawler 1964b: 21).

Many errors have been made by writers on the dance who have tried to interpret Greek art without knowing how to do so. How does Lawler suggest we deal with the created dance forms and techniques of Isadora Duncan[5] and the Denishawn school,[6] who "devoted considerable attention to dances built upon Greek and Cretan painting and sculpture" (Lawler 1964: 24)? Emile Jaques-Dalcroze's method of rhythmic gymnastics was influenced by ancient Greek art and Greek authors.

The key words are "influenced by" as the author so plainly points out:

> Isadora Duncan, for example ... often said, 'We are not Greeks, and therefore cannot dance Greek dances'. Her aim was to draw the dance *back to nature*. Ruth St. Denis and Ted Shawn ... sought *to suggest the pictorial effect* of the ancient art representations rather than to restore by scientific scholarship the actual choreography or movements of any particular dance. Emile Jaques-Dalcroze ... carefully avoided giving the impression that he was seeking to *reproduce* any Greek dance (Lawler 1964b: 24 - italics added).

Rovik provides present-day students with sources for Lawler's critical assessments of interpretations of the Greek dance, saying that

> Isadora Duncan, Maude Allen and the Denishawns, who were cult figures of the contemporary dance world, [met] with young Lillian's disapproval for their lack of attention to archæological and literary sources in their avowed aim to restore in visible form the spirit of Greek dance, but she also castigates dance lexicographers for uncritical and inadequate coverages of the subject and archæologists for their "obvious lack of familiarity with the technique of dancing" (Rovik 1991: 159).

Influence or Reconstruction or Cultural Translation?

Although her aim was "to draw the dance back to nature," Isadora Duncan's dancing was interpreted by many as actual Greek dancing. Duncan was *influenced by* Greek art and culture. She did not perform Greek dancing, ancient or modern. But, an artist who is influenced by the art of another culture produces different work from one who sets out (as Glasser did) to achieve an accurate *cultural translation* of meaning. A great deal hangs on the difference, not only for the artist but for critics and for the traditions of the people whose work was 'borrowed'.

There were (and probably still are) many people who mistakenly saw St. Denis's and Shawn's interpretations of the effects of Greek art as 'the real thing' and there are others who believe that Duncan, Shawn, St. Denis and Dalcroze attempted the same kind of work that modern historical reconstructionists do with regard to, say, sixteenth-century Italian court dances.

Reconstructionists among dance historians aim, as far as possible, to "restore by scientific scholarship the actual choreography or movements of [a] particular dance" (Lawler 1964: 24).

In an interesting and informative essay on the subject of reconstruction, Archer and Hodson (1994) remark:[7]

> Prior to the widespread preservation of dance through modern recording methods, it was a maxim that ballets passed from one generation to the next via performers themselves. This kind of apostolic succession has prevailed throughout the history of dance despite periodic advances in notation [i.e. technologies of movement-writing].
>
> The systems of Raoul-Auger Feuillet and Pierre Beauchamp in the eighteenth century, or Arthur Saint-Léon, Friedrich Zorn and Vladimir Stepanov in the nineteenth, developed ever more precise ways of notating body movement, patterns in space, and time values in relation to music. These efforts culminated in the system of Rudolf Laban and that of Rudolf and Joan Benesh in the twentieth century, coinciding with the emergence of film and video technology. All the same, the presence of a ballet's original dancers, or their successors, is still taken by many as the guarantee of authenticity, notwithstanding progress in recording dance by camera or notation score (Archer and Hodson 1994: 100).

In anthropological terms, these authors make a point about 'oral history', i.e. *oral transmission of knowledge* which we shall later distinguish (however briefly) from *literate forms of transmission*.

Archer and Hodson ask interesting questions, for example, "The reconstructor's task hinges on how the terms 'lost' and 'found' are understood. Both concepts are relative. How much of a ballet has to be missing for it to be considered lost? And how much has to be recovered for it to qualify as found?" (1994: 99).

> [A] ballet has disappeared from repertory; none of the original performers or their successors survives; and neither a notation score nor a continuous visual record exists ... Need the ballet be gone for good, even though a wealth of other documentation may be retrievable?

Some Renaissance and Baroque dances are reconstructed under these circumstances; yet, for modern ballets, the given sources may strike us all as inadequate. Does this conclusion make sense? Or is it simply a response to the fact that recent works were created in the context of this century's high-tech computer notation and instant video replay? ... If conventional wisdom states that a ballet is lost, we query how lost it actually is. ...(1994: 100-101).

Movement Literacy and the
Credibility of Movement-Writing

In spite of the fact that movement-writing has had a long history of attempted solutions to the problem of nonliteracy and movement, there are widespread, deep misconceptions about movement-writing. The misconceptions are important, in particular regarding Laban's script (see Williams 1996). Archer and Hodson's (1994) essay forms a good descriptive account of how reconstruction is seen in general, and how reconstructionists accomplish what they do, but there is also much to be learned about movement-writing itself.[8] Page (1996) nails the essential problem with regard to movement writing:

It is as true of movement-writing scripts as of spoken language scripts that "[A] script is only a device for making examples of a language visible" (Sampson 1985: 21); but movement-writing has the same potency with regard to its literate applications that has been demonstrated for spoken language (Ong 1982: 194-199).

Movement literacy isn't usefully thought of merely as a means of recording human actions because its use is predicated on different conceptions of the categories and organizations of those actions. This is a literacy, then, which changes our thought processes (our "noetic habits") no less than it does for spoken languages (Ong 1982: 170, cited in Page 1996: 171).

Not only does movement-writing *change habits of thought* pertaining to space/time and movement for those who study the anthropology of human movement, it provides other advantages. In the *International Encyclopedia of Communication*, Farnell observes:

A system of notation is very important for the systematic study of the role of BODY MOVEMENT in communication. Once movements are transcribed into graphic form it becomes possible for an investigator to read and analyze those movements without being confined to the rapid flow of real space and time. In addition to being a recording device, a notation system provides for the development of important conceptual skills—ways of thinking with and about human movement (Farnell 1989: 203).

As a brief history of movement and gesture in the field of anthropology, students can do no better than to consult the citation above and the entry 'MOVEMENT AND GESTURE' in the recent *Encyclopedia of Cultural Anthropology*. "The development of an adequate writing system had already emerged as a formidable problem for the study of movement"(1966c). Farnell also observes, "Anthropologists ... use a movement script called Labanotation to create ethnographic records of movement events"(*Ibid.*). The importance of ethnographic records of this kind can hardly be overstressed.

Probably the most complete account of systems of movement-writing — its numerous forms throughout history and its problems — is to be found in Farnell (1996b). Relevant to the previous chapter regarding time, is a subsection dealing with how time is dealt with in Laban's system:

Scripts of all kinds deal with time by assigning a direction for reading—an axis for the sequential flow of sound or action. Labanotation reads from bottom to top. This was not an arbitrary choice for Laban: he originally devised a script that read from left to right but changed it in order to retain an iconicity between left and right sides of the reader's body and left and right sides of the written text of the action (Farnell 1996b: 873).

Because Laban's script is written from the standpoint of the person moving, rather than an observer's standpoint, the reader can imagine performing the written actions while reading the movement text.

This means that the sequential axis (see Fig. 1) aids reading because "the flow of time appears to move forward and up as one reads" and the "horizontal axis provides for actions that occur simultaneously" (Farnell 1996b: 873). Take the time to study Fig. 1 with these ideas in mind.

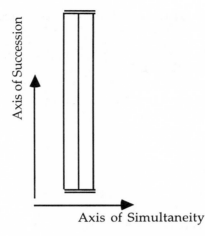

Figure 1. Reading Laban's script *sequentially* is 'vertical'.
Actions which occur simultaneously are found *across*
the staff on a 'horizontal' axis.

Williams first defended the credibility of movement-writing in Chapter 2, Section 3, of a B. Litt. thesis entitled *Social Anthropology and [the] Dance* (1972). Seven theoretical criteria from Nelson Goodman's *Languages of Art* (1969) were used to illustrate to examiners who knew nothing about movement-writing in any form that Laban's system was *not* merely a mnemonic device. Few people realize that if Laban's system is primarily iconographic in nature (a feature of visual mnemonics, as, for example, pictographs), then Laban's script cannot rightly be called a writing system at all, hence the need to defend the system's properties. Laban's script is alphabetic and, it is primarily ideographic, which makes it equal to writing systems for vocalized sound.[9]

For a long time, the lack of an adequate transcription system was a major contributing factor to the lowly status of body languages, but we can no longer use that excuse:

> When we are confronted with a movement text, we can no longer live solely in a notionally abstracted world of words. Movement texts force ... into consideration ... the relations between actions and bodies — our own bodies, and those of others (Williams 1996b: 202).

It is vitally important for students of this subject carefully to examine the cited texts regarding movement-writing. They must be able rationally to assess the importance of having texts of the results of fieldwork.

In our opinion, the importance of having texts of the results of fieldwork can be summed up in one word: *evidence.*

[The Editor]

PRECIS 9

[1]In the previous chapter, we learned that the Bushmen left a [2]legacy of hundreds of thousands of paintings and engrav-[3]ings in southern Africa in rock caves and shelters. Unfortu-[4]nately, many people still consider these 'primitive' in con-[5]tent as well as style. It takes a long time for attitudes rooted [6]in ethnocentrism and cultural superiority to change.

[7]It was the work of David Lewis-Williams, however, who con-[8]nected the strands [of evidence] and interpreted the rock art [9]as part of Bushmen's religious beliefs and ritual practices ... [10][He] connected [present day] trance-dancing with the rock-art.

[11]Lewis-Williams began his career as a social anthropologist, [12]turning to archæology when he became interested in the [13]idea of possible connections between prehistoric paintings [14]and engravings and some of the dances performed by Bush-[15]men today. He says "[S]ome [Bushmen] still cling to their [16]main religious ritual, the trance dance, [but] it will not save [17]their traditional way of life. As one woman put it, 'Death [18]is dancing with me'."

[19]It seems likely that shamans painted their pictures after [20]their trances -- an hypothesis confirmed by an old Bush-[21]man woman (the last survivor of the southern Drakensberg [22]Bushmen) in 1985. "She identified paintings done by her

[23]father and insisted that all the paintings had been done by
[24]shamans. Lewis-Williams discovered that the potency of
[25]animals such as the eland was stored and kept in the paint-
[26]ings. "This potency could flow from the paintings to the
[27]shamans while in trance and give them more power to heal,
[28]make rain, or have successful hunting expeditions."

[29]The fact that Lewis-Williams was able to incorporate both
[30]archæological and anthropological evidence is significant
[31]because it gives his work a sense of completeness and con-
[32]tinuity that few other works on dancing possess. For stu-
[33]dents, however, it is of equal importance to understand
[34]the nature of the archæological evidence Lewis-Williams
[35]relied upon to arrive at the date assigned to Bushman
trance-dancing ...

[36][T]he most recent paintings were done in the 1880s and 1890s,
[37]and perhaps even more recently by the few Bushmen who
[38]survived in the Drakensberg and Maluti mountains. Some
[39]of these paintings are easily dated because they depict white
[40]settlers and their horses. *The other end of the time scale is more*
[41]*difficult to define.*

[42]At present it is virtually impossible to date rock paintings
[43]by radiocarbon, the way organic finds are usually dated, but
[44]important work is being done on particles of carbon present
[45]in some black paints. These particles are so minute that an
[46]atomic accelerator has to be used to measure the amount of
[47]radioactive carbon present. Working with this sort of paint
[48]sample from the western cape, Nick van der Merwe and his
[49]fellow researchers obtained a date of approximately 500 B.P.
[50](years Before the Present) for paint taken from a human fig-
[51]ure that appears to have been drawn with a finger dipped in
[52]black paint ...

[52]Notice that rock paintings are not all ancient. Moreover,
[53]the farther one travels backwards in time, the more diffi-
[54]cult dating becomes:

[55]Until this dating technique has been more extensively ap-
[56]plied, we shall have to rely on painted and engraved stones

[57]retrieved from deposits in cave sites. These stones vary from
[58]about the size of a hand to about 30 cm. across. Some were
[59]placed in graves, but most were simply part of the accumu-
[60]lation of cave debris. Although neither the stone itself nor
[61]the paint on it can be dated, *carbon from the stratum in which*
[62]*they were found can be used.* Dates thus obtained show that
[60]painted mobile art, as these stones are called, was being made
[61]as long ago as 26,300 ([+]400) B.P. This astonishingly early date
[62]comes from Eric Wendt's excavation in the Apollo 11 shelter
[63]in southern Namibia. ... It means that at least some south-
[63]ern African rock art was contemporaneous with the Upper
[64]Palæolithic art of Western Europe. The most famous of the
[65]European painted caves, Lascaux, has been dated to about
[66]17,000 B.P., ten thousand years later than the Apollo 11 art.

[67]There are six important points to be remembered in the
[68]above passage.

[69]1. Rock art paintings aren't all the same age;
[70]2. some are easy to date because they include drawings
[71]of horses and white settlers;
[72]3. it is extremely difficult to carbon-date rock paintings,
[73]but work on paint particles, using an atomic accelera-
[74]tor have dated some paintings at 500 B.P.
[75]4. Until more of the kind of dating described in item 3
[76]can be done, dates are obtained from the *stratum* in which
[77]the stones were found;
[78]5. the 'stratum-dates' show that rock art was being made
[79]as long as 26,000 years ago (plus or minus 400 years)
[80]and that it was made by Bushmen.
[81]6. Finally, Wendt's research in Namibia indicates that
[82]some southern African rock art was made 10,000 years
[83]earlier than the Lascaux cave paintings in western Europe.

[84]There is a seventh point as well: notice that the dating tech-
[85]niques pertain to paint, rocks and geological strata. There
[86]is no 'dating' of the actual movement or the action-signs
involved.

[87]Archæological evidence itself is constantly being re-evalu-
[88]ated. Because of new evidence and new technology, ideas
[89]are abandoned from time to time, for example, diffusionist
[90]theories of the spread of ideas:

[91]The great age of the Apollo 11 mobile art counts against the
[92]belief that the practice of painting on rocks spread by diffu-
[93]sion from Europe, through East Africa to southern Africa.
[94]Southern African rock art is more probably an independent
[95]tradition, and *today archæologists believe that there is little or no*
[96]*evidence for the diffusionist explanation.* Other painted stones,
[97]notably from Hilary and Janette Deacon's excavation at
[98]Boomplaas, near Oudtshoorn, have been dated to 6,400 B.P.
[99]and 2,000 B.P. Still other, from Ronald Singer and John
[100]Wymer's excavation at Klasies River Mouth, have been
[101]dated to 2,285 and 4,110 B.P. ... The paintings on the Apollo
[102]11, Oudtshoorn and Klasies river stones show animals and
[103]geometric forms. Significantly, one of the Apollo 11 animals
[104]has been painted in two colours. *This calls in question the*
[105]*commonly held belief that the oldest art is monochrome* and that
[106]bichrome and polychrome paintings are much later de-
[107]velopments. It seems more likely that people used more
[108]than one colour from very early times.

Find Definitions

•potency [lines 19, 20]; •eland [line 19]; •shaman(s) [lines 19, 22];
•strata (-um) [lines 46, 59, 60]; •diffusionist [lines 72, 75]; •mono-
chrome (bichrome, polychrome) [line 80].

Answer These Questions

I. What is it that David Lewis-Williams did that was so different
from anything that preceded his research? [lines 7-10]. Use your
own words.

II. There is nothing explicit in the précis text that explains the difference between archæological and social anthropological evidence,
but from the reading as a whole, it should be clear that there *is* a
difference. In a few words, *explain* the differences you perceive.

III. Why are some rock paintings easy to date? [lines 29-35]

IV. Can rock paintings be dated in the same way that most organic finds are dated? [lines 42-52].

V. In line 61-2, we read, *"carbon from the stratum in which they were found can be used.."* To what does the word, 'they' refer?

VI. What does the date 26,300 B.P. *mean*? [line 61].

VII. Although not included in the précis text, the whole chapter explains what diffusionist theory amounts to [pp. 201-202, i.e. 'Powerful Outdated Theories]. How would you explain diffusionist theory to someone who asked you about it? Be brief.

VIII. How, *in your own words*, would you summarize the six points outlined in lines 69-83?

IX. What is the *seventh* point about the passage that you are asked to remember? [lines 84-86].

X. "Archæological evidence itself is constantly being re-evaluated." [lines 87-8]. Discuss.

Thought Exercises

1. On pages 205-6 of the chapter text, we read that Lillian Lawler believed archæological evidence to be of great importance with reference to the study of dances, but she adds: *"…no sources are so capable of serious misinterpretation."* Why?

2. On p. 207, we find this quotation:

> Isadora Duncan, Maude Allen and the Denishawns, who were cult figures of the contemporary dance world, [met] with young Lillian's disapproval for their lack of attention to archæological and literary sources in their avowed aim to restore in visible form the spirit of Greek dance, but she also castigates dance lexicographers for uncritical and inadequate coverages of the subject and archæologists for their "obvious lack of familiarity with the technique of dancing" (Rovik 1991: 159).

In your own words, summarize the significance of Rovik's statement to the modern dance world.

SECTION III
INTELLECTUAL RESOURCES
[Evidence]

Chapter 10

Movement Literacy

CHAPTER 10

Movement Literacy

Evidence as Written Texts

The word 'evidence'[1] points to the available facts and circumstances that support (or, in their misapplication or absence, *do not* support) a proposition, hypothesis, claim or belief. Evidence indicates whether a thing is "true" (i.e. valid or invalid). Evidence can take many forms: facts,[2] circumstances, proofs, documentation, grounds and/or data, support, sign(s), testimony, statement(s), and assertions.

A little-known fact regarding evidence and the study of dances or dancing has to do with the generally assumed nature of movement itself, which boils down to the question of *the existence of movement*. That is, movements (hence, dance steps, gestures, signs, etc.) are commonly considered ephemeral. Now you see the gestures — now you don't. Do they exist, or don't they? Did they exist in the exact forms the investigator claims they existed or were they figments of his or her imagination?

The best evidence that can be produced about a dance, a sign language, an exercise technique, a set of greeting gestures (or any other movement-based phenomena) is a written text of the movements themselves.

The most widely used system of movement-writing is based upon a script developed by Rudolf Laban in the 1920s. It is the script used in connection with Farnell's essay in this volume (and movement writing figures, pp. 255-262).[3] To illustrate, readers are asked to examine the transcription of actions on page 219.[4]

Notice that the transcription is identified not by the words 'bowing from the waist' (a gross physical movement having no indexical[5] features) but by the phrase, 'I bow from the waist' (the description of an action performed by a moving, human *social* being).[6] This means that the action is *intentional*. It also means that, because the transcription is done from the actor's perspective, it has a built-in assumption of *agency*.[7]

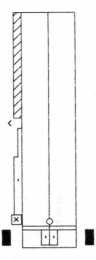

Figure 1. A transciption of the action 'I bow from the waist' using Laban's movement script.

Fig. 1 records the action 'I (the person acting) bow from the waist', rather than the movement generalization, 'bowing from the waist' which eliminates the person.

A movement researcher finds this kind of description inadequate, especially if the movement system that includes the 'bow' is, for example, a Catholic mass, a stretch from the exercise technique T'ai Chi Ch'uan, or the ballet, *Checkmate*.

To specify 'bowing' in those movement contexts, Fig. 1 would be amended as in Fig. 2 on p. 220.

Reading from the bottom of the staff to the top, we see that the starting position, ⌐·⌐·⌐, for the feet is designated as 'feet

pointing straight ahead'. The arms no longer simply hang straight down by the sides. Here, the upper arms hang straight down ■■, but the *lower arms* are raised diagonally

forward; i.e. .

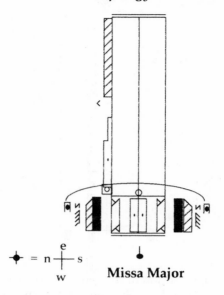

Missa Major

Figure 2. A transcription of a 'bow' before the altar by
a celebrant of the Latin High Mass.

In Fig. 2, we see the additional symbols, 𝄞𝄞 which indicate
'hands', with the symbol '𝓌' above each symbol, telling us
that the fingers are stretched. Finally, we see the symbol, ⊓,
telling us that the *palms* of the hands are pressed together,
indicated by a connecting symbol across the whole staff:
⌒ .
We would say, "The celebrant is standing with feet pointing straight ahead, with his arms and hands in a prayer position in front of his body."

In Fig. 1, we see that the actor bows from the waist, ⊠, but
in Fig. 2, the celebrant bows from the upper body — only his
chest is involved: ⊠ . The chest moves forward, ⌐⌐, return-
ing to 'normal', ⧄ . Notice, however, that many of the signs
in Figs. 1 and 2 are the same. Notice, too, that some of the
symbol-shapes are the same in Fig. 3: but are in a lower position, ▮.

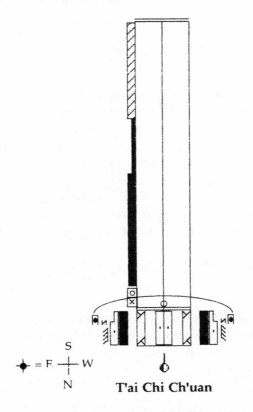

S

 = F. ─┼─ W

N   **T'ai Chi Ch'uan**

Figure 3. A transcription of a 'bow' at the beginning of a 'short form' of the exercise technique, T'ai Chi Ch'uan.

Again, reading from the bottom of the staff to the top, we see that the starting position of the feet, ⬚⬚, is the same as that for the celebrant, but in Fig. 3, the upper arm hangs straight down, but the arms are raised in a more directly forward

We see that the hands, ⬚⬚ , are the same as in Fig. 2, and the palms are similarly joined. We would say, "The performer is standing with feet pointing straight ahead, with his arms and hands in a [modified] prayer position."

However, in Fig. 2 (Missa Major), the celebrant's bow involved only the chest, ⬚, but in Fig. 3 (T'ai Chi Ch'uan), the bow includes *the whole torso* from the hips: ⊟. Remember that in Fig. 1 (an 'ordinary' bow), the bow was from the waist, ⊠ .

Another significant difference between Figs. 2 and 3 has to do with the symbols on the left side of the staff, known as the 'body column'.[8] They are *joined* in Fig. 3, but *not joined* in Fig. 2. In T'ai Chi, all the moves beginning with the initial bow are continuous. In the High Mass, the moves have pauses (separations of different durations), as they do in Fig. 4 (p. 223) which is a bow the Red Knight (in the ballet Checkmate) makes to the Red King apologizing for his inability to kill the Black Queen because of the rules of a chivalric code of honor that he follows.

In Fig. 4, we see that the position of the Knight's feet is different. They are slightly 'turned out', i.e. ⏅, approximately 45° indicated by the directional symbol, ⏇. We see that his arms hang straight down at his sides (as in Fig. 1), but the palms of his hands are turned diagonally forward toward the Red King. He bows from the waist, as in Fig. 1, but his head is bowed forward: it is not simply carried as part of the torso. There is no special move of the head [C] in Figs. 2 and 3, such as we find in Fig. 4.

The 'ad lib' symbol in the center of the staff (taken from musical symbols) shows that the Knight has some latitude in how long he holds the forward position of the body before straightening his body and proceeding with the dance. Finally, the performers of each bow *are not bowing to the same entities or for the same reasons.*

We don't know to whom the 'self' of the actor in Fig. 1 addresses his or her bow. The celebrant of the Mass bows to a monotheistic Divinity. The T'ai Chi executant acknowledges the Tao and the Red Knight bows to another performer who represents an earthly King.

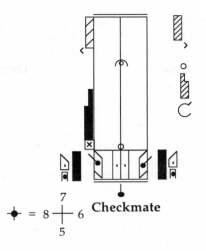

$$\blacklozenge = 8 \underset{5}{\overset{7}{+}} 6 \quad \text{Checkmate}$$

Figure 4. A transcription of a 'bow' made by the
Red Knight to the Red King.

Like the linguistic sign, the action sign has a performer and
a 'watcher' -- someone who sees the act and responds to its
meaning.

Spatial Orientation

In ordinary life, each individual's orientation to his or her
personal space and to the physical spaces which are shared
with others (home, school, work place, town or city, etc.) are
taken for granted. One's education in spatial orientation tends
simply 'to happen' or 'to grow' somehow along with learning the language into which one was born. The point is that
whatever we grow up with is just 'there'. What we learned
(and then later, perhaps, amended through travel or study)
is what we settle for, partly because nothing else is available
and because spatial orientation has not achieved a promi-
nent place in the educational scheme of things.

With regard to movement-writing (and to movement texts
used as evidence for research), spatial orientation is fundamental. For a start, it forms the core of intersubjective understanding. It provides the groundwork for intelligent

intersubjective relations with other people. It provides clues to understanding the meanings of the three human action-sign systems to which the 'bows' in Figs. 2, 3, and 4 belong. It is just here that we can see the sense in Urciuoli's description of the properties of action signs and their relation to conventional language:

> The property that [spoken] language shares with all sign systems is its indexical nature; its maintenance and creation of social connections, anchored in experience and the sense of the real. ... The structure of action fans out from the center, the locus of *I* and *you*, to delineate where and when everything happens relative to the central actors: *he* and *she* versus *I* and *you, there* versus *here, then* versus *now*, present versus non-present (past or future). This is the structure of parole in language, the structure of each situation of speaking ... In short, indexes make the social person (Urciuoli 1995: 189-190).

Of what kind of elements do these 'indexes' consist?

Spatial Context

In Fig. 2, we see signs *below* the staff. These pertain to constituent elements of the *spatial* context of the celebrant's movement circumstances. That is, the symbol ♦ tells us that these moves in the *Missa Major* (the Latin high mass) can only be performed by men.

The 'standard cross of axes' symbol, ✦ , tells us that the celebrant faces the *liturgical direction* 'east' (with 'west' behind him, 'south' to his right and 'north' to his left). A celebrant in the Latin High Mass performed the ritual actions in the spatial context of an *embedded* set of liturgical directions that pertained specifically to the mass and no other actions that may have occurred before or after it.

In Fig. 3, we see the standard cross of axes again, but this time, it is accompanied by a familiar set of symbols [N,S,E,W], indicating the actual geographical directions of north, south, east and west. In China, people face *south* to perform the exercise technique.

In Fig. 4, we see the standard cross of axes accompanied by a set of numbers [5,6,7,8]. This set is part of the set diagrammed below:

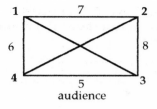

Figure 5. The system of numbering corners and walls of a room (or stage) used by ballet dancers to locate themselves in space in accordance with the rules for the idiom of movement they use.

Meaningful human movements do not happen in a vacuum. There is always and everywhere some spatial schema (usually out of awareness to performers) that, apart from supplying direction and purpose to the moves that human actors make, adds vital dimensions of meaning to signifying acts.

Many little known and less undertood facts about movement study belong to the spatial contexts in which these human actions take place. In a summary of some significant spatial differences between the Roman Mass, the exercise technique T'ai Chi Ch'uan and the ballet *Checkmate* (Williams 1995: 68-69), several elements of spatial orientation are emphasized, some of which are these:

T'AI CHI uses actual geographical space and directions, with south the dominant facing in China. The performer imagines the space as if standing in the center of a compass on the ground. The technique is tied to an ancient Chinese cosmological system based on the *I Ching* (Book of Changes) and it is a form of Taoist meditation.

MISSA MAJOR is an embedded liturgical space using cardinal directions that do not necessarily correspond to geographical directions. In this rite, the high altar *is* liturgical east. The whole set of liturgical directions derive from Christian theological concepts.

CHECKMATE is an embedded space based on a performer-audience relationship standard to all ballets (Fig. 5). Geographical directions are irrelevant. The spatial arrangement of the ballet is based on a chess game and the choreographer's usage of the game as an allegory.

In other words, "Each bow unfolds a different reality, a universe peculiar to its own system" (Urciuoli 1995: 194).

Williams directly links the unfolding of space and time to an unfolding of person. There is no such thing as space or time in a simple sense. Time and space are conceptual, moral, and ethical before they are physical. If the selection of [time/space] indexes is reduced to the utilitarian (as it usually is), the actor is essentially disembodied, at best one-dimensional, with no real motive ... Williams makes it clear that cosmological space or metaphysical space or dramatic space all emerge performatively from *the enactment of self*, just as a promise or threat unfolds from the words, nuances and intonations of the self in the moment of utterance, enclosing a world of action. *The meaning of all subsequent action—the Mass, the tai chi, the ballet—flows from that moment* (Urciuoli 1995: 194-95 - italics added).

Meaning only emerges in significant actions in ways that are systematically linked to a person's relation to an audience, perhaps to a Divinity, but in any case, *to an addressee.* There are always links from performed gestures and actions *to* someone or something. There is always more than an existential connection. *Human actions do not happen in isolation.* They always occur within a spatial context, and they are always included in some larger cultural construct of meaning.

Movement Literacy

To become literate in movement is to have developed the skills to read and write movement so that *translation into the medium of words is unnecessary* for creating appropriate descriptions of actions, except in cases like this chapter, where translation is necessary because most readers cannot read movement-writing texts.

Today, the majority of movement-writers use Laban's script. It is a script that (a) provides the means to become literate in movement, and (b) provides an "alphabetic script" (instead of pictographs, photographs or other iconic devices) for recording movement. (See Farnell 1994: 937*ff* for complete discussion). The writing of conventional languages performs a real (and very important) function in human life. Movement-writing is no different. We need to know as much about the components of human actions as we know about speech components. To acquire such knowledge we must, as Farnell suggests, "remove them from the flow of 'real time' by writing them down" (1994: 937).

[The Editor]

PRECIS 10

[1]The word 'evidence' points to the available facts and cir-[2]cumstances that support (or, in their misapplication or ab-[3]sence, *do not* support) a proposition, hypothesis, claim or [4]belief. Evidence indicates whether or not a thing is true or [5]valid. Evidence can take many forms: facts, circumstances, [6]proofs, documentation, grounds and/or data, support, [7]sign(s), testimony, statement', and/or assertions.

[8]A little-known fact regarding evidence and the study of [9]dances or dancing has to do with the generally assumed [10]nature of movement itself, which boils down to the ques-[11]tion of *the existence of movement*. That is, movements (hence [12]dance steps, gestures, signs, etc.) are commonly considered [13]ephemeral. Now you see the gestures — now you don't. [14]Do they exist, or don't they? Did they exist in the exact [15]forms the investigator claims they existed, or were they [16]figments of his or her imagination?

[17]*The best evidence that can be produced about a dance, a sign* [18]*language, an exercise technique, a set of greeting gestures (or* [19]*any other movement-based phenomena) is a written text of the* [20]*movements themselves.*

[21]The most widely used system of movement-writing is [22]based upon a script developed by Rudolf Laban in the [23]1920s. It is the script used in connection with Farnell's es-[24]say in this volume.
[25]To illustrate, readers are asked to examine the following [26]transcriptions of actions:

•SEE FIG. 1, PAGE 219•

[27]Notice that the transcription is identified, not by the words [28]'bowing from the waist' (a gross physical movement hav-[29]ing no indexical features), but by the phrase, 'I bow from [30]the waist' (the description of an action performed by a mov-[31]ing, human *social* being). This means that the action is *in-*[32]*tentional*. It also means that that, because the transcription [33]is done from the actor's perspective, it has a built-in as-[34]sumption of *agency*.

[35]Fig. 1 records the action 'I (the person acting) bow from [36]the waist' rather than the movement generalization, 'bow-[37]ing from the waist' which eliminates the person. To a move-[38]ment researcher, however, this description is inadequate, [39]especially if the movement system that includes the [40]'bow' is, for example, a Catholic mass, a stretch from the [41]exercise technique T'ai Chi Ch'uan, or the ballet, *Check-mate*.

Find Definitions

•exist (-ed; -ence; -ential) [lines 9, 11, 12]; •ephemeral [lines 10-11]; •transcription(s) [lines 20, 21, 25 and caption, 'Figure 1']; •agent (-cy) [line 26]; index (-ical, -icality) [line 22].

N.B. 1. The word, 'existential' is not in the précis text, however, it is found in the Chapter. Do you know what it means and how it is related to the word, 'exist'? For the full meaning of 'existential', you may have to consult a dictionary of philosophy. **2.** Do you know what 'ephemera' means? **3.** If you know what a 'transcription' is, do you also know what 'translation', 'transposition' and 'transliteration' mean? **4.** A definition of what 'agency' means in this context, will be found in Angeles (1981). **5.** You may find that collegiate dictionaries (in contrast to international or 'complete' versions) will *not* suffice to explain the word, 'index', as it is used in this context. Search until you find a *linguistic* definition of the term. Endnote #5 on p. 269 is helpful as a beginning.

Answer These Questions (Précis Text)

I. What is the best evidence for dances, sign languages, etc.? [lines 14 - 16]. Would you agree or disagree? In either case, briefly explain why.

II. Why does the author use the words, 'I bow from the waist' in Figure 1 instead of the words, 'bowing from the waist'? [lines 21 - 29].

III. What do you think the phrase, "gross physical movement" means? [line 22].

Answer These Questions (Chapter Text)

IV. In your view, what are some of the important features behind the statement (p. 225), *"Meaningful human movements do not happen in a vacuum."*

V. What is the significance of the comparisons on p. 225?

VI. It is commonplace for many people to think of movement (gestures, dances, etc.) as ephemeral. In your opinion, why is sound (speech, music, etc.) not thought of in the same way?

Thought Exercises

1. Alfred Gell (1985) wrote about his objections to movement notation in an essay about *Umeda* dancing from the West Sepik Province in Papua, New Guinea. For example, he says,

> One of the difficulties that has prevented progress in the field of the anthropology of dance being as rapid as that in, say, the anthropology of visual art, has been the need for a notation of dance movement that combines accuracy with some degree of readability for the non-dance expert. Art objects, such as the masks mentioned in the previous section, can be simply reproduced, but this simple graphic reduction is not feasible where dance movements are concerned. Labanotation and Benesh notation both have their

advocates, but are equally incomprehensible to the rest of the anthropological profession, who are unlikely to undertake the task of learning complicated systems of hieroglyphics lightly. (Gell 1985: 187).

a. What *claims* does Gell make in this passage?

b. After reading the whole section of Gell's essay in which this passage is included, do you think the author's claims are well-supported?

c. In the above passage, Gell compares "art objects" (e.g. masks) with dance movements. Do you think this is a fair comparison?

2. In a later section of his essay entitled 'Dance and nondance', the author says,

There is not, in Umeda or perhaps anywhere, a clear boundary between dance and nondance; we always find the self-consciously graceful walk that seems continually to refer to the dance without quite becoming it, and the half-hearted dance that lapses back into the security of mere locomotion. Yet it also remains true that there is a gap, a threshold however impalpable, that is crossed when the body begins to dance, rather than simply move. This gap is less a matter of movement *per se* than of meaning, for what distinguishes dance movements from nondance movements is the fact that they have dance meanings attached to them. But here is a paradox, fundamental to the whole question of dance, because what source can these dance meanings possibly have except the patterned contrasts, the intentional clues, embodied in everyday, nondance movement? Dance seems to separate itself from nondance by its atypicality, its nonnormal, nonmundane character, but dance acquires its meaning by referring us back always to the world of mundane actions, to what these performers would be doing, were they doing anything but dance ... (Gell 1985: 190-191).

    a. In simple terms, state the central *issue* in this passage.

    b. What do you think Gell means by "mundane" actions?

    c. Based on the material in this chapter about the mass, t'ai chi and the ballet Checkmate, how do you think Gell would deal with the Mass and with T'ai Chi? Here are two systems of movement that are "nondance." How do they acquire meaning, and do you think the meanings in T'ai Chi and the Mass have *the same meanings* to everyone?

    d. Gell may be able to speak about Umeda dancing as culture-specific. Could he talk about the ballet *Checkmate* in the same way? (Remember that he is trying to define 'dance and nondance' in all cultures everywhere). Checkmate is a dance. How well do you think it (or any ballet) fits into his scheme of classification?

3. Gell later goes on to say,

> Dance meanings originate through a process whereby elements, or components, of nondance motor patterns are seized upon, stereotyped (usually with some degree of formalisation and exaggeration), and are set within a particular context. The logic of dance is, in this respect, highly akin to the logic of play; the message 'this is dance' (like the message 'this is play': *cf.* Bateson 1972: 151) is a meta-message, one that sets the subsequent communicative transaction in its correct logical context (I am going to pretend to stab you with this knife, but only in play, really we are the best of friends ...). The function of style in dance, the immediately recognisable but usually very impalpable mannerism that colours the complete gamut of dance forms in a specific culture, is to mark this logical boundary between dance and nondance, ambiguous though it may become in particular instances. We may profitably begin our analysis

of Umeda dance, therefore, by seeking out the motor ste-
reotype that conveys this context shift, that establishes the
category of dance as one with ground rules that are distinc-
tively different from those that govern the interpretation of
behaviour in the nondance context (Gell 1985: 192).

a. According to Gell, how does "dance meaning"
originate?

b. Gell claims that "the logic of dance" is akin to the
"logic of play." What *evidence* does he use to support
the claim?

c. Gell claims that "the function of style in dance" is
"to mark [the] logical boundary between dance and
nondance." Do you think this claim is valid? Why?

SECTION III
INTELLECTUAL RESOURCES
[Rational Justification]

Chapter 11

Basic Structures of Argument

CHAPTER 11

Basic Structures of Argument

Arguments vs. Quarrels

No matter how well students may ultimately write movement and regardless of how much evidence they gather, everything they want to say can come to nothing because their evidence is not well supported.

My colleagues and I have known many students who possessed excellent *data* who did not have the required skills for presenting lucid, well-structured arguments in support of their data. We find that sometimes, they do not really understand what 'argument' means with reference to research.

The word 'argument' comes from the Latin *arguere*, which means 'to make clear'. An argument comprises the reasons, proofs and evidence offered in support or denial of something — 'something' being one or more *claims* that have been made by an author about the subject of the investigation. In formal logic, an argument consists of a series of statements called *premises* that are related in specific ways to a further statement called the *conclusion*. In general, arguments are of two types, deductive and inductive, but these categories need not detain us further here.[1] For our purposes, we will make a distinction between arguments and quarrels.

Quarreling is an altercation between individuals that frequently disrupts friendly -- even civil -- relations. Basically, to *quarrel* is to find fault — *to complain* against a person or a person's actions. The word 'quarrel' also partially derives from the Latin *querel(l)*: a complaint.

It is safe to say that nearly everyone knows what quarreling is. However, not everyone knows of what *argument* consists — even at a graduate level — hence the need for this chapter about relevant intellectual resources that will go some way toward producing rational arguments rather than ill-disguised quarrels about any given subject.

Although we risk offending some readers by including such discussion, it is a calculated risk, weighed against the prevailing undeniable evidence (especially visible on television talk shows, panels, etc.) that many people these days -- some of them highly educated professionals -- *do not know the difference between quarrels and arguments*. If they do, they do not publicly display their knowledge.

What is the major difference between an argument and a quarrel? *An argument is based on sound reasoning rather than rhetoric, emotion and charisma.*

We are mainly concerned in this chapter with *invalid* arguments — with inadequate statements or claims that are based upon faulty ('weak') justification and corroboration. We will avoid arguments that depend upon little more than the ability to interrupt, to declaim, or to cause an opponent to capitulate through emotional appeals and/or grumbling.

In contrast to invalid argument, *valid* argument is 'strong', meaning that *it is adequately justified and supported*. In other words, it is founded on 'fact' and/or 'truth'.

Ad Hominem Argument

An argument that deteriorates into a shouting match or a vulgar display of verbal aggression ceases to be an argument and becomes a quarrel. An argument that disintegrates into complaints about a person or his or her actions is called an *ad hominem* argument. The fallacy of *argumentum ad hominem* (argument against the man) means that someone argues against, or rejects another's views by attacking or abusing his or her personality, character, motives, intentions, qualifications, and such -- in contrast to providing evidence and solid reasons *why* his or her views are misguided or misconceived. How is *ad hominem* argument avoided?

A familiar example to most students of anthropology and human movement is analyzed below with a view toward revealing its structure:

CLAIM: [Walter Sorell] claims that [primitive dancers] have "complete freedom" but that men and women can't dance together. He qualifies this statement by saying that men and women dance together after the dance "degenerates into an orgy!" (1997: 18).

SUPPORT: Reveals the contradictions with which Sorell supports his claim.
WARRANT: Knowledge of the rules of fallacies in argument which make claims unsound, therefore unbelievable.

Keali'inohomoku sets about proving that Sorell's many claims about so-called "primitive dances" are full of contradictions, stereotypes and fallacies and shouldn't be taken seriously. Nowhere in her essay does Keali'inohomoku say, (for example) "Sorell is an ignoramus," or "Sorrell loves the ballet -- no wonder he doesn't understand any other form of dancing." Had she made this kind of statement, she would have committed a fallacy of *ad hominem* argument. She avoids the pitfall by revealing the contradictions in Sorell's statements by quoting what the author himself said.

Sorrell repeatedly contradicts himself, i.e. if "primitive" dancers have complete freedom then they must be able to dance together. If they cannot dance together, then they do not have complete freedom, contrary to Sorell's claim. None of the claims Sorrell makes about "primitive" dances are accurate because his claims are contradictory and he lacks concrete evidence in the form of fieldwork data to prove his argument.

If readers wish (or if they don't believe Keali'inohomoku's account of Sorell's claims) they can go to the source and discover the validity of her arguments for themselves.

Claims

Confronted by a claim, students are meant to ask, "What is this person trying to prove?" because that's what a claim is. Claims always say something that someone is trying to prove. Generally speaking, there are three different kinds of claims: claims of *fact*, claims of *value* and claims of *policy*. In everyday life and in most popular writing, claims aren't made separately, but together, so that readers must sort them out for themselves.

• **Claims of** *fact*, i.e. attempts to prove that a condition exists (has existed or will exist or that something is true or not true).

These claims must be supported *by* facts and data that are acceptable to the intellectual discipline to which they belong.

• **Claims of *value*** attempt to prove that something is more or less desirable.

• **Claims of *policy*** are claims attempting to prove why one course of action should be instituted over another with reference to a specific problem.

In rational arguments, *all of these claims must be supported.* Sufficient evidence must be presented so that the entire argument and each claim that is made are sound.

Warrants

In addition, any claims that are made must have a warrant. *A warrant is an inference or an assumption, a belief or principle that is taken for granted.*[2]

In an illuminating essay, *The Dance in Anthropological Perspective* (1978), Adrienne Kaeppler claims that Tongan, Aboriginal or African dances *are not* earlier stages of Western dance forms. As we have seen, there is a widely held misconception among many dance educators and historians that these dances *are* earlier stages of Western dance forms.

CLAIM: "[T]here is no reason to believe that non-Western dance represents earlier stages of western dance" (1978: 33).
SUPPORT: Shows how Sachs's book is based on unilineal evolutionary theory taken from the German *Kulturkreis* school which is based on diffusionist theory.
WARRANT: Unilineal evolutionary theory has been abandoned by anthropologists and archæologists, and the *Kulturkreis* school of thought is no longer credible.

Kaeppler refutes one of the claims Curt Sachs makes in his book *The World History of the Dance* (1937) by citing evidence in support of her claim that unilineal evolutionary theory is not only outdated but inaccurate based on recent advances in anthropological understanding.

In Kaeppler's argument (both the quoted section and the essay from which the passage was cited), Kaeppler doesn't *state* the warrant for the claims she makes about Sachs's book because, unlike claims and their supports, *warrants can be (and often are) unstated.*

Warrants are usually unstated because *they provide the grounds for what we claim* which makes them seem so obvious that we think they don't need to be made explicit. Notice, too, that both Kaeppler and Keali'inohomoku refrain from making explicit *claims of value.*

Kaeppler says, "there is no reason to believe" — that is, there are no facts to support the claim that non-Western dances are "earlier stages" of Western dances. She doesn't say, "Sachs was a poor writer" or "Sachs doesn't know what he's talking about" (*ad hominem* arguments). Kaeppler assumes that when readers discover that Sachs's claims are without rational and/or disciplinary support they will reject them, as she did.

Keali'inohomoku claims that Sorell's claims are contradictory. Because they are, we can't believe what he says about dancing. She *doesn't* say, "Sorell is wrong" because Sorell wasn't 'wrong' in everything he said — just what he said about alleged 'primitive' dancing. Basically, she assumes that Sorell is an intelligent and reasonable man who made some mistakes. His mistakes were (1) he didn't really know anything first-hand about the "primitive dance" he writes about and (2) he didn't attempt to learn anything about archæological records so that he could back the claims he made with evidence — if such evidence actually existed.

So far, we have briefly dealt with a tripartite structure of argumentation that encourages students to ask three questions:

1. What are the claims made by the author?
2. What evidence does the author provide in support of his or her claims?
3. What warrant(s) subsist "behind" the claims and their supports?

In other words, we claim (and this is an example of a 'claim of value') that this structure of questions is useful to students who are expected to write papers about the essays of received authorities in the anthropology of human movement.

We support this claim by producing evidence that at least two authors have made claims and supported them in such a way that they have avoided certain fallacies of argument by doing so.

The warrant for our claim of value (i.e. that the structure we provide is useful) is that students should be supplied with enough available intellectual resources to assist them to write better-than-average essays, which leads to getting good marks in their course of study.

The unstated assumption is three-fold: (1) students write essays as part of course-work; (2) students want to write "good" essays and get good marks; (3) students need adequate intellectual resources in order to write good essays.

Assumptions

In connection with argument, the word, 'assumption' (Latin *assumere*, "to take," "to adopt," "to accept") means a statement (idea or belief) that is accepted as true without clear proof or without presenting an argument to support it (Angeles 1981: 19).

In Section I of this book, Baynton provides a clear example. Speaking about E.B. Tylor, he says that "[Tylor] held to *the prevailing evolutionary assumption* that sign language was a primitive — and therefore inferior — form of communication" (p. 32 - italics added). Later on, Baynton speaks of "a long-held assumption" that has been corrected; the assumption that Plains Indian Sign talk functioned only as a *lingua franca* for intertribal communication. He cites Farnell (1995: 1-3) as the authority.

Farnell discusses an assumption at the beginning of her essay, i.e. "*the general assumption* was that those [Native American] cultures were doomed to extinction or assimilation given the inevitable onslaught of 'progress' (see p. 78 - italics added). Under the subheading, 'The Rhetoric of Demise', Farnell presents sound arguments, counter-claims and evidence that the assumption about doomed Native Americans who will become extinct is not only inaccurate but ungrounded. The activities of Native American cultures for the past few hundred years provides ample contrary evidence.

Unexamined Assumptions

It is not easy to correct unexamined assumptions. In fact, unexamined assumptions can be liabilities of an especially pernicious kind. For example, David Best speaks of *the difficulty of making an argument clear because of the many prevailing unquestioned assumptions that exist regarding the subject under discussion.* He begins by telling us that "There are two technical terms I cannot avoid: dualism and behaviourism" (1998: 16). He then explains:

> Dualism has been for hundreds of years, and still is, the dominant doctrine of the relationship between body and mind. The dualist conception is that there are two basic and distinct entities in which human beings consist, a mind and a body, or mental stuff and physical stuff. The self, and all mental experience, such as sensations, emotions and thoughts, are assumed to be independent of the physical behaviour by which they may be expressed. These experiences are assumed to take place in the mind, and to be directly known only to me, while other people, it is believed, can be aware of them only indirectly by observing my physical behaviour and inferring from it what is going on inside my mind (Best 1998: 16).

The dualist position is "beset by fatal flaws" which Best points out in some detail. He then introduces the behaviorist's position, saying that

> They rightly repudiate the notion of an unverifiable inner 'self', and unverifiable mental experiences, which are distinct from any overt actions. They ask what can be verified and seen. There answer is, not this 'inner' nonsense, but the physical behaviour which can be scientifically quantified. That is, retain only the other, the physical body and its movements. So, for the behaviourist, mental experience just is, or an be reduced to, physical behaviour (1998: 17).

But, another problem looms: when thinking becomes polarized into two opposing 'positions', we are usually assumed to hold one or the other of the two available positions:

> [I]t is almost universally assumed that these are the only two possibilities ... if you criticise one you must be an adherent of the other. ...

[S]ince I have written and spoken a good deal criticising dualism, I have often been assumed to be a modified or even a radical behaviourist. This assumption, that if you are not X you must be Y, is very common — it is what I call the disease of the dichotomous mind. The dichotomous presupposition is often built into questions. ... [I]f I criticise dualism I am assumed to be a behaviourist, and if I criticise behaviourism I am assumed to be a dualist. In fact I am equally opposed to each. *It is worth emphasising too that my position is not midway between them, but is a different position altogether.* (Best 1998: 17-18 - italics added)

I know of no more concise statement of the problems surrounding assumptions. And, the problems exist in any situation where there is an 'X' and a 'Y'. Like Best, *one may be opposed to both X and Y* and be obliged, because of this, to take on advocates of both views.

Earlier on, students were encouraged to ask three questions about spoken or written arguments. We will now add another:

1. What are the claims made by the author?
2. What evidence does the author provide in support of his or her claims?
3. What warrant(s) subsist 'behind' the claims and their supports?
4. What are the assumptions (also called 'presumptions') upon which claims, evidence and warrants rest?

Students will be expected to identify these four elements of a arguments in other reading material in the interests of being absolutely clear about each element.

Fallacies

Angeles lists forty informal fallacies (1981: 95-100) including the *argumentum ad hominem*. Seven of the most common of these are the

1. Fallacy of *argumentum ad baculum* (argument from power or force). The Latin means "an argument according to the stick" ... Arguing to support the acceptance of an argument by a threat, or use of force. Reasoning is replaced by force, which results in the termination of logical argumentation and elicits other kinds of behavior such as fear, anger, reciprocal use of force, etc. (1981: 95-6).

Often, the force (or power) used in formal argument or debate is not physical force (hitting someone or threatening to strike them if they are not in agreement with the claims that are made), but *verbal* force. That is, *bullying* of some kind, that manifests itself as shouting, interrupting, name-calling — or simply a refusal on the part of the speaker to cease talking so that another person may speak.

> 2. Fallacy of *argumentum ad misericordiam* (argument to pity). Arguing by appeal to pity in order to have some point accepted. Example: "I've got to have at least a B in this course, Professor Angeles. If I don't, I won't stand a chance for medical school, and this is my last semester at the university." Also called the *appeal to pity* (1981: 96).

Nearly everyone at some time or another has used an 'argument to pity' and some arguments of this kind are legitimate. If a student says, "I couldn't finish the required term paper because of a death in the family. Will you give me an incomplete and an extension (of time) in order to finish the paper?" the student is appealing to the instructor's pity by asking him or her to understand circumstances that do not often arise and that certainly call for special consideration. On the other hand, the student who says "I couldn't finish the required term paper because I just didn't feel like writing," is less likely to be successful because he or she asked for pity based on an obvious inability to exercise the self-discipline required to finish the course.

> 3. Fallacy of begging the question. (a) Arriving at a conclusion from statements that themselves are questionable and have to be proved but are assumed true. Example: the universe has a beginning. Everything that has a beginning has a beginner. Therefore the universe has a beginner called God. This assumes (begs the question) that the universe does indeed have a beginning and also that all things that have a beginning have a beginner. (b) Assuming the conclusion or part of the conclusion in the premises of an argument. Sometimes called *circular reasoning*, ... Example: "Everything has a cause. The universe is a thing. Therefore, the universe is a thing that has a cause." ... (c) Arguing in a circle. One statement is supported by reference to another statement which statement itself is supported by reference to the first statement. Example: "Aristocracy is the best form of government because the best form of government is that which has strong aristocratic leadership" (1981: 97).

Examples of 3 **(b)** and **(c)** common to the dance world are these:

> [1] "All human beings move. All dance is movement. Therefore, all human beings dance." or,
> [2] "All dancing is movement. All human beings move. Therefore, all human beings dance."

These disguised syllogisms sound suspiciously like the basis for American post-modernist notions about dancing that originated from the Judson Theater Group. The circular reasoning in both should be obvious.

> **4.** Fallacy of *ignoratio elenchi* (irrelevant conclusion). An argument that is irrelevant; that argues for something other than that which is to be proved and thereby in no way refutes (or supports) the points at issue. Example: A lawyer in defending his alcoholic client who murdered three people in a drunken spree argues that alcoholism is a terrible disease and attempts should be made to eliminate it (1981: 98).

A further example: A bored (and obviously puzzled) observer of impressionist and surrealist paintings in an art museum says, "I don't understand why everyone talks about the aesthetic and/or artistic value of these paintings. I don't know anything about painting, impressionism or surrealism, but *I know what I like* — and I don't like these." *Question:* What is fallacious about this statement? *Answer:* The observer's like and dislikes are irrelevant to questions about the aesthetic or the artistic value of the paintings.

> **5.** Fallacy of *post hoc ergo propter hoc*. The Latin means "after this, therefore the consequence (effect) of this," or "after this therefore because of this." Sometimes simply called the *fallacy of false cause*. Concluding that one thing is the cause of another thing because it precedes it in time. A confusion between the concept of succession and that of causation. Example: "A black cat ran across my path. Ten minutes later I was hit by a truck. Therefore, the cat's running across my path was the cause of my being hit by a truck."

There is a sense in which the fallacy of false cause is at the bottom of most of the origins arguments one finds in the literature on dancing. That is, because most of the so-called "primitive" African or Australian Aboriginal dances *preceded* other dance forms in time, they are assumed somehow to have *caused* those dances to be what they are.

No one would argue that, for example, Bushman trance-dancing *preceded* many other dance forms in the world in time. In terms of a concept of *succession,* there is no doubt that Bushman trance-dancing is one of the oldest dance forms in the world. However, to conclude that Bushman trance-dancing was (or is) in any way, shape or form the *cause* of dance forms that succeeded it in time is mistaken.

> 6. Genetic Fallacy. **(a)** Arguing that the origin of something is identi-cal with that from which it originates. Example: "Consciousness origi-nates in neural processes. Therefore, consciousness is (nothing but) neural processes." Sometimes referred to as the nothing-but fallacy, or the REDUCTIVE FALLACY. **(b)** Appraising or explaining some-thing in terms of its origin, or source, or beginnings. **(c)** Arguing that something is to be rejected because its origins are known and/or are suspicious (Angeles 1981: 100).

Probably the most famous example of the genetic fallacy in the literature on dancing and drama was expressed by Harrison in her book *Ancient Art and Ritual* (1913[1948]). In her attempts to establish the origins of ritual and drama, this author assigns three types of prior existence to the dance:

> But historically and also genetically or logically the dance in its in-choateness, its undifferentiatedness, comes first. It has in it a larger element of emotion, and less of presentation. It is this inchoateness, this undifferentiatedness, that apart from historical fact, makes us feel sure that logically the dance is primitive (Harrison 1913[1948]: 171).

Here, we are told that dancing is "nothing but" inchoate, undifferentiated movement and because of that it is the "first," i.e., the most "primitive" of the arts.[3] Some of Harri-son's claims about the primitiveness of dancing are based on its presumed genetic source.

> 7. *The fallacy of division.* Arguing that what is true of a whole is **(a)** also necessarily true of its parts and/or **(b)** also true of some of its parts. Example: "The community of Pacific Palisades [in Los Angeles, Cali-fornia] is extremely wealthy. Therefore, every person living there is (must be) extremely wealthy (or therefore Adam, who lives there, is [must be] extremely wealthy)." Inferring that the parts of a collection have certain characteristics merely on the basis that the collection has

them [is a] notion that erroneously proceeds from regarding the collection collectively [instead of] regarding it distributively (Angeles 1981: 98). This fallacy is also called the *pars pro toto fallacy.*

In *Theories of Primitive Religion,* Evans-Pritchard provides an excellent example, i.e. "In classing primitive peoples with children, neurotics, &c., the mistake is made of assuming that, because things may resemble each other in some particular feature, they are alike in other respects, the *pars pro toto* fallacy" (1965: 46).

In a chapter entitled 'Natural Response and Action' (1992: 16-27), Best discusses two fallacies that underlie subjective-objective dualisms, so prevalent in all of the arts:

> Resort to subjectivism is largely a consequence of basic philosophical confusions, such as the definitional fallacy (that meaning is given by definition); the essentialist fallacy (that where the same term refers to various instances there must be some underlying common and distinctive essence); and the pervasive misconception that it is the main function of linguistic expressions to *name objects,* including supposed 'inner' occult mental processes. (This last has its equally pervasive counterpart in the misconceived notion that works of art in general stand for, symbolise, represent, or picture, objects or private mental states. ... (1992: 17).[4]

Summary

Learning to recognize the difference between arguments and quarrels, being able to decipher the claims that are made by speakers and writers about dancing, and understanding the warrants (the unquestioned assumptions) about art and human beings are not easy, but the rewards for the required effort are well worth it. To a large extent, the necessary effort is involves introspection. That is, we must abandon assumptions that seem so natural that *they don't appear as assumptions.* They appear to be obvious points of departure.

Many people tend to assume, for example, that science is 'objective' and art is 'subjective'. There are still those who assume that dancing is the most 'primitive' of the arts. Or, they assume that when all is said and done, the best explanation for dancing lies in its entertainment value.

In sum, examining one's assumptions about dancing (or any of the arts) is an act that permits examination of the nature of the lenses through which one sees and understands everything. It is not a process that happens quickly, by any means, but the examination will *never* happen unless a beginning is made.

[The Editor]

PRECIS 11

[1]The word, 'argument' comes from the Latin *arguere*, which [2]means 'to make clear'. An argument consists of the reasons [3](proofs, evidence) offered in support or denial of something [4]— some *claim* that has been made by someone about some-[5]thing. In logic, an argument consists of a series of statements [6]called *premises* that are logically related to a further state-[7]ment called the conclusion. In general, arguments are of two [8]types, deductive and inductive, but these categories need [9]not detain us further here. For our purposes, we will make [10] a distinction between arguments and quarrels.

[11]*Quarreling* as an altercation between individuals that fre-[12]quently disrupts friendly... relations.... To *quarrel* is to find [13]fault — *to complain against a person or a person's actions.* The [14]word, 'quarrel' also partially derives from the Latin *querel(l)*: [15]a complaint. It is safe to say that nearly everyone knows [16]what quarreling is. Not everyone knows of what *argument* [17]consists — even at a graduate level — hence the need for [18]this chapter about relevant intellectual resources that will [19]go some way toward producing rational arguments rather [20]than ill-disguised quarrels about any given subject.

[21]Although we may risk offending some readers of this book [22]by including discussion of this kind, it is a calculated risk, [23]weighed against the prevailing undeniable evidence (es-[24]pecially visible on television talk shows, panels, etc.) that [25]there are many people these days — some of them highly [26]educated professionals — who *don't know the difference be-*[27]tween quarrels and arguments, or if they do, they do not

^{28}publicly display their knowledge. *An argument is based on* ^{29}*sound reasoning rather than rhetoric and charisma.*

^{30}We are mainly concerned ... with *invalid* argument — with ^{31}inadequate statements or claims that are based upon faulty, ^{32}('weak') justification and corroboration. We will avoid ar-^{33}guments that depend upon little more than the ability to ^{34}interrupt, to declaim or to cause an opponent to capitulate ^{35}through emotional appeals and/or grumbling.

^{36}In contrast to invalid argument, *valid* argument is 'strong', ^{37}meaning that it is adequately justified and supported. In ^{38}other words, it is founded on 'fact' and/or 'truth'.

^{39}An argument that deteriorates into a shouting match or ^{40}vulgar displays of verbal aggression ceases to be an ar-^{41}gument and becomes a quarrel. An argument that disinte-^{42}grates into *complaints* about a person or his or her actions ^{43}is called an *ad hominem* argument. The fallacy of *argumentum* ^{44}*ad hominem* (argument against the man) means that some-^{45}one argues against, or rejects a person's views by attack-^{46}ing or abusing his or her personality, character, motives, ^{47}intentions, qualifications, etc. as opposed to providing evi-^{48}dence why his or her views are incorrect. How is this ^{49}kind of argument avoided? ...

^{50}Confronted by a claim, students are meant to ask, "What is ^{51}this person trying to prove?" because that's what a claim ^{52}is. Claims always say something that someone is trying to ^{53}prove. Generally speaking, there are three different kinds ^{54}of claims: claims of *fact*, claims of *value* and claims of *policy*. ^{55}In everyday life and in most popular writing, claims aren't ^{56}made separately, but together, so that readers must sort ^{57}them out for themselves.

^{58}**Claims of *fact*,** i.e. attempts to prove that a condition exists ^{59}(has existed or will exist or that something is true or not true). ^{60}These claims must be supported *by* facts and data that are ^{61}acceptable to the intellectual discipline to which they belong. ^{62}**Claims of *value*** attempt to prove that something is more or ^{63}less desirable.

[64]Claims of *policy* are claims attempting to prove why one [65]course of action should be instituted over another with ref-[66]erence to a specific problem. ...

Find Definitions

•rhetoric [line 29]; •charisma [line 29]; •fact(s) [lines 38, 54, 58, 60]; •deductive [line 8]; •prove [lines 51, 53]; •inductive [line 8]; •declaim [line 34].

Answer These Questions

I. *In your own words,* how would you explain the difference between an argument and a quarrel? [lines 1-20].

A. From your own experience, describe a quarrel you recently heard. Why was it a quarrel, not an argument?
B. From your own experience, describe an argument you recently heard. Why was it an argument, not a quarrel?

II. What role do *claims* play in an argument? [lines 50-57]

A. From your own experience, state some of the claims you have heard about some form of dancing.
B. From your own experience, state some of the claims you have heard about a sign language.

III. What is an *ad hominem* argument? [lines 41-49].

IV. Give examples of the three kinds of claim listed in lines 58-66.

V. On p. 239 in the essay text (not the précis text), 'Assumptions' are discussed. What is the relationship between an assumption and an argument?

VI. On pp. 240-41 in the essay text (not the précis text), 'Unexamined Assumptions' are discussed. Why do you think unexamined assumptions are *liabilities* of a special kind? What makes them "special problems" in the cases Best describes where there are two opposing positions involved?

ENDNOTES

Editor's Preface [pp. 1-18]

[1] I refer to the books mentioned in Keali'inohomoku's bibliography, among them Sorell (1960), Martin (1939 and 1963), Sachs (1937) and others. A recent book that does *not* follow this format is Adshead-Lansdale and Layson (1994 - 2nd Ed.).

[2] I've written about those elsewhere. When teaching, I'm more interested in helping students develop their own points of view.

[3] Some people think it unnecessary to deal with problems from the past. We can only answer them with Santayana's words: "Progress, far from consisting in change, depends on retentiveness ... Those who cannot remember the past are condemned to fulfil it" (*Life of Reason*, 1905-6. Vol. I, ch. xii: 'Flux and Constancy in Human Nature').

[4] Like Farnell (1995: 107), I use an upper-case letter with the word 'Deaf'. See her Note 3, p. 252.

[5] [Fairbank's Note]: This research project, initiated in 1981, proposed to document much of China's ethnic and folk dance materials by the year 1990. The project was sponsored by the Ministry of Culture and organized by the Arts Research Institute (Yishu Yenjiusu).

[6] Aspects of the transformation process called *xheng-li* involve categorization and elimination. Those dances and elements of the idiom considered to be 'unhealthy', 'in bad taste', 'feudal' and/or 'uncharacteristic of the people' will not be included in the official collection project either as material for the stage or the archives. "Unhealthy" elements include those movements and stylistic aspects which the government considers lewd, provocative or "politically backwards." For example, a shaman's ecstatic movements during a trance would likely be considered "unhealthy" because of their seemingly unrestrained quality and their associations with spiritual concepts — notions that are contradictory to the People's Republic of China viewpoint. (Fairbank 1985: 179).

[7] [Fairbank's Note]: The questions being raised at this time [early 'eighties] concerning China's culture turn around this question: 'What is the history of Chinese art and what should the national style of contemporary China be?' ... It is believed that China's rich cultural legacy should not be overlooked, while at the same time new models and forms must be developed in order to represent the multi-ethnic society and political ideology of modern China.

Since the devastating effects of the cultural revolution and subsequent reforms, pressure has been placed on the artistic community to create contemporary forms and fill the 'gap' of culture. In recent years, controversy has arisen over whether this contemporary dance style should illustrate the "spirit of the 1980s" ... or continue in its present course and focus on the indigenous movement traditions found throughout China.

Glasser [pp. 19-38]

[1] In this context, the word means "mixed blood" — persons of mixed black and white parentage.

[2] The 'golden period' of ballet in England is thought by many to have occurred between 1820 and 1850 — a period largely influenced by Jean Georges Noverre (Williams 1991: 28).

[3] See Franken (1997) for the Swahili language definition of *ngoma*.

[4] From Afrikaans language, the word meant "a policy of segregation or discrimination on grounds of race." (ODT)

[5] Although the term, 'non-verbal' is commonly used to describe dancing, we make a distinction between the truly 'non-verbal', i.e. animal communication, and human *non-vocal* communication when dancers, signers, and others use the medium of movement as their instrument for expression [The Editor].

•Suggested further readings in connection with Glasser's essay•

Bozzoli, B. [Ed.] 1983. History, Experience and Culture. IN *Town and Countryside in the Transvaal.* Johannesburg: Ravan.
Denisoff, S. 1968. Protest Movements: Class Consciousness and the Propaganda Song. *Sociological Quarterly* 9: 228-47.
Hall, S. and T. Jeffersen (Eds.) 1976. *Resistance Through Rituals.* London: Hutchinson.
Modisane, B.1963. *Blame On Me History.* Johannesburg: Donker.

Baynton [pp. 39-74]

[1] Within forty years there would be twenty residential schools in the United States; by the turn of the century, more than fifty (*Annals:* 46-7). The first two successful oral schools were both founded in 1867: The New York Institution for the Improved Instruction of Deaf Mutes, and the Clarke Institution for Deaf-Mutes in Northhampton, Massachusetts. On the early schools for the deaf, see Van Cleve and Crouch (1989: 29-59), Lane (1984: 206-251), and Valentine (1991: 355-375).

2 For an overview of the oralist movement, see Van Cleve and Crouch (1989: 106-141), Lane (1984: 339-414) and Winefield (1987).

3 See Hall (1956: 9) for a brief description of a battle between the Iowa Association of the Deaf and the Iowa School for the Deaf in the 1950s over this issue. See also Van Cleve (1984: 195-220) and Van Cleve and Crouch (1989: 128-141).

4 Ellegard's exhaustive review of the British popular press shows that the basic idea of evolution was accepted in Britain by 1870.

5 The literature is vast, but see Gilman (1988) on images of illness; Russett (1976) and Roberts (1988) on sin as reversion; Gould (1981) on criminology; and Levine (1971: 94), who wrote, "social Darwinism was not so much a conservative doctrine as a *universal* doctrine. The analogy found a home in America with amazing speed and ubiquity." However, in the light of Bowler's recent work (1988) Levine's statement should be amended to say that is was *social evolutionism*, not Darwinism *per se*, that became ubiquitous.

6 This section of my account of Condillac relies upon Stam (1976: 45-52).

7 See Pettingill (1873: 9) and Valade (1873: 31). Also see Wilkinson (1881: 167-168), Peet (1855: 10), Robinson (1890: 216) and Covell (1890: 133-36). Gallaudet claimed that sign language was "the mother language of mankind" (*n.d.*: 17) which statement is quoted in Winzer (1981: 118).

8 [Editor's Note]: Because British and American anthropology developed as academic disciplines in very different ways, confusion often arises. Although E.B. Tylor is considered by many on both sides of the Atlantic to be the father of the modern discipline, most of Tylor's theories of the origins of language and primitive religion (i.e. 'animism') have long been abandoned. Nevertheless, there are still existing terminological difficulties. In Britain, 'anthropologist' means social anthropologists who study people, their institutions and systems. In America, 'anthropologist' can mean physical anthropologists (primates and gene pools), archæologists (fossil remains, ancient artifacts, early 'digs', etc.), or cultural anthropologists ('people' anthropologists) most closely resembling social anthropologists. Baynton seems to use the all-inclusive American convention in this passage. It also seems necessary to say that attitudes toward language have changed drastically within sociocultural anthropology over the years on both sides of the Atlantic, but popular consciousness of the problems of sign languages and dancing still tend to be rooted in concepts generated during the times Baynton analyzes.

9 Sacks (1989: 75) notes Tylor's knowledge of sign language and friendships with deaf people. Also see the work of early sociologist Cooley (1909:

67), who thought it "probable that artificial gesture language was well organized before speech had made much headway."

[10] See Mallery (1880a: 1-3 and 6), and for the sources of Mallery's views, (1882: 69). See also Tylor (1878[1865]: 77-8).

[11] For other accounts of such visits, see Anonymous (1874: 48-9), Wilkinson (1881: 171) and Mallery (1882: 77-8).

[12] See Robinson (1890: 216) and T.H. Gallaudet (1847: 59).

[13] See entries under 'Tabular Statement ...' in reference list for 1920 and 1921. The figures are taken from the 1919 report because Texas and Maryland did not submit reports in 1920.

[14] Flowers's draft of an essay entitled *Life After Graduation* is undated and unsigned, but the body of the letter identifies it as his, written in 1908. His school file identifies him as "partially deaf," and "able to hear loud tones from those he is accustomed to hear speak," thus there would have been no question about his suitability for an oral education.

Farnell [pp. 75-100]

[1] See Clark (1885) and Mallery (1880a and 1881). La Mont West attempted a dialect survey across the Northern Plains in 1956 and concluded that there was a "standard" dialect known by fluent and well-traveled sign talkers, as well as regional variations. This is certainly a reasonable suggestion. West's conclusions, however, are based upon statistics drawn from problematic descriptions in the 19th century documentation plus his detailed work with one Arapaho consultant, not upon his own survey (West 1960). Sign talkers among the Assiniboine today recognize dialect variations that belong to neighboring groups.

[2] The film of the council and Scott's film dictionary are housed in the National Archives, Washington D.C., Video and Sound Branch, nos. 106.3, 106.4 and 106.5.

[3] The use of an upper case letter with the word "Deaf" is a convention recently established by deaf and hard-of-hearing Americans who identify themselves as members of the Deaf Community, a distinct sub-culture whose language is ASL.

[4] Ardener (1989: 18) suggests that Saussure's complex notion of the arbitrariness of the linguistic sign was clearly designed to answer adherents of the view—supported by Tylor—that all language had a representational origin.

5 This woman was Mrs. Rose Weasel [The Editor].

6 See Herzfeld (1987: 137) for discussion of Tylor's view of gesture as a sort of "expressive incontinence" and further discussion in Farnell (1995).

7 I have attempted to use word glosses (in upper case letters) and descriptions of signs for those readers unable to read the Labanotated texts enclosed in the figures. this is not easy because descriptions in words are always inadequate as well as lengthy, and photographs or pictures are only static, hence the need for the script, of course. See Farnell (1984) and Williams and Farnell (1990) for discussion of the notion of literacy in relation to movement.

8 ASL is the acronym for American Sign Language, also called Ameslan, which is the sign language used by Deaf communities in America. Linguistic research into ASL has blossomed over the past thirty years since the pioneering work of William Stokoe at Gallaudet University. Stokoe was the first to insist and demonstrate that ASL as a sign language was a real language in every sense of the word "real," and not a primitive substitute for speech (see Stokoe 1972).

9 Ray De Mallie: Personal communication and Buechel's *Lakota Grammar* (1983[1939]: 72).

10 The word "deixis" is a technical term in linguistics, used to handle those features of language that are relative to the place and time of the spoken utterance. They include personal pronouns and adverbials of time and space such as "here" and "there," and "now" and "then," as well as demonstratives and tense. "Deixis" is a Greek word meaning "pointing" or "indicating," which is somewhat ironic given the exclusion of the act itself from Western definitions of language and language-in-use. For introductions to deixis in general see Lyons (1977) and Buhler (1934).

11 Recent work on deixis in linguistics and psycholinguistics can be found in collections edited by Jarvella and Klein (1982) and Pick and Acredolo (1983). Important exceptions to this general neglect of the body in deixis are Sherzer (1973), McNeill and Levy (1982), McNeill (1985a and 1990) and Haviland (1986 and 1993). See also Bellugi and Klima (1982) on ASL and deixis. Hanks (1990) also aims to accomplish an embodiment of deixis in his masterful study of Mayan deictics.

**[For Nakota Words with diacritical marks,
see next page.]**

Page 82: When I asked how to say in Nakota that someone has a good mind, I was taught the phrase *t'awačį wašte* ... I [moved] a pointed index finger from the heart away from the chest with the finger pointing straight forward, then [added] the sign GOOD, a flat hand with the palm down moving from the center of the chest diagonally to the right. ... There is *no reference to head* as a place where mind is located, and second, emphasis is on the *movement* not on a location.

Page 83: To say "She thinks clearly," one would use the same work in the phrase *tayą t'awačį* and the sign was almost the same. consistent with an apparent lack of distinction between verbs and nouns ...*Wačį* "to think;"... *t'awačį mneha,* "strong-willed;" *t'awačįknuhana* "undecided." The phrase *t'awačį wašte* seems to indicate a general disposition ...

Page 84: *t'a* [possessional prefix] ...Your thinking and thoughts (*mit'awačį*) while certainly yours, are separable — they can be shared.

Page 85: *Ž ęįš oyate ka t'ipi hųšta kan.*

Page 86: *Wi ne eyaš kahąkeya t'ipi hųšta*

Page 87: *étų* or 'close', *ésten* meaning "soon/right away," *t'éhą,* "far away, " *t'éhą* refers to invisible rather than to visible distance; *wanąkaš* "a long time ago."

Page 88: *t'atetopa* the "four winds" or *t'ateoyétópa* "the four tracks of the winds." *Wiyota(hą)* is translated as 'south' but refers to "sun in the middle" and "noon." *Wiyohpe,* "west." *Waziyata,* "north." *Wíhinąp'e* "east."

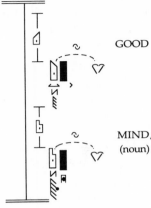

GOOD

MIND/THOUGHTS/DISPOSITION
(noun)

a) T'awac'į waśte.
"She/he has a good mind."

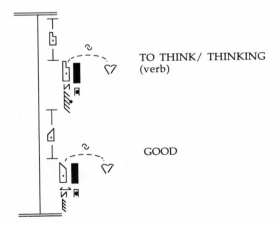

TO THINK/ THINKING
(verb)

GOOD

b) T'awac'į waśte.
"She/he thinks clearly."

Figure 1. Assiniboine/Nakota Embodiment of Mind

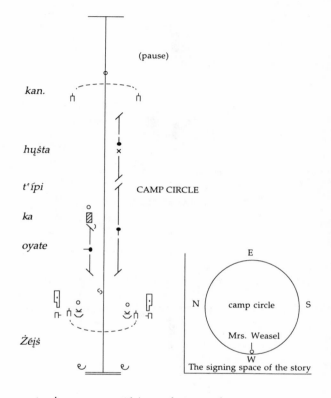

1. *Zéįš,   oyate   ka   t'ípi   hųśta   kan.*
    That one   tribe   over there   they live   it is said   over there
    So, the people were camped over yonder they say, over yonder.

Figure 2. The First Sentence from the Movement
Text of "The Star Children."

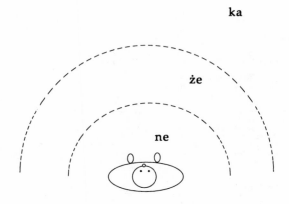

ne - near space/time (here/now)

że - farther space/time (there/then)

ka - far and visible space/time

Figure 3. Deictic co-ordinates shared by
Nakota and Plains Sign Talk.

HERE (near space and time)		THERE (medium distance away)		YONDER (far but visible space)	
ne	this, this one	zéi	that, that one	ka	(that) over there
nejs	this, this one	zéjs	that, that one (it)	kejs	that over there
nen	here	żen	there	kan	over there
néc'i	here, over here, this	żéc'i	there	kák'i	over yonder
néc'iya	this way, towards this place over here	żéc'iya	that way, in that direction, over there	kakiya	yonder, towards yonder place
néc'iyataha	through here, from (over) here	żéc'iyataha	from (over) there (ya/u—going/coming)	kakiyataha	from yonder, over there in that direction
néc'en	here, over here, thus, this way, like this, in this manner	żéc'en żetam żéc'etu	then, so, after, that over there, that way like that	kák'en (ken) katam kana	over there over that way those there
netam	over here, this way	żéc'a	that kind, thus		
néc'etuħ	so, this way	żéc'a ų	so it was,		
néc'a	then (near time), this kind one like this, similar to	żéna	(thus + to be) those		
		żetamya	thus, (use) that kind)		
néna	these here (pl. of ne)	że ų	go that way		
netamya	go this way	żéc'enżeha	then		
netam u	come this way	żeha	that, then		
netaha	from here (this time/place)	etaha żeha	from then, after that		
		żehata	then, after that (time)		
nétu	right here	żehac'eha	then, in those times		
nétun(a)	near here	żetaha	from there (that time/place)		
ąpa ne(n)	today, this day				
éstena nen	soon	żena (k'o)	those (too)		
n(e) iyuha	all of these	żehakam-nikte	I'm going that far		
nehakam-nikte	I'm going this far				

Figure 4. Deictical Terminology in Nakota

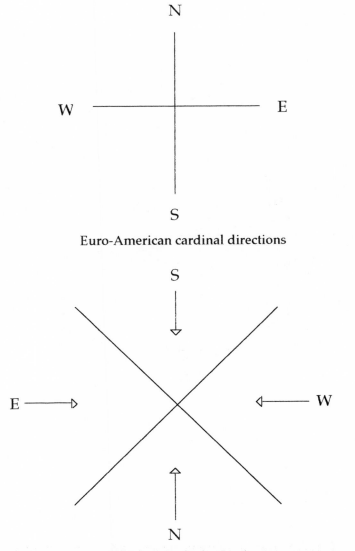

Euro-American cardinal directions

Assiniboine cardinal directions

Figure 5. Two different cultural conceptions of
the cardinal directions.

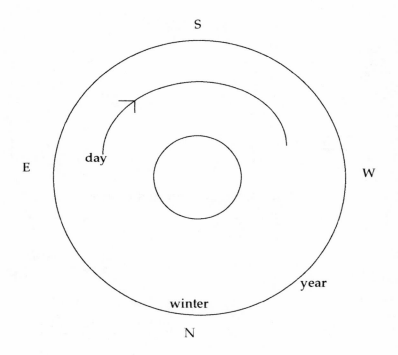

Figure 6. Time in space in Nakota and Plains Sign Talk

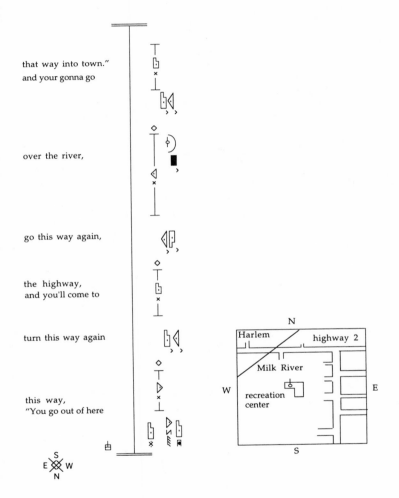

Figure 7. Route directions given by Fort Belknap resident

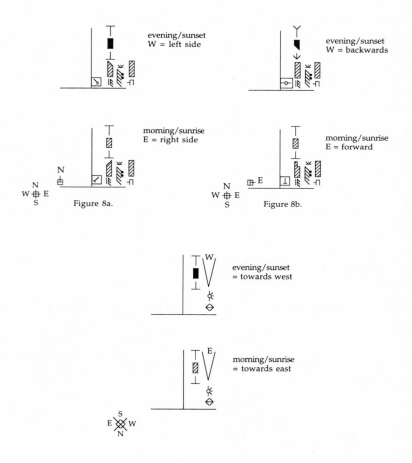

Figure 8. Assiniboine/Nakota Spatial Orientation

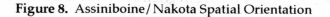

Chapter 5 [pp. 121-136]

[1] Of North American Indian descent, Maria Tallchief was born Jan. 24, 1925 in Fairfax Oklahoma. She was noted for her fine technique and was considered one of the United States' greatest ballerinas. She danced with the Ballet Russe de Monte Carlo (1942) and was guest artist at the Paris Opera (1947) She also danced with the New York City Ballet, where she was until she retired in 1965. Her sister, Marjorie Tallchief (b. 1927) — also a distinguished ballerina — danced with several companies: American Ballet Theatre - 1944-46; Grand Ballet du Marquis de Cuevas - 1947-57; Chicago Opera Ballet - 1956-58; Paris Opéra Ballet - 1957-62 and the Harkness Ballet - 1964-66. The Tallchief sisters founded the Chicago City Ballet in 1980.

[2] A German royal balletmaster, writing *circa* 1841-1869, who cites 'definitions' taken from sixteenth and seventeenth-century clerics: "Dancing is a lewd movement and a disgraceful spectacle by which one is annoyed." "Dancing is a sin." "Dancing is a heap of filth." "Dancing is a rotten tree." "Dancing is a frivolous disgrace, wickedness and vain darkness." "Dancing is a hideous monstrosity, a tiresome dishounourable, disgraceful and wanton abuse." "Dancing is a tinder of wickedness." (Voss 1869: 15 - Trans: Anne Oppenheimer, Oxford, 1972).

[3] Some students may want to see what has been written in the *Encyclopedia Americana* since 1830 and the *Encyclopædia Britannica* since 1768 to study of the ways in which dances and dancing have been described over the years. (See Williams 1991: 58 for further comment).

[4] Glasser (1993), Youngerman (1974), Keali'inohomoku (1997[1969] and 1980), Williams (1974) and others.

[5] Other classical forms are *Odissi, Kuchipudi, Kathak, Manipuri* and *Kathakali.*

[6] For a detailed treatment of the *Sadir Nac,* see Marglin (1980) who deals with the ritual role of the *devadasis* at the temple of Jagannatha in Orissa.

[7] Ethnic: [adj. or n.]. **1a:** (of a social group) having a common national or cultural tradition. **1b:** (of clothes, etc.) resembling those of a non-European exotic people. **2.** denoting origin by birth or descent rather than nationality (i.e. ethnic Turks). **3.** relating to race race or culture (ethnic group; ethnic origins). **4.** Archaic pagan; heathen. •n. **1** a member of an (esp. minority) ethnic group. **2.** (in pl., usu. treated as sing.) = ethnology. ❑ **ethnic cleansing** *euphem.* the practice of mass explusion or killing of people from opposing ethnic or religious groups within a certain area. **ethnic minority** a (usu. identifiable) group differentiated from the main population of a community by racial origin or cultural background.

[8] In fact, the word *nautch* (a corruption of the word *nac*) was originally derived from *nrtya* and *nrtta*, but today, it is a derogatory term for those dances that do not maintain the aesthetic standards of *natya* and *nrtya*. Both *abhinaya* and *nrtta* are included in *nrtya*, the word that is closest to the idea of 'dance' in India. And, *nrtya* is the main vehicle of *natya* (theatre).

One of the major points made by the Madras scholars who promoted the present popularity of Bharatanatyam was that far from being *nautch* in the derogatory sense, this idiom was a paradigm of *natya*. Common to all forms of *natya* and *nrtya* is the use of an elaborate gesture language which includes facial expressions, *and hasta mudras*, as well as movements of the whole body. A principle by which an idiom is classified as 'classical' is the extent to which the gesture-language of that idiom is elaborated. The use of gestures is not, however, considered enough in itself, unless they are used in accordance with the aesthetic ideals of classical Indian dramaturgical theory.

[9] The opposition *margi/desi* operates much more widely, as for example, in indigenous linguistic theory. *Margi* is virtually synonymous with *samskrta* which means 'highly elaborated' and 'well or completely formed' in contrast to *prakrta* which means 'normal', 'ordinary' and 'natural'. The latter word (*prakrta*) is the generic name given to the local vernaculars of the Gupta Empire, the languages of the market-place and of everyday discourse. Many plays of the Gupta period are actually written both in Sanskrit and in different *prakrits*, the former language being spoken by 'elevated' characters and the latter by 'lesser' characters and women. For more information, see Puri (1983: 45ff).

[10] Perhaps there is no satisfactory solution if one is writing for a reference book where one is obliged to use terms that are communly understood, however, it would have been possible to acknowledge the problems generated by 'Tribal Dance', saying that 'Traditional Dance' would be used instead.

[11] Detailed discussions of "the old record" and early theories of the dance (e.g. 'Substitution', 'magical' and 'imitation' theories can be found in four chapters of Ten Lectures on theories of the dance, i.e. Chap. 3-Emotional, Psychologistic, and Biological explanations; Chap. 4-Intellectualistic and Literary explanation; Chap. 5-Religious and Quasi-Religious Explanations; Chap. 6-Functional Explanations (Williams 1991: 41-150).

Chapter 6 [pp. 137-154]

[1] Reprinted by permission from the Editors of *JASHM*, who were grateful to the editors of *Curriculum*, Vol. 15, No. 1, 1994, for permission to reprint the essay in *JASHM* 9(1): 1-14. David Best is a Professor in the Department of Philosophy, University of Wales, Swansea. He was Visiting Professor, School of Theatre, Manchester Metropolitan University, and has held other important appointments as well. Recently, he was Professor of Philosophy at Birmingham Institute of Art and Design, and he acted as consultant for the National Department of Education and Science for England and Wales. His book, *Rationality of Feeling* (1993,) won the award for best book of the year in England. He is a contributor to *Anthropology and Human Movement, 1: The Study of Dances* (1997).

[2] The paragraphs are not numbered in the original essay. They are numbered here for ease of reference and for teaching purposes.

[3] [Best's Note]: For a more extended account of the general damage caused in educational policy by underlying positivism, please see especially chapter 2, pp. 11-15, and chapter 3 of my book *The Rationality of Feeling*. But discussion of the issue appears in various places throughout the book. see also "Learning from the Arts," *Reflections in Higher Education*, Vol. 2, No. 1.

[4] [Best's Note]: For a further account of the important similarities between sciences and arts, please see the works to which I refer in Note 3.

[5] Merleau-Ponty, together with Jean Paul sartre, founded existential philosophy. Merleau Ponty's constant target was the subject-object dualism of Cartesianism, which arguably still continued to dominate existentialism.

[6] That is not the only point he makes, of course. The essay from which the citation is taken is rich. It is a goldmine of information for undergraduate and graduate students who are interested in exploding the myth of a value-free science [The Editor].

[7] For students who want further information about these tables and the discussion that led to them, see farnell (1994) and Varela (1996).

[8] South African names and terminology for indigenous peoples are problematic, because the words, 'San', 'Bushmen' and 'Bushman' have all been used in a derogatory manner. I use the same conventions as Glasser and Lewis-Williams, i.e. (1) 'San' or 'Bushmen' are used in this book with no derogation intended. They are conceived to be synonyms for the former hunter/gatherers in southern Africa. (2) 'Bushmen' used by itself is a noun, whereas 'Bushman' is used as an adjective, as in "Bushman beliefs," or "Bushman dances" etc. (CF. Glasser 1996: 308 - note 2).

[9]About the dating of San rock-art, Lewis-Williams declares: "Dates thus obtained show that painted mobile art, as these sstones are called was being made as long ago as 26,300 (+400) B.P. ('Before Present'). This astonishingly early date comes from Eric Wendt's excavation in the Apollo 11 shelter in southern Namibia. It means that at least some southern African rock art was contemporaneous with the Upper Palæolithic art of Western Europe. The most famous of the European painted caves, Lascaux, has been dated to about 17,000 B.P., ten thousand years later than the Apollo 11 art (Lewis-Williams and Dowson 1989: 21).

Chapter 7 [pp. 155-174]

[1] The Tiv are a people living on both sides of the Benue River in Nigeria. They speak a language of the Benue-Congo branch of the Niger-Congo family. Thanks to missionaries, the language became literate around 1920. The Tiv are mainly susbsistence farmers. The main crops are yams, millet and sorghum. Although goats and chickens are plentiful, few cattle are kept because of the tsetse fly. The polygynous Tiv family occupies a cluster of round huts surrounding a reception hut and brothers usually live next to one another. Tiv social organization is based upon patrilineages. In the late 20th century, the Tiv numbered about 2,500,000.

[2] 'Sororate' is a word designating the marriage of one man with two or more sisters, usually successively, after the first wife has been found to be barren or after she has died.

[3] [Farnell's Note]: These points do not, although they might in some cases, correspond with true geographical directions—an important analytical consideration, marking the distinction between a ritually "embedded space" and one that is not; (see comparison between T'ai Chi and Catholic Mass; Williams 1995: 68-69).

[4] The high case locutions are taken from Lakoff and Johnson (1980).

Chapter 8 [pp. 175-196]

[1] The Temne are a people who live in Sierra Leone, West Africa.

[2] Lewis-Williams is head of the Rock-art Research Unit at the University of the Witwatersrand, Johannesburg, South Africa. Among others, he wrote two books that are relevant to the subject in hand: *Discovering Southern African Rock Art*, (1990), published by David Philip, Cape Town, and *Im-*

ages of Power (1989). Southern Book Publishers, Johannesburg. [N.B.: *Images of Power* is now out of print but has been recently republished under the same name by Southern Book Publishers, a member of the New Holland Struik Publishing Group, 1999].

[3] A Nilotic people of the southern Sudan. See Evans-Pritchard (1940).

[4] It is interesting to know that he was ordained a priest in 1530 and became a canon of the church at Langres in 1574 where he was encouraged to pursue his studies of the dance by the Jesuits, who considered it to be an educationally important art form.

[5] Arbeau's book isn't the sole source of information. There are the works of Robert Copland (*The maner of dauncynge of Bace daunces after the use of fraunce*, 1521), Fabritio Caroso da Sermoneta (*Il Ballarino*, 1581) and Cesare Negri (*Nuove Inventioni di balli*, 1604).

[6] These are Basse Danse, Gaillarde, Volte, Courante, Canaries, Bouffons, Morisque, Pavane d'Espagne and twenty three varieties of the Branle.

[7] These positions were codified by Pierre Beauchamp *circa* 1680 and set down in a book by Pierre Rameau [*Le Maitre à danse*, 1725]. Rameau's book was published in English as *The Dancing Master* in 1931.

[8] The heelless courtier's shoe which *preceded* the *pointe* shoe, was introduced *circa* 1740-50 by another Italian ballerina, Maria Carmago, who also shortened her skirts to a length above the ankle so that she could move more easily.

[9] It was also at the end of the nineteenth century that scenarios for ballets began to be devised by professional writers and librettists.

[10] Although I have drawn attention to Arbeau's book as the 'beginning' of the ballet, an Italian, Dominico da Piacenza (in service to the Estes family of Ferrara) is credited with writing one of the earliest known treatises on dancing (see Clarke and Crisp 1981 - cited in Durr 1985: 31).

[11] The oldest document that refers to Indian danced and dramatic forms in explicit terms is dated approximately to the third century (Jairazbhoy 1971 and Puri 1983).

[12] It may not be considered necessary for laypersons to make such connections at all, and it may be considered to be sufficient for reasonably educated graduate students to *know about* such connection — and of what 'evidence' consists — but neither of these approaches to the subject are

adequate for serious students at any level who are interested in 'doing' (rather than knowing about) the subject.

Chapter 9 [pp. 197-216]

[1] Often, students don't immediately grasp what is important about a passage, especially if they are unfamiliar with the activities that are described. They may not know *why* they are meant to understand what appear to be "technical details," which is why a list of important points have been added to the cited passage. *The list is meant to be used as a model for other citations.* There are some who might ask, "why not summarize the quotations so that the lists aren't necessary?" The answer: 1. *learning how to summarize* is built into the reading process, and 2. it is important to read the words of the original author.

[2] Sachs depended heavily on the German *Kulturkreis* school of thought which was based on diffusionist method. The *Kulturkreis* school of thought held that it is possible to trace the paths along which culture complexes have diffused by plotting the geographical points at which the constituent elements are found. Diffusionism was considered by its adherents to be more than a theory — it was a method.

[3] 'The Dance in Ancient Crete' is in *Studies Presented to David Moore Robinson*, Vol. I (St. Louis, 1951: 23-50) and 'Terpsichore: The Story of Dance in Ancient Greece' is in *Dance Perpectives* 13 (Winter 1962).

[4] [Lawler's Note]: A failure to observe and interpret properly various chronological and conventional aspects of Greek art has led on occasion to fantastically impossible theories with respect to the Greek dance—particularly those of Maruice Emmanuel. See, e.g. his *Essai sur L'Orchestique Greque*, Paris, Hachette, 1895, and the English translation by Harriet Jean Beauley, New York and London, John Lane, 1916. (Cf. Lillian B. Lawler, 'The Mænads', *Memoirs of the American Academy in Rome*, VI, 1927, 70-73).

[5] The American woman to whom the origins of modern American concert dance forms is attributed. She was born May 26, 1877, and died September 14, 1927.

[6] The Denishawn school of Dancing and Related Arts was founded by Ruth St. Denis in 1915 with her husband, Ted Shawn. Martha Graham was probably the most famous of its many illustrious students.

[7] At least some of the 'Select bibliography' at the end of this essay (pp. 115-16) should be examined. Archer and Hodson are careful scholars. In particular, Everett-Green's essay (1991): 'Dance Notation: Ballet's Missing Link' should be read by anyone unfamiliar with movement writing.

[8] For example, the Laban script is popularly believed to be just another complicated mnemonic device that is primarily iconographic in nature. Unlike the Benesh system, which is primarily iconographic, the Laban script is *ideographic*, but these are problems that are too complex and require to much space to explain to include in this book. Interested students can, however, consult Page (1990 and 1996) for further information.

[9] See Williams (1996) for complete discussion.

Chapter 10 [pp. 217-232]

[1] From Middle English, from Old French, from Latin: *evidentia*, as EVIDENT.

[2] 'Facts' in one academic discipline or methodology do not necessarily constitute 'facts' in another. The clearest example is the distinction between 'biological facts' and 'social facts', illustrated in social anthropology by 'mating' (biological fact) and 'marriage' (social fact).

[3] Farnell (1994) should be used as a supplementary text with this chapter, not only because she explains many of the basic features of Labanotation in greater detail, but because she explains why movement texts are preferable to photographs, pictographs, word glosses and diagrams.

[4] I am indebted to Farnell for the approach to these illustrations: I followed her format in the essay, *Ethno-graphics and the Moving Body* (1994).

[5] The property that [spoken] language shares with all sign systems is its indexical nature; its maintenance and creation of social connections, anchored in experience and the sense of the real. ... The structure of action fans out from the center, the locus of *I* and *you*, to delineate where and when everything happens relative to the central actors: *he* and *she* versus *I* and *you*, *there* versus *here*, *then* versus *now*, present versus non-present (past or future). This is the structure of parole in language, the structure of each situation of speaking ... In short, indexes make the social person (Urciuoli 1995: 189-190).

[6] This transcription could also be identified as 'she bows from the waist', 'he bows from the waist' or 'you bow from the waist'. The usage of plural pronouns ('we' or 'they') would require two writing staves — one for each person.

7 We know it is a human *agent* that is acting in the context of a situation.

8 Explanation of Laban's movement-writing staff is in Farnell (1994: 940).

Chapter 11 [pp. 233-248]

1 Students can easily discover the meanings of these terms by consulting a standard dictionary of philosophy, e.g., Angeles (1981).

2 In commercial transactions a warrant is a guarantee of reliability. Here, the warrant *guarantees the soundness of the relationship between the support and the claim.*

3 For further discussion, see Williams (1991: 76-79).

4 See Best (1974) for further discussion of these questions.

NAME INDEX

SUBJECT INDEX

BIBLIOGRAPHY

Acronyms

- **ASA**: Association of [British] Social Anthropologists
- **DRJ**: Dance Research Journal (CORD)
- **ILAM**: International Library of African Music at Rhodes University, South Africa
- **JASHM**: Journal for the Anthropological Study of Human Movement
- **JDE**: Journal of Dance Ethnology (U.C.L.A.)
- **JEFDSS**: Journal of the English Folk Dance and Song Society
- **JHMS**: Journal of Human Movement Studies
- **OCD**: Oxford Concise Dictionary
- **ODT**: Oxford Dictionary and Thesaurus
- **WID**: Webster's International Dictionary

Adshead-Lansdale, Janet, and June Layson (Eds.)
1994. *Dance History: An Introduction*, [2nd Edition]. London: Routledge.

Agar, M.H.
1980. *The Professional Stranger: An Informal Introduction to Ethnography*. New York and London: Academic Press.

Angeles, Peter A.
1981. *Dictionary of Philosophy*. New York: Harper & Row.

Anonymous (Annals)
1873. A Disgusted Pedagogue. The Perversity of Deaf-Mutism. *American Annals of the Deaf* 18, October. 1874. Institution Items: Pennsylvania Institution. *American Annals of the Deaf* 19, January. 1882. Institution Items. *American Annals of the Deaf* 27, April. 1898. Tabular Statement of Schools for the Deaf, 1897-98. *American Annals of the Deaf* 43, January. 1920. Statistics of Speech Teaching in American Schools for the Deaf. *Volta Review* 22, June.

Arbeau, Thoinot
1925[1588]. *Orchesography* (C. Beaumont, Trans.). Brooklyn, NY: Dance Horizons.

Archer, Kenneth, and Millicent Hodson
1994. Ballets Lost and Found. IN *Dance History. An Introduction* [2nd Edition] (J. Adshead-Lansdale and June Layson, Eds.). London and New York: Routledge, pp. 98-116.

Ardener, E.W.
> 1989 [1971]. Social Anthropology and Language. IN *The Voice of Prophecy and Other Essays/Edwin Ardener* (M. Chapman, Ed.). Oxford: Blackwell, pp. 1-44.
> 1989[1977]. Comprehending Others. IN *The Voice of Prophecy and Other Essays/Edwin Ardener* (M. Chapman, Ed.). Oxford: Blackwell, pp. 159-185.
> 1989[1985]. Social Anthropology and the Decline of Modernism. IN *The Voice of Prophecy and Other Essays/Edwin Ardener* (M. Chapman, Ed.). Oxford: Blackwell, pp. 191-210.

Ayres, J.A.
> 1848. An Inquiry Into the Extent to Which the Misfortune of Deafness May be Alleviated. *American Annals of the Deaf* 1, April.

Bacon, Lawrence
> 1974. *A Handbook of Morris Dances*, n.p., The Morris Ring.

Baker, C ., and D. Cokely.
> 1980. *American Sign Language: A Teachers Resource Text on Grammar and Culture.* Silver Spring, MD: T.J. Publishers.

Bateson, Gregory
> 1972. *Steps to an Ecology of Mind.* New York: Chandler.

Baynton, Douglas
> 1995. Savages and Deaf-Mutes. Evolutionary Theory and the Campaign Against Sign-Language. *JASHM* 8(4): 132-172.
> 1996. *Forbidden Signs: American Culture and the Campaign Against Sign Language.* Chicago: University of Chicago Press

Beaumont, Cyril (Trans.)
> 1968. *Orchesography* [Arbeau]. Brooklyn, NY: Dance Horizons.

Bell, Alexander G.
> 1884. *Proceedings of the Fifth National Conference of Principals and Superintendents of Institutions for Deaf-Mutes.* St. Paul, Minnesota.
> 1899. Address of the President. Association Review, 1, October [N.B. the Association Review was the official journal of the American Association to Promote the Teaching of Speech to the Deaf. The journal was renamed *Volta Review* in 1910].

Bell, Charles
> 1886[1842]. *The Anatomy and Philosophy of Expression as Connected with the Arts* [7th Ed. revised]. London: Bell and Sons.

Bellugi, U., and E.S. Klima
1982. From Gesture to Sign: Deixis in a Visual Gestural Language. IN *Speech, Place and Action: Studies in Deixis and Related Topics* (R.J. Jarvella and W. Klein, Eds.). Chichester, UK: Wiley & Sons, pp. 297-313.

Best, David
1992. *The Rationality of Feeling*. London: Falmer Press.
1993. Mind, Body and Sport. *JASHM* 7(4): 201-218.
1996. Educating Artistic Response: Understanding is Feeling. *JASHM* 9(1): 1-14 [Reprinted from *Curriculum*, Vol. 15, No. 1, 1994].

Bingham, Katherine T.
1900. All Along the Line. *Association Review* 2, February.

Blacking, John
1981. Political and Musical Freedom in the Music of Some Black South African Churches. IN *The Structure of Folk Models* [ASA Monograph 20] (L. Holy and M. Stucklik, Eds.). London: Tavistock.
1983. Movement and Meaning: Dance in Social Anthropological Perspective. *Dance Research* 1(1): 89-99.

Blundell, Nicholas
1712. *The Great Diurnal of Nicholas Blundell of Little Crosby, Lancashire*. Vol. 2. (J.J. Bagley, Ed. 1970). Chester: n.p., The Record Society of Lancashire and Cheshire [See entries for 3, 7, 8, 9 July, pp. 25-6].

Boas, Franz, and E. Deloria.
1941. *Dakota Grammar. Memoirs of the National Academy of Sciences*. Vol. xxiii. Washington DC: U.S. Government Printing Office.

Bohannan, Laura
1967. Miching Mallecho: That Means Witchcraft. IN *Magic, Witchcraft and Curing* (J. Middleton, Ed.). Austin: University of Texas Press, pp. 44-54.

Boller, Paul
1970[1850]. The New Science. IN *The Gilded Age: A Reappraisal* (H.W. Morgan, Ed.). Syracuse, NY: Syracuse University Press.

Bolton, W. F.
1994. Language: An Introduction. IN *Language Introductory Readings* (V.P. Clark, P.A. Escholz, and A.F. Rosa, Eds.). New York: St. Martin's Press.

Bowler, Peter J.
1988. *The Non-Darwinian Revolution: Reinterpreting a Historical Myth*. Baltimore: Johns Hopkins University Press.
1989. *Evolution: the History of an Idea*. Berkeley: University of California Press.

Brierley, Ben
> 1884a. Trevor Hall. IN *Tales and Sketches of Lancashire Life: The Chronicles of Waverlow*. Manchester: Heywood & Son and London: Simpkin, Marshall [See especially pp. 126-132].
> 1884b. Christmas at Ringwood Hall. IN *Tales and Sketches of Lancashire Life: The Chronicles of Waverlow*. Manchester: Heywood & Son and London: Simpkin, Marshall [See especially pp. 148-149].

Brown, J.E. (Ed.)
> 1953. *The Sacred Pipe: Black Elk's Account of the Seven Rites of the Oglala Sioux*. Norman: University of Oklahoma Press.

Buckland, Theresa
> 1982-8. (Ed.) Traditional Dance, 1-6. *Proceedings of the Traditional Dance Conferences held at Crewe and Alsager College of Higher Education*. Alsager: Crewe and Alsager College of Higher Education.
> 1983. Definitions of Folk Dance: Some Explorations. *Folk Music Journal* 4(4): 315-332.
> 1991. Institutions and Ideology in the Dissemination of Morris Dances in the Northwest of England. *1991 Yearbook for Traditional Music* 23: 53-67.
> 1994. Traditional Dance: English Ceremonial and Social Forms. IN *Dance History. An Introduction* [2nd Ed.] (J. Adshead-Lansdale and J. Layson, Eds.). London: Routledge, pp. 45-58.

Burton, A.
> 1891. *Rush Bearing*. Manchester: Brook & Crystal.

Buechel, E.
> 1983[1939]. *A Grammar of Lakota*. Saint Francis, South Dakota: Rosebud Educational Society.

Bühler, Karl
> 1934. *Sprachtheorie*. Jena, Germany: Fischer.

Camp, Henry
> 1848. Claims of the Deaf and Dumb Upon Public Sympathy and Aid. *American Annals of the Deaf*, 1, July.

Carter, Paul A.
> 1971. *The Spiritual Crisis of the Gilded Age*. DeKalb: Northern Illinois University Press.

Cawte, E.C.
> 1983. *An Index to Cecil J. Sharp The Morris Book 5 Volumes 1911-1924*. Sheffield: The Morris Ring and the Centre for English Cultural Tradition and Language, University of Sheffield.
> 1960. (with A. Helm, R.J. Marriot, and N. Peacock). A Geographical Index of the Ceremonial Dance in Great Britain. *JEFOSS* 1(1): 1-41.

Cawte, E.C. (continued)
    1961. Addenda and Corrigenda. *JEFDSS* 9(2): 93-95.

Chandler, K.
    1993. *Ribbons, Bells and Squeaking Fiddles: the Social History of Morris Dancing in the English South Midlands, 1660-1900.* (The Folklore Society, Tradition I, Enfield Lock) Middlesex: Hisarlik Press.

Chapman, Malcolm
    1982. "Semantics" and the "Celt." IN *Semantic Anthropology* [ASA 22] (D. Parkin, Ed.). London: Academic Press, pp. 123-144.

Clark, M. *et al.*
    1976. Subcultures, Cultures and Class. IN *Resistance Through Rituals* (S. Hall and T. Jefferson, Eds.). London: Hutchinson.

Clark, V.P., P.A. Escholz, and A.F. Rosa (Eds.)
    1994. *Language Introductory Readings,* New York: St. Martin's Press.

Clark, W.P.
    1885. *The Indian Sign Language.* Phildelphia: L.R. Hammersley.

Clegg, Jonathan
    1981. Towards an Understanding of African Dance: the Zulu *Isishameni* Style. Papers Presented at the *Second Symposium on Ethnomusicology,* ILAM October, 1980 [ILAM is located at Rhodes University in Grahamstown, South Africa].

Condillac, Etienne Bonnot de
    1971[1746]. *Essay on the Origin of Human Knowledge.* Gainesville, Florida: Scholars Facsimilies and Reprints.
    1986[1775]. *Grammaire.* Stuttgart-Bad Connstatt: Frommann-Holzberg.

Cooley, Charles H.
    1909. *Social Organization: A Study of the Larger Mind.* New York: Scribner.

Coplan, David
    1982. African Class Formation - Culture and Consciousness, 1870-1930. IN *Industrialisation and Social Change in South Africa* (S. Marks and R. Rathbone, Eds.) London: Longman Group, Ltd.
    1985. *In Township Tonight.* London: Ravan.

Corrsin, S.D.
    1990. *Sword Dancing in Central and Northern Europe: An Annotated Bibliography,* n.p., distributed by Country Dance and Song Society of America, Haydenville, MA.

Covell, J.C.
1870. *The Nobility, Dignity and Antiquity of the Sign Language*. Proceedings of the Seventh Convention of American Instructors of the Deaf, Indianapolis.

Crick, Malcolm
1976. *Explorations in Language and Meaning. Towards a Semantic Anthropology*. London: John Wiley & Sons.

Crouter, A.L.E.
n.d. [Pamphlet] 'The Development of Speech in the Deaf Child'. Gallaudet Archives, Box PSD: 'Dr. Crouter's Speeches' [Reprinted from the Transactions of the American Laryngological, Rhinological and Otological Society, 1910].

Darwin, Charles
1965[1872]. *The Expression of the Emotions in Man and Animals*. Chicago: University of Chicago Press.
1981[1871]. *The Descent of Man and Selection in Relation to Sex*. Princeton: Princeton University Press.

Deloria, E.
1940. *Lakota-English Lexicon*. [Manuscript] American Philosophical Society Library, Philadelphia, PA.

Demangles, Leslie G.
1992. *The Faces of the Gods: Vodou and Roman Catholicism in Haiti*. Chapel Hill: University of North Carolina Press.

Diamond, A.S.
1959. *The History and Origin of Language*. New York: Philosophical Society.

Discussion
1882. *Proceedings of the Tenth Convention of American Instructors of the Deaf*, Jacksonville, IL.

Dodds, R.W.
1899. The Practical Benefits of Methods Compared. *American Annals of the Deaf* 44, February.

Dudley, Lewis J.
1882. Address of Mr. Dudley in 1880. *Fifteenth Annual Report of the Clarke Institution for Deaf-Mutes*. Northampton, MA.
1884. Report of the Corporation. *Seventeenth Annual Report of the Clarke Institution for Deaf-Mutes*, Northampton, MA.

Dumont, Louis
1987. *Essays on Individualism. Modern Ideology in Anthropological Perspective*. Chicago: University of Chicago Press.

Dunley, T.W.
1982. *Wolves for the Blue Soldiers*. Lincoln: University of Nebraska Press.

Durr, Dixie
1985. The Structure of Ballet-Dancing, With Special Emphsis on Roles, Rules, Norms and Status. *M.A. Thesis*, New York University.

Ellegard, Alvar
1990[1958]. *Darwin and the General Reader: The Reception of Darwin's Theory of Evolution in the British Periodical Press, 1859-1892*. Chicago: University of Chicago Press.

Engelsman, B.
1890. Deaf Mutes and Their Instruction. *Science* 16, October.

Erlmann, Veit
1982. Black Political Song in South Africa: Some Research Perspectives. *Popular Music Perspectives* 2.
1987. Singing Brings Joy to the Distressed. *History Workshop, University of the Witwatersrand*, Johannesburg. [Later published in 1991 as A Feeling of Prejudice: Orpheus M. McAdoo and the Virginia Jubilee Singers in South Africa, 1890-1898. IN *Regions and Repertoires in South African Politics and Culture* (S. Clingman, Ed.). Braamfontein, South Africa: Ravan Press].

Evans-Pritchard, E.E.
1940. *The Nuer*. Oxford: Oxford University Press.
1965. *Theories of Primitive Religion*. Oxford: Clarendon.

Fairbank, Holly
1985. Chinese Minority Dances: Processors and Preservationists - Part I. *JASHM* 3(4): 168-189 [Also see Chinese Minority Dances: Processors and Preservationists - Part II. *JASHM* 4(1): 1-13, 1986].

Farnell, Brenda
1984. Visual Communication and Literacy: An Anthropological Enquiry Into Plains Indian and American Sign Languages. *M.A. Thesis*, New York University.
1989. Body Movement Notation. IN *International Encyclopedia of Communication* (D. Barnauw, Ed.). London: Oxford University Press with the University of Pennsylvania, Philadelphia.
1994. Ethno-graphics and the Moving Body. *MAN* (n.s.) 29: 929-974.
1995. Foreward. *JASHM* 8(4): 135-138.
1995a. Introduction. IN *Human Action Signs in Cultural Context. The Visible and the Invisible in Movement and Dance*. (B. Farnell, Ed.). Metuchen, NJ: Scarecrow Press, pp.1-28.
1995b. Where Mind Is a Verb: Spatial Orientation and Deixis in Plains Indian Sign Talk and Assiniboine [Nakota] Culture. IN *Human*

Farnell, Brenda (continued)
>   *Action Signs in Cultural Context. The Visible and the Invisible in Move-
>   ment and Dance* (B. Farnell, Ed.). Metuchen, NJ: Scarecrow Press,
>   pp. 82-111.
>
>   1995c. *Do You See What I Mean? Plains Indian Sign Talk and the Embodi-
>   ment of Action.* Austin: University of Texas Press.
>
>   1996a. Metaphors We Move By. *Visual Anthropology* 8(2-4): 311-336.
>
>   1996b. Movement Notation Systems. IN *The World's Writing Systems*
>   (P.T. Daniels and W. Bright, Eds.). Oxford and New York: Oxford
>   University Press.
>
>   1996c. Entry: Movement and Gesture. IN *The Encyclopedia of Cultural
>   Anthropology.* Lakeville, CT: Academic Reference Publishing Co.

Fischer, Renate
>   1993. Language in Action. IN *Looking Back: A Reader on the History of
>   Deaf Communities and their Sign Languages* (R. Fischer and Harlan
>   Lane, Eds.). Hamburg: Signum.

Flowers, Thomas
>   1915. Education of the Colored Deaf. *Proceedings of the Twentieth Con-
>   vention of American Instructors of the Deaf,* 1914, Washington DC.

Fowler, L.
>   1987. *Shared Symbols, Contested Meanings. Gros Ventre Culture and His-
>   tory 1778-1984.* Ithaca, NY: Cornell University Press.

Fox, Thomas
>   1897. Speech and Gestures. *American Annals of the Deaf* 42, November.

Franken, Marjorie A.
>   1997. The Dance and Status in Swahili Society. IN *Anthropology and
>   Human Movement, 1: The Study of Dances* (D. Williams, Ed.).
>   Lanham, MD: Scarecrow Press, pp. 202-218.

Frazer, J.G.
>   1890. *The Golden Bough: A Study in Comparative Religion* [2nd Ed. - 3
>   Vols.] London: Macmillan.

Gallaudet, Edward M.
>   1881. How Shall the Deaf Be Educated? *International Review* Decem-
>   ber [Reprinted in Gordon, J.C. (Ed.), 1892: 101].
>
>   *n.d.* Speech for the Deaf: Essays Written for the Milan International
>   Congress on the Education of the Deaf, Milan, Italy, September
>   n. p. [N.B.: Copy located in the *Volta Bureau* archives, Washing-
>   ton DC and cited in Winzer 1981].

Gallaudet, Thomas H.
> 1847. On the Natural Language of Signs—I. *American Annals of the Deaf* 1, October
> 1848. On the Natural Language of Signs—II. *American Annals of the Deaf* 1, January.

Garrett, Emma
> 1883. Report of the Teacher in Charge; Branch for Oral Instruction [Pennsylvania Institution for the Deaf and Dumb], January 1. *Gallaudet Archives*, Box: PSD Sundry Reports, Communications, etc. dating prior to 1890].

Gell, Alfred
> 1985. Style and Meaning in Umeda Dance. IN *Society and the Dance* (P. Spencer, Ed.). Cambridge, UK: Cambridge University Press, pp. 183-205.

Giddings, Franklin H.
> 1916[1898]. *The Elements of Sociology*. New York: Macmillan.

Gilman, Sander L.
> 1988. *Disease and Representation: Images of Illness from Madness to Aids*. Ithaca, NY: Cornell University Press.

Glasser, Sylvia
> 1991. Is Dance Political Movement? *JASHM* 6(3): 112-122
> 1993. On The Notion of "Primitive" Dance. *JASHM* [Special Issue on Editorial Policies] 7(3): 183-196.
> 1996. Transcultural Transformations. *Visual Anthropology* ('Signs of Human Action', D. Williams, Guest Ed.) 8(2-4): 287-310.

Goldstein, K.S.
> 1964. *A Guide for Fieldworkers in Folklore*. Hatboro, PA: Folklore Associates; London: Herbert Jenkins.

Goodman, Nelson
> 1969. *Languages of Art*. London: Oxford University Press.
> 1984. *Of Mind and Other Matters*. Cambridge, MA: Harvard University Press.

Goodwin, Brian
> 1994. *How the Leopard Changed its Spots. The Evolution of Complexity*. New York: Simon & Schuster.

Gordon, Joseph C.
> 1899. Dr. Gordon's Report. *Association Review* 1, December.
> 1892. (Ed.) *Education of Deaf Children: Evidence of Edward Miner Gallaudet and Alexander Graham Bell Presented to the Royal Commission of the United Kingdom*. Washington DC: The Volta Bureau.

Gore, Georgiana
 1994. Traditional Dance in West Africa. IN *Dance History. An Introduction* [2nd Edition] (J. Adshead-Layson and June Layson, Eds.). London and New York: Routledge, pp. 59-80.

Gould, Stephen J.
 1981. *The Mismeasure of Man*. New York: W. W. Norton.

Grau, Andrée
 1983. Sing a Dance - Dance a Song. *Dance Research* 1(2): 32-44.

Greene, John C.
 1981. *Science, Ideology, and World View*. Berkeley: University of California Press.

Hall, W. Earl
 1956. To Speak or Not to Speak: That is the Question Behind the Bitter Deaf-Teaching Battle. *The Iowan* 4, February / March.

Hanks, William
 1990. *Referential Practice: Language and Lived Space Among the Maya*. Chicago: University of Chicago Press.

Hardy, Thomas
 1974[1872]. *Under the Greenwood Tree; or, the Mellstock Quire*. London: Macmillan [See especially pp. 52-59.]

Harris, Roy
 1981. *The Language Myth*. New York: St. Martin's Press.

Harrison, J.E.
 1948[1913]. *Ancient Art and Ritual*. London: Oxford University Press.

Hart-Johnson, Diana
 1997. A Graham Technique Class. *JASHM* 9(4): 193-214.

Haviland, J.B.
 1986. Complex Referential Gestures. Draft manuscript, Center for Advanced Study in the Behavioral Sciences, Stanford University, California.
 1993. Anchoring, Iconicity and Orientation in Guugu Yimithirr Pointing Gestures. *Journal of Linguistic Anthropology* 3(1): 3-45.

Hawking, Stephen
 1988. *A Brief History of Time*. London: Transworld Publishing [Bantam].

Heaney, M.
　　1985. *An Introductory Bibliography on Morris Dancing.* Vaughan Williams Memorial Library Leaflet no. 19, Addenda (1990). London: English Folk Dance and Song Society.
　　1991. (with J. Forrest). *Annals of Early Morris.* Sheffield: Centre for English Cultural Tradition and Language, University of Sheffield, in association with The Morris Ring.

Herzfeld, Michael.
　　1987. *Anthropology Through the Looking Glass: Critical Ethnography in the Margins of Europe.* Cambridge, UK: Cambridge University Press.

Hewes, Gordon W.
　　1973. Primate Communication and the Gestural Origin of Language. *Current Anthropology* 14, February-April.

Hofstadter, Richard
　　1955. *Social Darwinism in American Thought.* Boston: Beacon Press.

Horst, Louis
　　1937. *Pre-Classical Dance Forms.* New York: Dance Observer.

Howe, Samuel Gridley, *et al.*
　　1866. *Second Annual Report of the Board of State Charities.* Boston: [n.p.]

Hoxie, Frederick E.
　　1989. *A Final Promise: The Campaign to Assimilate the Indians.* Lincoln: University of Nebraska Press.

Hubbard, Gardiner G.
　　1868. [A Summary of the] Proceedings of the American [Social] Science Association. *National Deaf Mute Gazette* 2, January.

Hull, Susanna E.
　　1877. Do Persons Born Deaf Differ Mentally From Others Who Have the Power of Hearing? *American Annals of the Deaf* 22, October.
　　1898. The Psychological Method of Teaching Language. *American Annals of the Deaf* 43, April.

Huxley, Thomas
　　1906. *Man's Place in Nature.* London: Macmillan.

Ives, E.D.
　　1980. *The Tape-recorded Interview: A Manual for Field Workers in Folklore and Oral History.* Knoxville: University of Tennessee Press.

Jairazbhoy, N.A.
　　1971. *The Rāgs of North Indian Music.* London: Faber & Faber.

James, Deborah
1990. Musical Form and Social History: Research Perspectives on Black South African Music. *Radical History Review (History from South Africa)*, 46(7), Winter.

Jarvella, R. J., and W. Klein (Eds.)
1982. *Speech, Place and Action: Studies in Deixis and Related Topics.* Chichester, UK: Wiley & Sons.

Jastrow, Joseph
1886. The Evolution of Language. *Science* 7, June.

Judge, R.
1989. Mary Neal and the Esperance Morris. *Folk Music Journal* 5(5): 545-591.

Kaeppler, Adrienne
1978. The Dance in Anthropological Perspective. *Annual Review of Anthropology* 7: 31-39.
1985. Structured Movement Systems in Tonga. IN *Society and the Dance* (P. Spencer, Ed.). Cambridge, UK: Cambridge University Press, pp. 92-118.

Keali'inohomoku, Joann
1980. The Non-Art of the Dance. *JASHM* 1(2): 83-97.
1997[1969]. An Anthropologist Looks at Ballet as a Form of Ethnic Dance. IN *Anthropology and Human Movement, 1: The Study of Dances* (D. Williams, Ed.). Lanham, Maryland: Scarecrow Press, pp. 15-36.

Kirkhuff, J.D.
1892. Superiority of the Oral Method. *Silent Educator* 3, January.

Kroeber, Alfred
1958. Sign Language Enquiry. *International Journal of American Linguistics* 24: 1-19.

Kuhn, Thomas S.
1962. *The Structure of Scientific Revolutions.* Chicago: University of Chicago Press.

Lakoff, George, and Mark Johnson
1980. *Metaphors We Live By.* Chicago: University of Chicago Press.

Lane, Harlan
1984. *When the Mind Hears: A History of the Deaf.* New York: Random House.

Langer, Susanne
1942. *Philosophy in a New Key.* New York: Mentor Books.

Lawler, Lillian
   1964a. *The Dance of the Ancient Greek Theatre*. Iowa City: University of
      Iowa Press.
   1964b. *The Dance in Ancient Greece*. London: Adam & Charles Black.

Lee, Irving J.
   1950. How Do You Talk About People? *'Freedom Pamphlet'* [Booklet].
      New York: Anti-Defamation League.
Leeuw, Gerard van der
   1963. *Sacred and Profane Beauty. The Holy in Art* (D.E. Green, Trans.).
      New York: Holt, Rinehart & Winston.

Levine, Daniel
   1971. *Jane Addams and the Liberal Tradition*. Madison: University of
      Wisconsin Press.

Lewis-Williams, David
   1989. (with Thomas Dowson). *Images of Power. Understanding Bush-
      man Rock Art*. Cape Town: Southern Book Publishers.
   1990. *Discovering Southern African Rock Art*. Cape Town and
      Johannesburg: David Philip Publishers.

Lewontin, Richard
   1991. *Biology as Ideology. The Doctrine of DNA*. New York: Harper.

Littlejohn, James
   1967. The Temne House. IN *Myth and Cosmos: Readings in Mythology
      and Symbolism* (J. Middleton, Ed.). Austin: University of Texas
      Press, pp. 331-347.

Lomax, Alan
   1968. *Folk Song Style and Culture*. AAAS Publication #88, Washington
      DC.

Lyons, John
   1977. *Semantics, Volume 2*. London and New York: Cambridge Uni-
      versity Press.

Mallery, Garrick
   1880a. *Introduction to the Study of Sign Language Among the North Ameri-
      can Indians as Illustrating the Gesture Speech of Mankind*. Washing-
      ton DC: U.S. Bureau of Ethnology.
   1880b. *Introduction to the Study of Sign Language Among the North Ameri-
      can Indians as Illustrating the Gesture Speech of Mankind*. Washing-
      ton DC: U.S. Bureau of Indian Affairs [Reprinted in Sebeok, T.,
      and J. Umiker-Sebeok, 1978 (Vol.1): 1-76].
   1881. *Sign Language Among the North American Indians*. BAE Annual
      Report 1: 269-552. Washington DC: Smithsonian Institution.
   1882. The Gesture Speech of Man. *American Annals of the Deaf 27*, April.

Marglin, F.A.

1980. Wives of the God-King: The Rituals of Hindu Temple Courtesans. *Ph.D. Dissertaion.* Anthropology Department. Brandeis University.

Martin, John

1939. *Introduction to the Dance.* New York: Norton.

1963. *Book of the Dance.* New York: Tudor [first published as *The Dance,* 1947].

Martin, Lynn

1995. Symbolism and Embodiment in Six Haitian Dances. *JASHM* 8(3): 93-119.

1996. Six Haitian Vodou Dances. *Visual Anthropology* 8(2-4): 219-250.

McCowan, Mary

1907. How Best to Secure Intelligent Speech for Deaf Children. *Association Review* 9, February-April.

McNeill, David

1985. So You Think Gestures Are Nonverbal? *Psychological Review* 92(3): 350-371.

1982. (with E. Levy). Conceptual Representations in Language Activity and Gesture. IN *Speech, Place and Action: Studies in Deixis and Related Topics.* Chichester, UK: Wiley & Sons, pp. 271-295.

Mead, George H.

1933. *Mind, Self and Society.* Chicago: University of Chicago Press.

Metherell, C.

1993. *An Introductory Bibliography on Clog and Step Dance.* Vaughan Williams Memorial Library leaflet no. 22. London: English Folk Dance and Song Society.

Middleton, John

1967. (Ed.). *Magic, Witchcraft, and Curing.* Austin: University of Texas Press.

1985. The Dance Among the Lugbara of Uganda. IN *Society and the Dance* (P. Spencer, Ed.). Cambridge, UK: Cambridge University Press, pp. 165-182.

Midgely, Mary

1978. *Beast and Man: The Roots of Human Nature.* Ithaca, New York: Cornell University Press.

Mitchell, J.C.

1956. The Kalela Dance. *Rhodes Livingstone Institute Papers, Number 27.* Manchester, UK: Manchester University Press.

Moore, James R.
1979. *The Post-Darwinian Controversies: A Study of the Protestant Struggle to Come to Terms with Darwin in Great Britain and America, 1870-1900.* Cambridge, UK: Cambridge University Press.

Needham, J.
1936. The Geographical Distribution of the English Ceremonial Dance Traditions. *JEFDSS* 3(1): 1-45.

Needham, Rodney
1973. *Right and Left. Essays on Dual Symbolic Classification.* Chicago: University of Chicago Press.

Neihardt, J.G.
1972[1932]. *Black Elk Speaks: Being the Life Story of a Holy Man of the Oglala Sioux.* New York: William Morrow.

Oesterley, W.O.E.
1923. *The Sacred Dance.* Cambridge, UK: Cambridge University Press.

Oldroyd, D.R.
1980. *Darwinian Impacts: An Introduction to the Darwinian Revolution.* Milton Keynes, England: Open University Press.

Ong, Walter
1982. Reading, Technology, and Human Consciousness. IN *Literacy as a Human Problem* (J.C. Raymond, Ed.). Atlanta: University of Alabama Press.

Overton, Frank
1908[1891]. *Applied Physiology: Including the Effects of Alcohol and Narcotics, Advanced Grade.* New York: Macmillan.

Page, JoAnne
1990. Documentation of Danced Performances: Video-Recording and Movement Notation. *JASHM* 6(1): 21-29.
1996. Images for Understanding. Movement Notations and Visual Recordings. *Visual Anthropology* 8(2-4): 171-196.

Pearson, Norman
1916. *The Soul and Its Story: A Sketch.* London: Arnold.

Peet, Harvey P.
1850. On the Origin and Early History of the Art of Instructing the Deaf and Dumb. *Proceedings of the First Convention of American Instructors of the Deaf* New York.
1855. Notions of the Deaf and Dumb Before Instruction. *American Annals of the Deaf* 8, October.
1868. Preliminary Remarks—Signs versus Articulation. *National Deaf Mute Gazette* 2, February.

Peet, Isaac Lewis
    1851. Moral State of the Deaf and Dumb Previous to Education, and the Means and Results of Religious Influence Among Them. *American Annals of the Deaf* 3, July.
    1890. The Relation of the Sign Language to the Education of the Deaf. *Silent Educator* 1, January.

Pettingill, Benjamin D.
    1873. The Sign-Language. *American Annals of the Deaf* 18, January.

Pick, H.L. Jr., and L.P. Acredolo (Eds.)
    1983. *Spatial Orientation.* New York and London: Plenum.

Plot, Robert
    1973[1686]. *The Natural History of Staffordshire.* Oxford: [Theatre Facsimile], published in Didsbury: E.J. Morten.

Pocock, David
    1967. The Anthropology of Time Reckoning. IN *Myth and Cosmos* (J. Middleton, Ed.). Austin: University of Texas Press, pp. 303-14.
    1994[1973]. The Idea of a Personal Anthropology. *JASHM* 8(1): 11-42.

Polanyi, Michael
    1958. *Personal Knowledge.* New York: Harper & Row.

Porter, Sarah Harvey
    1894. The Suppression of Signs by Force. *American Annals of the Deaf* 39, June.

Puri, Rajika
    1983. A Structural Analysis of Meaning in Movement: The Hand Gestures of Indian Classical Dance. *M.A. Thesis,* New York University.
    1997. Bharatanatyam Performed: A Typical Recital. *JASHM* 9(4): 173-190.

Rae, Luzerne
    1853. The Philosophical Basis of Language. *Proceedings of the Third Convention of American Instructors of the Deaf,* Colombus, OH.

Richards, Robert J.
    1987. *Darwin and the Emergence of Evolutionary Theories of Mind and Behavior.* Chicago: University of Chicago Press.

Riden, P.
    1989. *Local History: A Handbook for Beginners.* London: B.T. Batsford.

Rippon, Hugh
    1993. *Discovering English Folk Dance.* Aylesbury, Bucks.: Shire Publications.

Roberts, John H.
1988. *Darwinism and the Divine in America: Protestant Intellectuals and Organic Evolution, 1859-1900.* Madison: University of Wisconsin Press.

Robinson, Warren
1890. Something About the Sign Language. *The Silent Educator* 1.

Rogers, A.
1977. *Approaches to Local History.* London and New York: Longman.

Rovik, Patricia
1991. Homage to Lillian B. Lawler With a Select Bibliography of Her Writings. *JASHM* 6(4): 159-168.

Russett, Cynthia E.
1976. *Darwin in America: The Intellectual Response.* San Francisco: W.H. Freeman.

Sachs, Curt
1937. *The World History of the Dance.* (B. Schöenberg, Trans.). London: Allen & Unwin.

Sacks, Oliver
1989. *Seeing Voices: A Journey Into the World of the Deaf.* Berkeley: University of California Press.

Sampson, Geoffrey
1985. *Writing Systems.* Stanford: Stanford University Press.

Sebeok, Thomas, and Jean Umiker-Sebeok (Eds.)
1978. *Aboriginal Sign Languages of the Americas and Australia.* Vols. 1 and 2. New York: Plenum Press.

Settles, Dr.
1940. Normal Training for Colored Teachers. *American Annals of the Deaf* 85, March.

Sharp, Cecil
1907-1914. *The Morris Book.* London: Novello [In Five Parts -- Complete listing of this collection, *The Country Dance Books* and *The Sword Dances of Northern England,* in Buckland (1994: 58)].

Sherzer, Joel.
1973. Verbal and Nonverbal Deixis: The Pointed Lip Gesture Among the San Blas Cuna. *Language in Society* 2: 117-131.

Singer, Peter.
1975. *Animal Liberation: A New Ethics for Our Treatment of Animals.* New York: Avon Books.

Sklar, Deborah
   1991. II. On Dance Ethnography. *CORD Dance Research Journal* 23/1 (Spring 1991).

Sommerfelt, Alf
   1954. The Origin of Language: Theories and Hypotheses. *Journal of World History* 1, April.

Sorell, Walter
   1960. *Dance Throughout the Ages*. London: Thames & Hudson.

Spencer, Paul
   1985. Dance as Antithesis in the Samburu Discourse. IN *Society and the Dance* (P. Spencer, Ed.). Cambridge, UK: Cambridge University Press, pp. 140-164.

Stam, James H.
   1976. *Inquiries Into the Origin of Language: The Fate of a Question*. New York: Harper and Row.

Stanner, W.E.H.
   1979. *White Man Got No Dreaming*. Canberra: Australian National University Press [Special reference to 'Religion, Totemism and Symbolism', pp. 106-143].

Steiner, Franz
   1967[1956]. *Taboo*. London: Pelican.

Stokoe, William
   1972. *Semiotics and Human Sign Language*. New York: Humanities Press.

Stone, Collins
   1848. On the Religious State and Instruction of the Deaf and Dumb. *American Annals of the Deaf* 1, April.

Sughrue, C.M.
   1987. Proceedings of the Contemporary Morris and Sword Dancing Conference, University of Sheffield, 1988. *Lore and Language* 6(2).

Tabular Statement of American Schools for the Deaf October 20, 1919. *American Annals of the Deaf* 65, January, 1920.

Tabular Statement of American Schools for the Deaf October 20, 1920. *American Annals of the Deaf* 66, January, 1921.

Themba, Can
   1972. *The Will To Die*. Johannesburg and Cape Town: David Philip Publishers.

Thomas, Keith
1983. *Man and the Natural World.* New York: Pantheon Books.

Turner, Charles P.
1848. Expression. *American Annals of the Deaf* 1, January.

Turner, James P.
1980. *Reckoning with the Beast: Animals, Pain, and Humanity in the Victorian Mind.* Baltimore, MD: Johns Hopkins University Press.

Tyler, John M.
1899. The Teacher and the State. *Association Review* 1, October.

Tylor, Edward B.
1878[1865]. *Researches Into the Early History of Mankind* [3rd Ed.]. New York: Henry Holt.

Unsigned Excerpt
1890. Vulgarity in Signing [from *The Kentucky Mute*]. *Silent Educator* 1, January.

Urciuoli, Bonnie
1995. The Indexical Structure of Visibility. IN *Human Action Signs in Cultural Context: The Visible and the Invisible in Movement and Dance* (B. Farnell, Ed.). Metuchen, NJ: Scarecrow Press, pp. 189-215.

Valade, Remi
1893. The Sign Language in Primitive Times. *American Annals of the Deaf* 18, January.

Valentine, Phyllis Klein
1991. A Nineteenth Century Experiment in Education for the Handicapped: The American Asylum for the Deaf and Dumb. *New England Quarterly* 64: 355-375.

Van Cleve, John
1984. Nebraska's Oral Law of 1911 and the Deaf Community. *Nebraska History* 65.
1989 (with Barry Crouch). *A Place of Their Own: Creating the Deaf Community in America.* Washington DC: Gallaudet University Press.

Varela, Charles
1994. Pocock, Williams and Gouldner: Initial Reactions of Three Social Scientists to the Problem of Objectivity. *JASHM* 8(1): 43-64.
1995. Cartesianism Revisited: The Ghost in the Moving Machine or the Lived Body. IN *Human Action Signs in Cultural Context. The Visible and the Invisible in Movement and Dance* (B. Farnell, Ed.). Metuchen, NJ: Scarecrow Press, pp. 216-293.
1996. The Visual in Visual Anthropology. *Visual Anthropology* 8(2-4): 155-170.

Voss, Rudolph

1869(?). *Der Tanz und seine Geschichte, Einekulturhisotische-choregraphische Studie. Mit einem Lexicon der Tanze* [The Dance and Its History: a Cultural-Historical Choregraphic Study. With a Lexicon of Dances]. Berlin (N.B. There is disagreement over the dating of this work between London Library and British Museum Library).

Walker, J.R.

1980. *Lakota Belief and Ritual* (R.J. DeMallie and E.A. Jahner, Eds.). Lincoln: University of Nebraska Press.

West, La Mont

1960. The Sign Language: An Analysis. *Ph.D. Dissertation*, Indiana University, Bloomington.

Whitney, William D.

1876. *The Life and Growth of Language: An Outline of Linguistic Science*. New York: Appleton and Co.

Wilkinson, Warring

1881. The Development of Speech and of the Sign-Language. *American Annals of the Deaf* 26, January.

Williams, Drid

1972. Social Anthropology and [the] Dance. *B. Litt. Thesis*, Oxford, UK.

1974. Book Review of Francis Rust [*Dance in Society*]. *CORD Dance Research Journal* 6(2).

1976a. Deep Structures of the Dance. Part I: Constituent Syntagmatic Analysis. *JHMS* 2(2): 123-144.

1976b. Deep Structures of the Dance. Part II: The Conceptual Space of the Dance *JHMS* 2(3): 155-171.

1980. Taxonomies of the Body, With Special Reference to the Ballet: Part I, *JASHM* 1(1): 1-19 and Part II, *JASHM* 1(2): 98-122).

1990 (with Brenda Farnell). *The Laban Script: A Beginning Text on Movement Writing for Non-Dancers*. Canberra: Australian Institute for Aboriginal and Torres Strait Islander Studies.

1991. *Ten Lectures on Theories of the Dance*. Metuchen, NJ: Scarecrow Press.

1994. An Appreciation. *JASHM* 8(4): 174-189.

1995a. The Sokodae: A West African Dance. IN *Cultural Research: Papers on Regional Cultures and Culture-Mixing* (Tahir Shah, Ed.). London: Octagon Press.

1995b. Space, Intersubjectivity, and the Conceptual Imperative: Three Ethnographic Cases. IN *Human Action Signs in Cultural Context. The Visible and the Invisible in Movement and Dance* (B. Farnell, Ed.). Metuchen, NJ: Scarecrow Press, pp. 44-81.

Williams, Drid (continued)

1996a. The Credibility of Movement-Writing. *JASHM* 9(2): 73-89.

1996b. Ceci n'est pas un "wallaby." *Visual Anthropology* 8(2-4): 202.

Winefield, Richard

1987. *Never the Twain Shall Meet: Bell, Gallaudet, and the Communications Debate*. Washington DC: Gallaudet University Press.

Winzer, Margaret

1981. An Examination of Some Selected Factors That Affected the Education and Socialization of the Deaf of Ontario, 1870-1900. *Ph.D. Dissertation*, Canada: University of Toronto.

Wittgenstein, Ludwig.

1958. *Philosophical Investigations* [English text of 3rd edition] (G.E.M. Anscombe, Trans.). New York: Macmillan.

Woodruff, Lucius H.

1849. Grace of Expression. *American Annals of the Deaf* 2, July.

Wright, John D.

1897. Speech and Speech-Reading for the Deaf. *Century Magazine* January.

Yale, Caroline

1908. Letter to Mrs. Alexander Graham Bell. *In files stored in the President's Office*; Box labeled 'Dr. and Mrs. Alexander Graham Bell', Clarke School for the Deaf, Northampton, ME, May 19.

Youngerman, Susanne

1974. Curt Sachs and His Heritage: A Critical Review of *World History of the Dance* with a Survey of Recent Studies That Perpetuate His Ideas. *CORD News* 6(2): 6-19.